SILENCE ON THE WIRE

silence on the wire

a Field Guide to Passive Reconnaissance and Indirect Attacks

Michal Zalewski

NO STARCH
PRESS

♻ Printed on recycled paper in the United States of America

1 2 3 4 5 6 7 8 9 10 – 07 06 05 04

No Starch Press and the No Starch Press logo are registered trademarks of No Starch Press, Inc. Other product and company names mentioned herein may be the trademarks of their respective owners. Rather than use a trademark symbol with every occurrence of a trademarked name, we are using the names only in an editorial fashion and to the benefit of the trademark owner, with no intention of infringement of the trademark.

Publisher: William Pollock
Managing Editor: Karol Jurado
Production Manager: Susan Berge
Cover and Interior Design: Octopod Studios
Developmental Editors: William Pollock and John Mark Walker
Technical Reviewer: Solar Designer
Copyeditor: Pat Coleman
Compositor: Riley Hoffman
Proofreader: Stephanie Provines
Indexer: Ted Laux

For information on book distributors or translations, please contact No Starch Press, Inc. directly:

No Starch Press, Inc.
555 De Haro Street, Suite 250, San Francisco, CA 94107
phone: 415.863.9900; fax: 415.863.9950; info@nostarch.com; http://www.nostarch.com

Library of Congress Cataloging-in-Publication Data

Zalewski, Michal.
  Silence on the wire : a field guide to passive reconnaissance and indirect attacks / Michal
Zalewski.
      p. cm.
  Includes index.
  ISBN 1-59327-046-1
1. Computer networks--Security measures. I. Title.
  TK5105.59.Z35 2005
  005.8--dc22
                                        2004009744

For Maja

ABOUT THE AUTHOR

Michal Zalewski is a self-taught information security researcher who has worked on topics ranging from hardware and OS design principles to networking. He has been a prolific bug hunter and a frequent Bugtraq poster since the mid '90s and has authored popular security utilities such as p0f, a passive OS fingerprinter. He has also published a number of acclaimed security research papers. Michal has worked as a security expert for several reputable companies, both in his native Poland and the U.S., including two major telecoms. In addition to being an avid researcher and occasional coder, Michal dabbles in the fields of artificial intelligence, applied mathematics, and electronics, and is also an amateur photographer.

BRIEF CONTENTS

CONTENTS IN DETAIL

PART I: THE SOURCE

On the problems that surface long before one sends any information over the network

1
I CAN HEAR YOU TYPING   3

Where we investigate how your keystrokes can be monitored from far, far away

2
EXTRA EFFORTS NEVER GO UNNOTICED   21

Where we learn how to build a wooden computer and how to obtain information from watching a real computer run

3
TEN HEADS OF THE HYDRA   51

*Where we explore several other tempting scenarios that occur very early on in the process
of communications*

4
WORKING FOR THE COMMON GOOD   57

*Where a question of how the computer may determine the intent of its user is raised and
left unanswered*

PART II: SAFE HARBOR
On the threats that lurk in between the computer and the Internet

5
BLINKENLIGHTS
Where we conclude that pretty can also be deadly, and we learn to read from LEDs

6
ECHOES OF THE PAST
Where, on the example of a curious Ethernet flaw, we learn that it is good to speak precisely

7
SECURE IN SWITCHED NETWORKS
Or, why Ethernet LANs cannot be quite fixed, no matter how hard we try

8
US VERSUS THEM

103

What else can happen in the local perimeter of "our" network? Quite a bit!

PART III: OUT IN THE WILD

Once you are on the Internet, it gets dirty

9
FOREIGN ACCENT

113

Passive fingerprinting: subtle differences in how we behave can help others tell who we are

10
ADVANCED SHEEP-COUNTING STRATEGIES   151

Where we dissect the ancient art of determining network architecture and computer's whereabouts

11
IN RECOGNITION OF ANOMALIES   173

Or what can be learned from subtle imperfections of network traffic

12
STACK DATA LEAKS   189

Yet another short story on where to find what we did not intend to send out at all

13
SMOKE AND MIRRORS   193

Or how to disappear with grace

14
CLIENT IDENTIFICATION: PAPERS, PLEASE!   199

Seeing through a thin disguise may come in handy on many occasions

15
THE BENEFITS OF BEING A VICTIM   219

*In which we conclude that approaching life with due optimism may help us track down
the attacker*

PART IV: THE BIG PICTURE

Our legal department advised us not to say "the network is the computer" here

16
PARASITIC COMPUTING, OR HOW PENNIES ADD UP   227

*Where the old truth that having an army of minions is better than doing the job yourself
is once again confirmed*

17
TOPOLOGY OF THE NETWORK   243

On how the knowledge of the world around us may help track down friends and foes

18
WATCHING THE VOID   253

When looking down the abyss, what does not kill us makes us stronger

CLOSING WORDS   261

Where the book is about to conclude

BIBLIOGRAPHIC NOTES   263

INDEX   269

FOREWORD

What does it take to write a novel book on computer security? Or rather, what does it take to write a novel on modern computing?

A young yet highly experienced author with talents in many areas including many aspects of computing, mathematics, and electronics (and perhaps a hobby in robotics), as well as other seemingly unrelated interests (including, let's say, fatalistic erotic photography), and indeed with a talent and desire to write.

Once upon a time in a dark and largely unexplored forest, the magic chemistry of (brain cell) trees gave birth to a bit of information, only to let him sail his way down a quick river, into the vast sea (of the Internet), and ultimately find his new home, grave, or maybe a place in a museum.

And so the tale begins. Whether our little bit is good or evil, at a young age he will reach the stream flowing into a shiny castle made out of white-colored foil (yet regarded by many as a black box). He will pass through the entrance and approach the counter to check in. If he weren't so naïve and short-sighted, he could notice a group of evil-looking bits staring at the counter from a distance, taking note of the time bits check in and out; he would have no choice but to proceed to sign in, though.

Once rested, our hero might be asked to team up with his siblings or to join a group of other bits and bitesses, and together they would pack their bodies tightly onto a used inflatable boat. A careful bit could notice bits of garbage (or is that garbage?) in the boat, presumably left by a previous group.

Observing the traffic lights and squeezing through traffic jams, our bits enter a safe harbor and sail to the wharf. Will they be seen from nearby castles and lighthouses? Will someone track the traffic light switches to determine just when our group sailed? Will someone turn on lights at the wharf and take pictures? Will those other evil bits assume the identity of ours and sail away to the sea first? Our bits wouldn't know.

And so they change boats at the wharf and sail to the sea . . . The journey of our pet bits proceeds, with many dangers yet to come.

No, Michal's book does not hide technical detail behind a fairy tale as I have above. Rather, while a very entertaining read, it gets all the facts straight and promptly gives answers to most challenges introduced at the beginning of each chapter.

Silence on the Wire is unique in many aspects, but two stand out: First, it provides in-depth coverage of almost all essential stages of data processing that enable today's "internetworking"—from a keypress to the intended end result of that keypress. Second, it outlines the largely overlooked, under-researched, and inherent security issues associated with each stage of networking and with the process as a whole. The security issues covered serve well to demonstrate the art of vulnerability research from both the attacker's and the defender's perspective, and will encourage further research on the part of the reader.

Clearly, a computer security book can't be comprehensive. In *SotW*, Michal has provocatively chosen to leave out all the well known yet highly dangerous and widespread vulnerabilities and attacks being discussed and worked on today by most in the information security community. He will teach you about subtle keystroke timing attacks, but you will not be reminded that "trojan horse" software with key logging capabilities is currently both more common and easier to use than any of such attacks could ever be.

Why mention keystroke timings while leaving the trojans out? Because timing attacks are largely underappreciated and misunderstood even by information security professionals, whereas trojans are a widely known and obvious threat. Vulnerability to timing attacks is a property of the design of many components involved, whereas to implant a trojan requires either a software bug or an end-user error.

Similarly, and with few exceptions, you won't find the slightest mention in *SotW* of the widely exploited software bugs—or even generic software bug classes such as "buffer overflows." If you are not already familiar with the common computer security threats and would like to gain that knowledge, you will need to accompany yourself on your journey through this book with the perusal of less exciting material available on the Internet and in other books, and in particular with material pertaining to the specific operating systems that you use.

Why study silence, you may wonder—isn't that a nothing? Yes, in a sense. A zero is a nothing in that sense, too. But it is also a number, a concept we cannot really understand the world without.

Enjoy the silence—the best you can.

Alexander Peslyak
Founder and CTO
Openwall, Inc.

better known as

Solar Designer
Openwall Project leader

January 2005

INTRODUCTION

A Few Words about Me

I seem to have been born a computer geek, but my adventure with network security began only by accident. I have always loved to experiment, explore new ideas, and solve seemingly well defined but still elusive challenges that require innovative and creative approaches—even if just to fail at solving them. When I was young, I spent most of my time pursuing sometimes risky and often silly attempts to explore the world of chemistry, mathematics, electronics, and finally computing rather than ride my bike around the block all day long. (I probably exaggerate a bit, but my mother always seemed to be worried.)

Shortly after my first encounter with the Internet (in the mid '90s, perhaps eight years after I coded my first "Hello world" program on a beloved 8-bit machine), I received an unusual request: a spam letter that, hard to believe, asked me (and a couple thousand other folks) to join an underground team of presumably malicious, black hat hackers. This did not drive me underground (perhaps due to my strong instinct for self-preservation, known in certain circles as cowardice) but somehow provided a good motivation to explore the field of computer security in more detail. Having done plenty of amateur programming, I found it captivating to look at code from a different perspective and to try to find a way for an algorithm to do something more than it was supposed to do. The Internet seemed a great resource for the challenges I craved—a big and complex system with only one guiding principle: You cannot really trust anyone. And so it all began.

I do not have the background you might expect from the usual computer security specialist, a profession that is becoming commonplace today. I have never received any formal computer science education, nor do I hold an impressive-sounding set of certifications. Security has always been one of my primary passions (and is now my living). I am not the stereotypical computer geek—I do get up once in a while to look at my work from a sane distance or to get away from computers altogether.

For good or bad, all this has affected the shape of this book and its message. My goal is to show others how I view computer security, not how it is usually taught. For me, security is not a single problem to be solved nor a simple process to follow. It is not about expertise in a specific field. It is an exercise in seeing the entire ecosystem and understanding its every component.

About This Book

Even in the dim light of our monitors, we are still only humans. We were taught to trust others, and we do not want to be too paranoid. We need to find a sensible compromise between security and productivity to live comfortably.

The Internet is, nevertheless, different from a real-world society. There is no common benefit from conforming to the rules, and there is seldom any remorse for virtual misdeeds. We cannot simply trust the system, and our attempts to come up with a single rule that can be applied to all problems will fail miserably. We instinctively draw a straight line to separate "us" from "them" and call our own island safe. Then, we look out for rogue ships on the horizon. Soon, security problems start to appear as localized abnormalities that can be easily defined, diagnosed, and resolved. From that perspective, attackers appear to be driven by clear motives, and if we are vigilant, we can see them and stop them as they approach.

Yet, the virtual world is quite different: security is not the absence of bugs; safety does not lie in being beyond the reach of attackers. Just about any process involving information has inherent security implications, which are visible to us the moment we look beyond the scope of the goal the process tries to achieve. The art of understanding security is simply the art of being able to cross the line and look from a different perspective.

This is an unconventional book, or so I hope. It is not a compendium of problems or a guide to securing your systems. It begins with an attempt to follow the story of a piece of information, from the moment your hands touch the keyboard, all the way to the remote party on the other end of the wire. It covers the technology and its security implications, focusing on problems that cannot be qualified as bugs, with no attacker, no flaw to be analyzed and resolved, or no detectable attack (or at least not one that we can distinguish from legitimate activity). The goal of this book is to demonstrate that the only way to understand the Internet is to have the courage to go beyond the specifications or read between the lines.

As the subtitle suggests, this book focuses on privacy and security problems inherent to everyday communications and computing. Some of them have profound implications, while others are simply interesting and stimulating. None will have an immediate damaging impact on your environment or destroy the data on your disk drive. The information here is useful and valuable to IT professionals and seasoned amateurs who want to be challenged to exercise their minds and who want to learn about the nonobvious consequences of design decisions. This is a book for those who want to learn how to use these subtleties to take control of their environment and gain an advantage over the world outside.

The book is divided into four sections. The first three cover stages of data flow and technologies deployed there. The last section focuses on the network as a whole. Every chapter covers relevant elements of the technology used to process the data at each stage, a discussion of security implications, a demonstration of its side-effects, suggestions on how to address the problems (if possible), and recommendations for how to further explore the subject. I do my best to avoid charts, tables, pages of specifications, and so forth (though you will find numerous footnotes). Since you can easily find plenty of good reference materials online, my focus is on making this book simply enjoyable.

Shall we begin?

PART I

THE SOURCE

On the problems that surface long before one sends
any information over the network

1

I CAN HEAR YOU TYPING

*Where we investigate how your keystrokes can be monitored
from far, far away*

From the moment you press the first key on your keyboard, the information you are sending begins a long journey through the virtual world. Microseconds before packets speed through fiber-optic links and bounce off satellite transceivers, a piece of information goes a long way through an amazing maze of circuits. Prior to your keystrokes being received by the operating system and any applications it might be running, many precise and subtle low-level mechanisms are engaged in a process that is of interest to all sorts of hackers and has proven to be of significance to the security crowd as well. The path to user land has many surprises lurking along the way.

This chapter focuses on these early stages of moving data and on the opportunities that arise for your fellow (and possibly naughty) users to find out way too much about what you are doing in the comfort of your own terminal.

A prominent example of a potential information disclosure scenario related to the way a computer processes your input is associated with a subject that, at first glance, appears to be unrelated at best: the difficult task of producing random numbers on a machine that behaves in a fully predictable manner. It is difficult to imagine a less obvious connection, yet the problem I mention is very real, and may allow a sneaky observer to deduce much of a user's activity, from his passwords to private email that he is typing.

The Need for Randomness

Computers are completely deterministic. They process data in a way that is governed by a well-defined set of laws. Engineers do their best to compensate for imperfections associated with the manufacturing process and the properties of the electronic components themselves (interference, heat noise, and so on), all to ensure that the systems always follow the same logic and work properly; when, with time and stress, components refuse to act as expected, we consider the computer to be faulty.

The ability of machines to achieve this level of consistency, combined with their marvelous calculation capabilities, is what makes computers such a great tool for those who manage to master and control them. Naturally, one thing has to be said: not all is roses, and those who complain of computers being unreliable are not all that mistaken. Despite the perfect operation of the equipment, computer programs themselves do misbehave on various occasions. This is because even though computer hardware can be and often is consistent and reliable, you typically can't make long-term predictions about the behavior of a sufficiently complex computer program, let alone a complex matrix of interdependent programs (such as a typical operating system); this makes validating a computer program quite difficult, even assuming we could come up with a detailed, sufficiently strict and yet flawless hypothetical model of what the program should be doing. Why? Well, in 1936, Alan Turing, the father of modern computing, proved by *reductio ad absurdum* (reduction to the absurd) that there can be no *general* method for determining an outcome of *any* computer procedure, or algorithm, in a finite time (although there may be *specific* methods for *some* algorithms).[1]

This in practice means that while you cannot expect your operating system or text editor to ever behave precisely the way you or the author intend it to, you can reasonably expect that two instances of a text editor on systems running on the same hardware will exhibit consistent and identical behavior given the same input (unless, of course, one of the instances gets crushed by a falling piano or is otherwise influenced by other pesky external events). This is great news for software companies, but nevertheless, in some cases we, the security crowd, would prefer that the computer be a bit less deterministic. Not necessarily in how it behaves, but in what it can come up with.

Take data encryption and especially that mysterious beast, public key cryptography. This novel and brilliant form of encryption (and more), first proposed in the 1970s by Whitfield Diffie and Martin Hellman, and shortly thereafter turned into a full-blown encryption system by Ron Rivest, Adi Shamir, and Len Adleman, is based on a simple concept: some things are more difficult than others. That seems obvious, of course, but just throw in several higher math concepts, and you're all set for a groundbreaking invention.

Traditional, symmetrical cryptography called for an identical shared "secret" value (a key) to be distributed among all parties involved in a secret communication. The key is required and sufficient to encrypt and later decrypt the information transferred, so that a third-party observer who knows the encryption method still cannot figure out the message. The need for a shared secret made the entire approach not always practical in terms of computer communications, primarily because the parties had to establish a secure exchange channel prior to communicating; transferring the secret over a nonsecure stream would render the scheme vulnerable to decryption. In the world of computers, you often communicate with systems or people you have never seen before and with whom you have no other affordable and secure communication channel.

Public key cryptography, on the other hand, is not based on a shared secret. Each party holds two pieces of information: one (the public key) useful for creating an encrypted message, but next to useless for decryption, and the other (the private key) useful for decrypting a previously encrypted message. The parties can now exchange their public keys using an insecure channel even if it is being snooped. They provide each other with the information (meaningless to an observer) needed to encrypt messages between parties, but they keep the portion needed to access the encrypted data private. All of a sudden, secure communications between complete strangers—such as a customer sitting on a sofa in his apartment and an online shopping server—became closer to reality.

Fundamentally, the original RSA (Rivest, Shamir, and Adleman) public key cryptosystem is based on the observation that the computational complexity of multiplying two arbitrarily large numbers is fairly low; it is directly proportional to the number of digits to be multiplied. On the other hand, the complexity of finding factors (factorization) of a large number is considerably higher, unless you are a mythical crypto-genius working for the National Security Agency. The RSA algorithm first chooses two arbitrary, very large primes, [*] p and q, and multiplies them. It then uses the product along with a coprime, [†] $(p-1)(q-1)$, to construct a public key. This key can be used to encrypt information, but it alone is not sufficient to decrypt that information without resorting to factorization.

And the catch: Factorization of products of two large prime numbers is often impractical, foiling such attacks. The fastest universal integer factorization algorithm on traditional computers, general number field sieve (GNFS), would require over a thousand years to find factors of such a 1,024-bit

---

[*] A prime number is a positive integer that divides only by 1 and itself.
[†] A number that is *coprime to x* (also called *relatively prime to x*) shares no common factors with *x*, other than 1 and -1. (Their greatest common divisor is 1.)

integer, at a rate of one million tests per second. Finding two primes that yield a product that big is, on the other hand, a matter of seconds for an average PC.

As indicated before, in RSA, in addition to your public key, you also produce a private key. The private key carries an additional piece of information about the primes that can be used to decrypt any information encrypted with your public key. The trick is possible, thanks to the Chinese Remainder Theorem, Euler's Theorem, and other somewhat scary but fascinating mathematical concepts a particularly curious reader may want to explore on his own.[2]

Some other public key cryptosystems that rely on other hard problems in mathematics were also devised later on (including elliptic curve cryptosystems and so on), but all share the underlying concept of public and private keys. This method has proved practical for securing email, web transactions, and so forth, even if two parties have never communicated and do not have a secure channel to exchange any additional information prior to establishing a connection.[*] Almost every encryption design that we use everyday, from Secure Shell (SSH) and Secure Sockets Layer (SSL) to digitally signed updates or smart cards, are here thanks to the contributions of Diffie, Hellman, Rivest, Shamir, and Adleman.

Automated Random Number Generation

There is only one problem: When implementing RSA on a deterministic machine, the first step is to generate two very large primes, p and q. It is simple for a computer to find a large prime, but there is a tiny issue: the primes also must be impossible for others to guess, and they cannot be the same on every machine. (If they were, the attack on this algorithm would not require any factorization, and p and q would be known to anyone who owns a similar computer.)

Many algorithms have been developed over the past few years to quickly find prime number candidates (pseudo-primes) and to perform rapid preliminary primality tests (used to verify pseudo-primes).[3] But to generate a truly unpredictable prime, we need to use a good dose of entropy or randomness in order to either blindly choose one of the primes within a range, or start at a random place and pick the first prime we stumble upon.

Although the need for some randomness at the time of key generation is essential, the demand does not end there. Public key cryptography relies on fairly complex calculations and is thus fairly slow, particularly when compared with the traditional symmetric key cryptography that uses short shared keys and a set of operations machines that are known to execute very fast.

---

[*] For the sake of completeness, it should be noted that ad-hoc public key cryptography is, among other things, vulnerable to "man in the middle" attacks, where an attacker impersonates one of the endpoints and provides its own, fake public key, in order to be able to intercept communications. To prevent such attacks, additional means of verifying the authenticity of a key must be devised, either by arranging a secure exchange or establishing a central authority to issue or certify keys (public key infrastructure, PKI).

To implement functionality such as SSH, in which reasonable performance is expected, it is more sensible to establish the initial communication and basic verification using public key algorithms, thus creating a secure channel. The next step is to exchange a compact, perhaps 128-bit symmetric encryption key and continue communicating by switching to old-style symmetric cryptography. The main problem with symmetric cryptography is remedied by creating an initial (and slow) secure stream to exchange a shared secret, and then switching to faster algorithms, hence enabling the user to benefit from the higher performance without sacrificing security. Yet, to use symmetric cryptography in a sensible way, we still need to use a certain amount of entropy in order to generate an unpredictable symmetric session key for every secured communication.

The Security of Random Number Generators

Programmers have invented many ways for computers to generate seemingly random numbers; the general name for these algorithms is pseudorandom number generators (PRNGs).

PRNGs suffice for trivial applications, such as generating "random" events for computer games or meaningless subject lines for particularly obtrusive unsolicited bulk mailings. For instance, take the linear congruent (aka power residue) generator,[4] a classic example of such an algorithm. Despite its obscure name, this random number generator performs a sequence of simple operations (multiplication, addition, and modulus[*]) every time it generates its "random" output. The generator uses its previous output r_t to calculate the next output value, r_{t+1} (where t denotes time):

$$r_{t+1} = (a \times r_t + c) \bmod M$$

The modulo operator controls the range and prevents overflows, a situation that occurs when the result at some point goes beyond the predefined range of values. If r_0, a, M, and c—a set of control variables for the generator—are all positive integers, all results of this equation fall in the range of 0 to $M-1$.

Yet, while the output of this algorithm may, with some fine-tuning, exhibit statistical properties that make it suitable for generating random number lookalikes, nothing is genuinely unpredictable about its operations. And therein lies the problem: An attacker can easily develop their own copy of the generator and use it to determine any number of results that our generator will produce. Even if we start with an initial generator state (r_0) that is unknown to the attacker, they can often successfully deduce important properties of this value by observing subsequent outputs of the victim's generator and then use this knowledge to tweak their version of it to mimic ours. In fact, a general method to reconstruct and predict all polynomial

---

[*] The modulo operator returns the remainder of an integer division of two numbers. For example, 7 is divided by 3 yielding an integer result of 2 and a remainder of 1 (7 = 2 * 3 + 1); 7 modulo 3 is thus 1.

congruent generators was devised over a decade ago,[5] and it would be quite unwise to ignore this little, perhaps somewhat inconvenient detail, as it creates a gaping hole in this algorithm when used for mission-critical purposes.

Over time, we have realized that the only sane way for a computer to produce practically unpredictable data, short of suffering a massive memory failure or processor meltdown, is to try to gather as much practically unpredictable information from its physical surroundings as possible and then use that as a value passed to any application that demands good randomness. The problem is, an average computer has no "senses" with which it could probe the environment for seemingly random external signals. Nevertheless, we know a fairly good way to work around this inconvenience.

I/O Entropy: This Is Your Mouse Speaking

On almost every computer system, external devices communicate relevant asynchronous events, such information being made available from the network card or the keyboard, using a hardware interrupt mechanism. Each device has an assigned hardware interrupt (IRQ) number and reports important developments by changing the voltage on a designated hardware line inside the computer, corresponding to this particular IRQ. The change is then interpreted by a device called a *programmable interrupt controller* (PIC), which serves as a personal butler for the main processor (or processors).

Once instructed by the CPU, the PIC decides if, when, how, and with what priority to deliver requests from the external devices to the main unit, which makes it easier for the processor to manage events in an efficient and reliable manner. Upon receipt of a signal from the PIC, the processor postpones its current task, unless of course the CPU had chosen to ignore all interrupt requests at the moment (if it's really busy). Next, it invokes a code assigned by your operating system to handle feedback from this device or group of devices. Once the program handles the event, the CPU restores the original process and its context—the information about the state of its environment at the time of the interruption—and continues as if nothing has happened.

Delivering Interrupts: A Practical Example

In practice, many additional steps are involved in detecting an external condition and then generating and receiving an IRQ. For example, Figure 1-1 shows the sequence of events triggered by pressing or releasing a key on the keyboard. Before you even touch a single key, a tiny microcontroller chip inside your keyboard, serving as a keyboard controller, is busy sweeping the keyboard for any changes to its state.

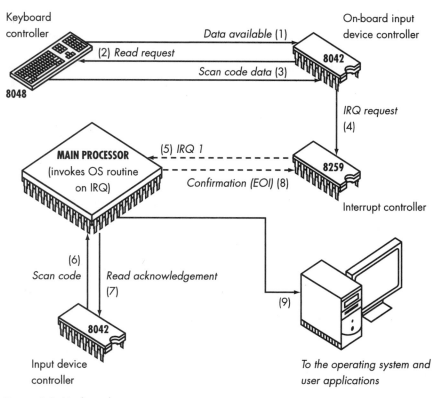

Figure 1-1: Keyboard-to-computer communications

The keyboard is organized as an array of horizontal and vertical wires. Keys (microswitches or pressure-sensitive membrane switches) are installed at the intersection of each row and column. The controller tests every row and column separately, at very high speed.

If, for example, the keyboard controller detects a closed circuit when testing row 3, column 5 (which is signified by low resistance when voltage is applied to these lines), it concludes that the key at this particular location (J) is pressed. When the keyboard controller senses a change, it converts row and column coordinates into a scan code, a value that identifies a key by its unique identifier. The scan code information is then queued in the internal buffer of a chip, which then tells the CPU that there's new data and goes back to minding its own business.

An input controller chip is the keyboard controller's counterpart on the motherboard. The input controller usually handles all basic input devices, such as the mouse and keyboard. It receives a single scan code from the keyboard chip and signals an appropriate interrupt to the CPU's butler, the PIC. As soon as the PIC determines that it can deliver this particular IRQ, the PIC passes this signal to the processor, which then usually interrupts its current task and invokes the interrupt handler installed by the operating system. The handler is expected to read the data and to tell the chip that it has read the scan code successfully. The input controller then resumes its normal operations and eventually reads another scan code from the keyboard if there is any data in the buffer.*

This scheme is important to random number generation, although its significance is indirect. The computer, using the asynchronous event notification scheme (interrupts), receives almost instantaneous and precise feedback about user activity—perhaps most interestingly, accurately measured delays between keystrokes. Although the information is not always unpredictable, it is perhaps the best source of external, measurable, somewhat indeterministic signal the machine can get. And so, in order to work around the deterministic nature of the computer and to insert randomness in their calculations, authors of secure PRNG implementations resort to gathering entropy from generally unpredictable behavior of certain devices, such as the mouse, keyboard, network interfaces, and sometimes disk drives. To do so, they add an extra code inside an interrupt handler for the operating system that records certain parameters for every acceptable event.

Although it can be argued that neither of those sources provide truly random feedback all the time—for example, it is likely that after the user types aardva, the next two characters are going to be rk—some of the behavior, such as my thinking of aardvarks to begin with, is indeed rather unpredictable, from a practical standpoint (and not getting into an academic discussion of free will and deterministic universes). This method of adding entropy works reason-ably well because it incorporates several factors that cannot be reasonably considered and monitored or predicted by an attacker while still maintaining their sanity. By gathering data from all those sources for an extended period of time, the laws of probability tell us that we will collect a certain amount of entropy. By collecting the data in a buffer, we construct an entropy pool that can be full or depleted, depending on the supply and demand for unpredict-able data. Unfortunately, these small bits of randomness within the pool—where our typing was influenced by cosmic events—is still mixed with plenty of easily predictable data and as such can't be immediately used for random number generation.

To ensure that the amount of actual entropy collected in the process of maintaining and replenishing the entropy pool is spread evenly over all PRNG output bits (with all unpredictable data expended), the pool has to be hashed; that is, it has to be stirred and mixed throughly so that no section of the data is easier to predict than any other. Every bit of the output must depend equally on all the input bits, in a nontrivial way. Achieving this without knowing which pieces of information are predictable and which are not (information that is not readily available to a computer monitoring keystrokes or mouse movements) can be a difficult task.

---

* On many architectures, it is necessary to manually instruct the PIC that the interrupt has been processed and that it should no longer block subsequent interrupts. This is done with the End of Interrupt (EOI) code.

One-Way Shortcut Functions

Luckily enough, secure one-way hashing ("message digest") functions, a flagship product of modern cryptography, can assist us with mixing data to get the most entropy into every bit of output, regardless of how nonuniform the input. These are functions that generate a fixed-length shortcut: a unique identifier of an arbitrary block of input data. But that is not all.

All one-way hashing functions have two important properties:

- It is easy to calculate the shortcut, but not possible to deduce the original message or any of its properties from the result. Any specific change to the message is just as likely to affect all properties of the output as any other change.

- The likelihood of two distinct messages having the same shortcut is determined only by the size of the shortcut. With a sufficiently large shortcut (large enough to make exhaustive searches impractical, nowadays set at around 128 to 160 bits, or circa 3.4E+38 to 1.46E+48 combinations), it is not possible to find two messages that would have the same shortcut.

As a result, shortcut functions provide a means for distributing entropy present in the input data in a uniform way over the output data. This solves the problem with generally random but locally predictable entropy sources: we gather an approximate amount of entropy from the environment, mixed with predictable data or not, and can generate a shortcut that is guaranteed to be just as unpredictable as the entropy collected in the first place, regardless of how the input entropy was distributed in the input data.

How do shortcut functions work? Some again rely on mathematical problems that are, as far as we know, very difficult to solve. In fact, any safe symmetrical or public key cryptography algorithm can be easily turned into a secure hashing function. As long as humanity does not come up with a really clever solution to any of these problems, relying on this approach should be fine.

Yet, by rolling out heavy artillery, we end up with slow and overly complicated tools to generate shortcuts, which is often impractical for compact implementations, particularly when integrating such a solution with an operating system. The alternative is to process the data so that the interdependency between all bits of input and output is sufficiently complex so as to fully obfuscate the input message and hope this is "good enough" to stop known cryptoanalysis techniques. Because "hopefully good enough" is actually the motto for a good chunk of computer science, we gladly accept this as a reasonable approach.

The advantage of the latter group of algorithms, which includes popular functions such as MD2, MD4, MD5, and SHA-1, is that they are generally , much faster and easier to use than their counterparts based on difficult mathematical challenges and, when well designed, are not susceptible to cryptoanalysis tricks of the trade. Their weakness is that they are not provably secure because none of them reduces to a classic, hard-to-solve problem. Indeed, some have been proved to have specific weaknesses.[6]

As suggested earlier, a great service of shortcut functions to pseudo-random number generation is that they can be run on a segment of data that contains n random bits, and any number of predictable bits, to produce a shortcut that will spread n bits of entropy evenly across all bits of the shortcut (thanks to the two fundamental one-way shortcut function properties discussed earlier). As a result, the shortcut function becomes a convenient entropy extractor. By running a sufficient amount of data collected from a generally unpredictable interrupt handler through a shortcut function, we can generate random numbers without disclosing any valuable information about the exact shape of the information used to generate the number, and without the risk of imperfect input affecting the output in any meaningful way. All we need to do is to ensure that there is a sufficient amount of entropy collected and feed into a shortcut function within a chunk of interrupt data, else we risk compromising the entire scheme. If the attacker can predict considerable portions of the data we use for random number generation, and the remainder has only a handful of possible combinations, they can throw a successful brute-force attack against our implementation by simply trying and verifying all possible values. If, for example, we use a shortcut function that produces 128-bit digests, no matter how much data we actually collected, be it 200 bytes or 2 megabytes worth of keyboard tapping, we must be sure that at least 128 of these input bits are unpredictable to the attacker before hashing it.

The Importance of Being Pedantic

As an example of when things can go wrong, consider a user who decides to write a shell script when a system entropy pool is empty, perhaps due to some random number-hungry operation that was performed a while ago. The attacker notices that the user is writing a script because vi delallusers.sh is being executed; they further assume that the script must have started with something along the lines of #!/bin/sh. Although they cannot be sure what is coming next, they can reasonably expect that the script will open with an invocation of a shell command and that it is somewhat less likely to continue with a tacky poem about aardvarks.

At this point, an encryption utility of some kind suddenly asks the system for a 128-bit random number to be used as a session key to protect communications. However, the system fails to correctly estimate the amount of entropy available in the buffer that recorded the process of writing the first lines of the script, and the attacker now has an easy task. The computer is devoid of the information whether this particular action performed by the user at the very moment is predictable to others or not. It can only speculate (aided by the assumptions made by the programmer) that, over the course of a couple of minutes or hours, users' actions will sum up to something that could not be precisely predicted and that, on average, this much of the input indeed would depend on factors unpredictable to the attacker.

The attacker, at this point, knows most of the entropy pool contents and is left with barely thousands of options to choose from when it comes to the unknown part—despite the fact that the operating system is convinced that there is far more entropy in the buffer. These thousands are hardly a big challenge for someone assisted by a computer. Consequently, instead of getting a 128-bit random number, which has a 39-digit number of combinations, an unsuspecting cryptography application ends up with a number generated from input that could have been only one of a couple thousand of options, easily verifiable by the attacker by trial and error, and the attacker can soon decrypt the information that was supposed to remain secure.

Entropy Is a Terrible Thing to Waste

Because it is next to impossible to accurately predict the amount of entropy collected from a user in a short run, in order to prevent the predictable PRNG output problem discussed previously, all implementations include the shortcut or internal PRNG state in the process of generating new output. The previous output becomes a part of the equation used to calculate the next PRNG value.

In this design, once a sufficient amount of entropy is initially gathered in the system, the most recent data used to replenish the entropy pool does not need to be fully random at all times in order to ensure basic security.

Yet, there is another problem. If the implementation runs for a prolonged period of time on old, inherited entropy, only hashed again and again with MD5 or SHA-1, it becomes fully dependent on the security of the shortcut algorithm, which cannot be completely trusted due to the performance and security trade-off discussed before. Moreover, the hashing functions have not necessarily undergone an appropriate evaluation of suitability for this particular use from competent cryptographers. The implementation no longer relies simply on the bit hashing properties of a shortcut function and now fully depends on its invulnerability to cracking attacks. If, with every subsequent step, a small amount of information about the internal state of the generator is disclosed, and no new unpredictable data is added to the pool, in the long run, the data may suffice to reconstruct or guess the internal state with reasonable certainty, which makes it possible to predict the future behavior of the device. On the other hand, if new random data is added at a rate that, at least statistically, prevents a significant reuse of the internal state, the attack becomes much less feasible even if the hashing function is fundamentally broken.

Many experts believe this level of trust and reliance on the hashing function should not be exercised for the most demanding applications. Hence, it is important for an implementation to keep track of an estimated amount of entropy collected in the system, which, even if not momentarily correct, reflects a general statistical trend we would expect from the sources used. Minor short-term fluctuations in the availability of external entropy, such as the script editing example discussed previously, may occur and will be compensated for by the output reuse algorithm. Still, it is necessary to make accurate long-term predictions to ensure frequent replenishing of the internal entropy pool and to minimize exposure should the hashing function turn out to leak internal state over time. As such, the implementation has to account for all entropy spent in data supplied to user processes and refuse to supply more random numbers until a sufficient amount of entropy is available.

A good example of a proper PRNG implementation that takes all the above into account is the excellent system devised and implemented in 1994 by Theodore Ts'o of the Massachusetts Institute of Technology. His mechanism, /dev/random, was first implemented in Linux and later introduced to systems such as FreeBSD, NetBSD, and HP/UX. Ts'o's mechanism monitors a number of system I/O events, measuring time intervals and other important interrupt characteristics. It also preserves the entropy pool during system shutdowns by saving it to disk, which prevents the system from booting up to a fully predictable state, making it even more difficult to attack.

Attack: The Implications of a Sudden Paradigm Shift

What could be the problem with this seemingly fool-proof scheme for supplying unpredictable random numbers to demanding applications? Nothing, at least not where you would expect it. The numbers generated are indeed difficult to predict.

There is, however, one slight but disastrous mistake in the reasoning of the designer of this technology. Mr. Ts'o's design assumes that the attacker is interested in predicting random numbers based on knowledge of the machine and its environment. But what if the attacker wants to do quite the opposite?

The attacker with an account on the machine, even though they have no direct access to the information the user is typing, can deduce the exact moment input activity is occurring in the system by emptying the entropy pool (which can be achieved by simply requesting random data from the system and discarding it) and then monitoring the availability of PRNG output. If there is no I/O activity, the PRNG will not have any new data available, because the entropy estimate won't change. If a keystroke or a key release occurs, a small amount of information will be available to the attacker, who may then deduce that a key was pressed or released.

Other events, such as disk activity, also generate some PRNG output, but the amount and timing patterns of entropy gathered this way differ from the characteristics of keyboard interrupt data. As such, it is possible and easy to discern events by the amount of data available at any given time. The data from keystrokes will look different from the data from disk activity.

In the end, a method for assuring the highest possible level of safety for secure random number generation actually results in degrading the privacy of the user: the availability of this mechanism to estimate the amount of entropy available from an external source can be abused and used to monitor certain aspects of input activities on the system. Although the attacker cannot detect exactly what is being typed, there are strong timing patterns for writing different words on the keyboard, especially if precise key press and release information is present, as it is in this case. By examining those patterns, the attacker can deduce the actual input, or at least guess it more easily.

A Closer Look at Input Timing Patterns

An in-depth analysis led by a team of researchers at the University of California[7] indicates that it is possible to deduce certain properties of user input, or even fully reconstruct the data, by looking only at inter-keystroke timing. The research concluded that, for seamless typing and a keyboard-proficient operator, there might be some variation in inter-keystroke timings, but dominant timing patterns for each key-to-key transition are clearly visible.

The reason is that our hands lie on the keyboard a certain way and that the key position on the keyboard affects how fast we can reach a key with our fingertips. For example, the interval between pressing e and n is generally different from the interval between m and l. In the first case, because one hand controls the left side of the keyboard, and the other controls the right side (see Figure 1-2), typing both characters requires almost no movement, and both keys are pressed almost simultaneously, with a time interval of less than 100 milliseconds. Typing m and l requires a fairly awkward fingering and takes much longer.

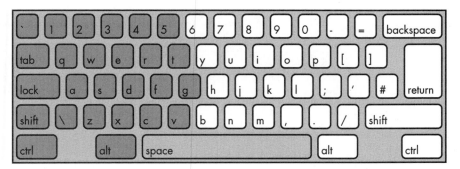

Figure 1-2: The usual territory for each hand. Dark-gray keys are usually controlled by the left hand, and white areas are controlled by the right hand.

After analyzing a number of samples, the authors of this research estimate that approximately 1.2 bits of information per key pressed can be acquired from the timing data. By observing sequence delays, it is possible to determine the set of keyboard inputs most likely to generate this pattern, thus making it easier to guess the exact sequence of keys pressed. The idea of counting fractions of bits may sound ridiculous, but what this really means is that the number of possibilities for every key can be reduced by $2^{1.2}$, or approximately 2.40 times. For a single regular keystroke, which usually carries no more than 6 bits of randomness to begin with, this reduces the option set from about 64 to 26 elements.

The net effect is that this reduces the level of search space; we can see that there's a way to limit the number of possibilities if we want to guess at what keys are being typed. Although this reduction may not be particularly impressive on its own, add to this that the data entered from the keyboard is not likely to be just random garbage to start with. The entropy of English text is estimated to be as low as 0.6 to 1.3 bits per character,[8] meaning that it on average takes approximately 1.5 to 2.5 attempts to successfully predict the next character. With a method to further reduce the search space, it is possible to find nonambiguous dictionary word matches for almost all the input data.

To verify their estimates and demonstrate the issue in practice, the researchers used the Hidden Markov Model and Viterbi algorithm to guess keystrokes. A Markov Model is a method for describing a discrete system in which the next value depends only on its current state, and not on the previous values (Markov chain). The Hidden Markov Model is a variant that provides a method for describing a system for which each internal state generates an observation, but for which the actual state is not known. This model is commonly used in applications such as speech recognition, in which the goal is to obtain pure data (a textual representation of the spoken word) from its specific manifestation (sampled waveform).

The authors conclude that the Hidden Markov Model is applicable to keystroke analysis, and they consider the internal state of the system to be the information about keys pressed; the observation in the Hidden Markov Model is the inter-keystroke timing.

It might be argued that this is an oversimplification, because, most notably in the situation pictured in Figure 1-3, there might be a deeper dependency.

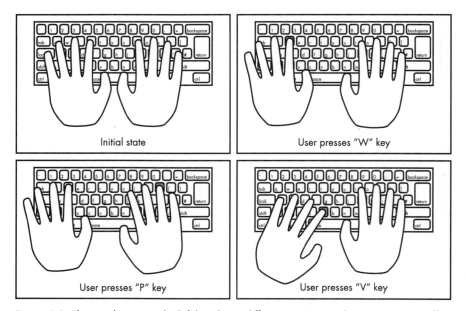

Figure 1-3: The need to move the left hand to a different position in the previous step affects the P-V timing. The Markov Model is unable to take a previous location of the hand on hand-switch scenarios into account.

The Viterbi algorithm is one way to solve Hidden Markov Model problems. The algorithm can be used to find the most likely sequence of internal states based on a sequence of observations. In this particular case, we use it to determine the most likely sequence of characters based on a sequence of timings.

The final result of applying the Viterbi algorithm is a reduction of the search space for nondictionary eight-character passwords by a factor of 50. For reconstruction of typed dictionary-based English text, the factor is likely to be considerably higher.

Now let's look at interrupt monitoring. The research we've just discussed focused on partial information available by snooping on Secure Shell (SSH) traffic patterns. In the case of interrupt monitoring, the attacker has considerably more information available. For one thing, keystroke duration information is available as well as inter-keystroke timings, with the duration of a single keystroke depending on the finger used. For example the index finger usually makes the shortest contact with the key, the ring finger is probably the slowest, and so on. This is valuable information, which makes it much easier to locate an approximate area of keys on the keyboard.

Second, the data also enables the attacker to monitor hand transitions, the moment when the first character is typed by the left hand, and the second by the right hand, or vice versa. Because each hand is controlled by a different hemisphere of the brain, almost all proficient keyboard users often press the second key before releasing the first when switching hands. Although key press and release events are indistinguishable as such, a particularly short interval of time between two keyboard events is a clear sign of this phenomenon. In some rare situations, particularly when the typist is in a hurry, the second key press occurs not only before the release, but even before the press of the first key. This results in popular typographic errors such as "teh" instead of "the."

Figure 1-4 shows a capture of sample keyboard timings. The user types the word *evil*. The middle finger of the left hand presses e for a medium period of time. Then, there is a considerable interval before the typist presses v due to the need to move the entire hand in order to reach v with the index finger. (The thumb cannot be used because the spacebar gets in the way.) "The v is pressed for a short period of time, as is i, with both accessed by the index finger. There is also a visible overlap: i is pressed before v is released due to a hand transition. Finally, the ring finger presses l after a while (there is no need to move the hand), and the contact is quite long.

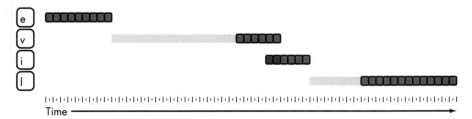

Figure 1-4: Key press and release timing for hand transitions

Hence, it is reasonable to expect that it is possible to achieve a much higher success ratio in this attack. (Most of this information was not available in the scenario discussed in the aforementioned white paper.)

Immediate Defense Tactics

Now that we know the potential for keyboard sniffing, how do we thwart it? The best way is to employ a separate keyboard entropy buffer of a reasonable size. The buffer is flushed and passed down to the core PRNG implementation only after it overflows or after a time interval considerably larger than the usual inter-keystroke delay (that is, at least several seconds) passes, thus eliminating the attacker's ability to measure timing.

With this solution, only two types of information are available to the attacker. The first results from the flush on overflow procedure and discloses to the attacker that a number of keys (depending on the buffer size) were pressed in a measurable period of time, but does not divulge exact key interval timings. The second possibility is a result of a timed flush sequence, and informs the attacker that a key or several keys were pressed during a fixed time frame, but does not provide any information about the number of events and their precise time of occurrence. The information provided in this way is of a marginal value for timing attacks and can only be used for generating general statistics of keyboard activity, the latter not posing a threat in most multiuser environments.

Hardware RNG: A Better Solution?

A number of today's hardware platforms implement physical random number generators, often referred to as TRNGs, or true random number generators. These devices provide a more reliable way of generating truly unpredictable data, as opposed to gathering information that is merely expected to be difficult to predict, and are a recommended way of acquiring entropy on all machines equipped with this hardware. Two popular solutions, as of this writing, are integrated circuits developed by Intel and VIA.

Intel RNG is integrated with chip sets such as i810 and uses a conventional design of two oscillators. The high-frequency oscillator generates a base signal, which is essentially a pattern of alternating logical states (010101010101...). The other oscillator is a low-frequency device, working at a nominal rate of 1/100 the frequency of the high-speed oscillator, but its actual frequency is modulated by a resistor, which serves as a primary source of entropy.

Certain measurable characteristics of a resistor change as a result of thermal noise and other random material effects. The low-frequency oscillator is used to drive sampling of the alternating signal at now random frequencies (falling edge of the oscillator output). The signal, after some necessary conditioning and "whitening" using von Neumann correction, is then made available to the outside world. A careful analysis of the design and actual output of the generator performed by Benjamin Jun and Paul Kocher of Cryptography Research[9] has shown that the quality of the output is consistently high and that the generator provides an estimated 0.999 bits of entropy per output bit.

VIA C3 "Nehemiah" RNG is based on a slightly different design that uses a set of oscillators, but not a separate source of noise, such as a special resistor hookup. Instead, it relies on the internal jitter of the oscillators, an effect that can be attributed to a number of internal and external factors and additionally controlled by a configurable "bias" setting.

In this case, a separate analysis led by Cryptography Research[10] indicated the generator apparently delivers a lower-quality entropy than its counter-part, ranging from 0.855 to 0.95 bits per output bit. This is a dangerous result if the RNG output is taken as fully random as-is and used for key generation or other critical tasks 1:1, because the amount of actual entropy is reduced accordingly. To solve this problem, we can acquire more data than necessary from the generator and then run the data via a secure hashing function, such as SHA-1, to eliminate any eventual bias or entropy deficiency. The solution is a general good practice for preventing TRNG issues, as long as these unde-sirable effects are within reasonable limits—that is, each bit still carries some useful entropy.

Several researchers have also suggested using certain nonspecialized input devices, such as webcams or built-in microphones, as a source of entropy: Charge Coupled Device (CCD) sensors in digital cameras tend to exhibit pixel noise, and a severely overamplified microphone signal is essentially a good source of random noise. However, there is no universal method for setting up such a generator due to the differences in circuits of popular media devices from various manufacturers, and as such the quality of "random" numbers generated this way cannot be assured. In fact, some devices pick up seemingly random but fully predictable radio interference or certain in-circuit signals. Additionally, some devices, in particular CCD sensors, exhibit static noise patterns. While seemingly random, this noise is not changing rapidly and may be dangerous to rely on.

Food for Thought

I have decided to omit in-depth discussion of a few interesting concepts, but these may be a valuable inspiration for further explorations.

Remote Timing Attacks

In theory, it might be possible to deploy the PRNG timing attack over a network. Certain cryptography-enabled services implement symmetrical cryptography. After establishing a slower asymmetric stream using public key infrastructure and verifying both parties, a symmetrical session key is generated, and both endpoints switch to a faster symmetrical alternative.

- It might be possible to time keystrokes by causing the application to exhaust an existing entropy pool in the system to the point that there is not enough entropy to seed a new session key, but only by a small fraction. The application will then delay generating a symmetrical key until enough entropy to seed the remainder of a key is available, and this will occur, among other possibilities, on the next key press or release.

- It is my belief that the attack is more likely to succeed in a laboratory setup than in any real-world practical application, although my technical reviewer disagrees with my skepticism, and so, consider it to be merely an opinion. An interesting analysis from the University of Virginia criticized the original SSH timing research discussed in the paper mentioned before on the grounds that network jitter is sufficient to render timing data unusable, although it is worth noting that if a specific activity is repeated over time (for example, the same password is entered upon every login), random network performance fluctuations may very well average out.[11]

Exploiting System Diagnostics

Some systems have better ways to recover the keystroke information and other timing data. After publishing my PRNG timing research, it was pointed out to me that Linux provides a /proc/interrupts interface that displays interrupt summary statistics, with the intention of providing some useful performance data. By examining interrupt counter changes for IRQ 1, it is possible to obtain the same timing information that is acquired via PRNG, already filtered of any eventual disk and network activity inclusions, thus causing a privacy exposure similar to the one discussed before.

Reproducible Unpredictability

Other issues worth considering are related to the PRNG implementation itself. Buying identical hardware in bulk and installing the same system on each device is a common practice and can be a problem for servers that do not experience heavy console activity. There is also a risk of mirroring an installation using specialized duplication tools and then propagating the image across a number of servers. In all situations, systems can end up with low real entropy for perhaps a bit too long.

2

EXTRA EFFORTS
NEVER GO UNNOTICED

*Where we learn how to build a wooden computer and how to
obtain information from watching a real computer run*

The data you entered is now safe in the hands of the
application you chose to run. The program will take its
time deciding what to do with the information, how to
interpret it, and which actions to take next.

In this chapter, we examine the low-level mechanics of data processing
in detail and explore some of the pitfalls that can lurk deep beneath the heat
sink of your processor. We pay particular attention to the information we can
deduce simply by observing how a machine executes given programs and
how much time it takes to complete certain tasks. As a bonus, we'll also build
a fully functional wooden computer.

Boole's Heritage

To understand the design of a processor, we must return to the days when
processors had not yet been dreamed of. It all started quite innocently back in
the 19th century, when self-taught mathematician George Boole (1815–64)
devised a simple binary algebra system intended to provide a framework for
understanding and modeling formal calculus. His approach reduced the

fundamental concepts of logic to a set of three, simple algebraic operations that could be applied to elements representing two opposite states, true and false. These operations are:

- The disjunction operator, **OR**. This is true when at least one of its operands[*] is true.[†]

- The conjunction operator, **AND**. This is only true when all its operands are true.

- The complement (negation) operator, **NOT**. This is true when its only operand is false.

Although simple in design, the Boolean algebraic model turned out to be a powerful tool for solving logic problems and certain other mathematical challenges. Ultimately, it made it possible for many brave visionaries to dream of clever analytic machines that would one day change our daily lives.

Today, Boolean logic is seldom a mystery for the experienced computer user, but the path from this set of trivial operations to today's computer often is. We'll begin exploring this path by first attempting to capture the essence of this model at its simplest.

Toward the Universal Operator

The path to simplicity often leads through a seemingly needless level of complexity—and this case is no exception. To even begin, we must consider the work of another 19th-century mathematician, Augustus DeMorgan (1806–71). DeMorgan's law states that "a complement of disjunction is the conjunction of complements." This infamous exercise in obfuscating trivial concepts has some profound consequences for Boolean logic and, ultimately, the design of digital circuits.

In plain English, DeMorgan's law explains that when any (or both) of two conditions is not satisfied, a sentence that claims that both conditions are met (or, in other words, a conjunction of conditions occurs) will be false as well—oh, and vice versa.

The law concludes that NOT OR (a, b) should be logically equivalent to AND (NOT a, NOT b). Consider a real-world example in which a and b represent the following:

a = "Bob likes milk"

b = "Bob likes apples"

The two sides of the DeMorgan's equation can be now written as:

OR (NOT a, NOT b) ⇔ Bob does NOT like milk OR does NOT like apples

NOT AND (a, b) ⇔ It is NOT true that Bob likes both milk AND apples

---

[*] The operand is something that is operated on by the operator.
[†] The meaning of logical OR differs from the common English understanding of this term: the resulting statement remains true both when only one of the OR parameters is true and when all are. In English, "or" typically means that *only* one option is true.

Both expressions are functionally equivalent. If it is true that Bob dislikes either milk or apples, the first expression is true; it is then also true that he does not like both, which means that the second expression is also true.

Reversing the situation also results in agreement: If it is not true that Bob dislikes at least one of the choices, he likes both (and the first expression is false). In that case, it is also not true that he does not like both (and the second expression is also false).

DeMorgan at Work

To evaluate logic statements beyond appeals to intuition and some hand waving, it helps to construct so-called truth tables that demonstrate all the results that can be calculated from all possible combinations of true and false operators.

The following two tables represent each expression from the previous example. Each table includes columns for both operators and the corresponding results for all possible true and false combinations. And so, in the first row, you can see that two first columns—both operands to NOT AND(a, b)—are false. This causes AND(a, b) to be false, as well, hence causing NOT AND(a, b) to be true. The outcome is denoted in the third column.

As you can see, the two expressions behave identically:

NOT AND(a, b): AND w/Result Negated		
Operand 1 (a)	**Operand 2 (b)**	**Result**
FALSE	FALSE	TRUE
FALSE	TRUE	TRUE
TRUE	FALSE	TRUE
TRUE	TRUE	FALSE

OR(NOT a, NOT b): OR w/Operands Negated		
Operand 1	**Operand 2**	**Result**
FALSE	FALSE	TRUE
FALSE	TRUE	TRUE
TRUE	FALSE	TRUE
TRUE	TRUE	FALSE

But why do computer designers care about Bob's food preferences? Because in the context of Boolean operators, DeMorgan's law means that the set of basic operations proposed by Boolean algebra is actually partially redundant: a combination of NOT and any of the two other operators (OR and AND) is always sufficient to synthesize the remaining one. For example:

OR (a, b) ⟺ NOT AND (NOT a, NOT b)

AND (a, b) ⟺ NOT OR(NOT a, NOT b)

This understanding reduces the set of operators to two, but the Boolean system can be simplified still further.

Convenience Is a Necessity

Several additional operators are not crucial for implementing Boolean logic, but complement the existing set of operations. These additional operators, NAND and NOR, are true only when AND and OR respectively are false:

NAND(a, b) ⇔ NOT AND(a, b) ⇔ OR(NOT a, NOT b)

NOR(a, b) ⇔ NOT OR(a, b) ⇔ AND(NOT a, NOT b)

These new functions are no more complex than AND and OR. Each has a four-state (four-row) truth table, and hence its value can determined with just as much effort.

NOTE   *NOR and NAND are not found in the basic set of operands because neither one corresponds to a commonly used, basic type of logical relation between sentences and has no atomic representation in the common language.*

I have just introduced a set of new operators, derived from the existing set, that seem to offer nothing but a dubious convenience feature for those wanting to express more bizarre logic dependencies or problems using formal notation. What for?

The introduction of NAND or NOR alone makes it possible to get rid of AND, OR, and NOT altogether. This furthers our goal of simplicity and affords us the ability to describe the entire Boolean algebra system with fewer elements and operators.

The importance of those negated auxiliary operators is that you can use any one of them to build a complete Boolean algebra system. In fact, you can construct all basic operators using NAND, as shown here (*T* stands for a true statement, and *F* stands for false[*]). How? Well, quite obviously, the following pairs of statements are equivalent:

NOT a ⇔ NAND(*T*, a)

AND(a, b) ⇔ NOT NAND(a, b) ⇔ NAND(*T*, NAND(a, b))

OR(a, b) ⇔ NAND(NOT a, NOT b) ⇔ NAND(NAND(*T*, a), NAND(*T*, b))

or, if we prefer to rely exclusively on NOR, rather than NAND, we can say

NOT a ⇔ NOR(*F*, a)

OR(a, b) ⇔ NOT NOR(a, b) ⇔ NOR(*F*, NOR(a, b))

AND(a, b) ⇔ NOR(NOT a, NOT b) ⇔ NOR(NOR(*F*, a), NOR(*F*, b))

---

[*]Purists may want to assume that *T* is equivalent to AND(a, a), for example, which is always true, and *F* is equivalent to NOT AND (a, a), which is always false. In other words, we do not introduce a new concept or equation element—we only simplify the notation a bit at this point.

Embracing the Complexity

It can be hard to believe that the essence of all computing can be captured within one of the universal logic operators. You can implement most complex algorithms, advanced computations, cutting-edge games, and Internet browsing using an array of simple circuits that involve one of the following truth tables, which convert input signals to output signals:

NAND State Table		
Operand 1	**Operand 2**	**Result**
FALSE	FALSE	TRUE
FALSE	TRUE	TRUE
TRUE	FALSE	TRUE
TRUE	TRUE	FALSE

NOR State Table		
Operand 1	**Operand 2**	**Result**
FALSE	FALSE	TRUE
FALSE	TRUE	FALSE
TRUE	FALSE	FALSE
TRUE	TRUE	FALSE

It would seem we are going nowhere, though. . . . How come this trivial set of dependencies make it possible to build a device capable of solving complex problems, such as rejecting your credit application in a tactful manner? And what does a piece of theory based on the states "true" and "false" have in common with digital circuits?

Toward the Material World

There is nothing complex about the mechanism devised by Boole: it calls for two opposite logic states, "true" and "false," 0 and 1, "cyan" and "purple," 999 and 999 ½. The actual meaning, the physical representation, and the medium are irrelevant; what matters is the arbitrarily chosen convention that assigns certain states of the medium to a specific set of logic values.

Computers as we know them use two different voltage levels in an electronic circuit and interpret them as values their designers refer to as 0 and 1. These values, which are carried through the electric circuit, represent two digits in the binary system—but nothing is stopping a person from using just about any method to convey the data, from water flow, to chemical reactions, to smoke signals, to torques transmitted by a set of masterfully crafted wooden gears. The information remains the same, regardless of its carrier.

The key to implementing Boolean logic in the physical world is simple, once we agree on the physical representation of logic values. Next, we need only find a way to arrange a set of components to manipulate those values in order to accommodate any task we want our computer to perform (but more about this later). First, let's try to find out how to manipulate signals and implement real-world logic devices, commonly referred to as gates. Wooden gates, that is.

A Nonelectric Computer

Moving from a set of theoretical operations spawned by the world of pure mathematics to a device that can moderate water flow, torques, or electrical signals in a way that mimics one of the logic operators appears to be a difficult task—but it isn't.

Figure 2-1 shows a trivial gear set mechanism that implements NOR functionality using torque-based logic. The "output" wheel at idle represents state 0; when a torque is applied to the wheel, its state is 1. The device transmits torque from an external source to the output *only* if no torque is applied to two control "input" wheels. In theory, there is no need for an external source of energy, and the design could be simpler; in practice, however, friction and other problems would make it fairly difficult to build a more complex set of fully self-contained gates.

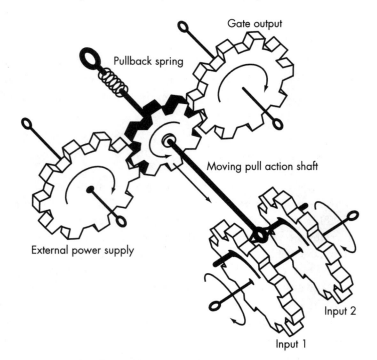

Figure 2-1: Mechanical NOR gate design

Applying a torque to either or both of the inputs will pull out the tiny connector gear and make the "output" gear idle. When inputs go idle, a spring pulls the connector gear back to its position. The truth table for this device is exactly what NOR should be.

As you will recall, NOR or NAND are all we need to implement any Boolean logic operator. Although adding the ability to implement other operators without recombining NAND and NOR gates would make our device smaller and more efficient, the device does not need this ability in order to work.

Assuming we skip the pesky detail of making all the gates work together in a way we are accustomed with, we can conclude that computers can be built with almost any technology.[*]

A Marginally More Popular Computer Design

Although the computer boom of the last several decades sprang from the ingenious transistor, our reliance on it is not associated with any magical value or unique quality. Quite simply, it is the most affordable, usable, and efficient design we have at the moment.

Unlike the possibly far superior wooden gear machine, the electronic computers we use relay electrical signals using transistors, which are tiny devices that let a current flow in one direction between two of their nodes (connection points) when a voltage is applied to the third node. Transistors can be miniaturized quite efficiently, require little power, and are reliable and cheap.

Logic Gates

The transistor is simple. In fact, it alone is too simple a device to implement any meaningful Boolean logic. Yet, when properly arranged in logic gates, transistors make it easy to perform all basic and supplementary Boolean algebra operations.

The AND gate can be implemented by arranging two transistors serially, so that both must have low resistance (be "on") before the voltage can flow to the output. Each transistor is controlled (activated) by a separate input line. The output is nominally "pulled down" using a resistor, so that it has the ground voltage 0 ("false"), but will go up past 0 once both transistors switch on and allow a slight current flow.

The OR gate is implemented by setting up a parallel transistor so that it is sufficient for any of the transistors to enable in order for the output to be set to a nonzero voltage, signifying "truth."

---

[*] And, needless to say, nonelectric computers are not a tall tale. Famous examples of such devices include Charles Babbage's Analytical Engine, and technologies such as nanotechnology also hold some promise. See Ralph C. Merkle, "Two Types of Mechanical Reversible Logic," *Nanotechnology* 4 (1993).

The last basic gate, NOT, is implemented using a single transistor and a resistor. "NOT" output is 1 in the idle state (pulled up through the resistor) and gets pulled down to 0 when the transistor opens.

Figure 2-2 shows the three most basic transistor gate designs: AND, OR, and NOT.

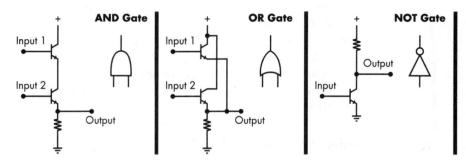

Figure 2-2: Transistor-based logic gates—construction and symbols

NOTE   *You might notice that both AND and OR gates can be turned into NAND and NOR without introducing additional components. It is sufficient to use a design observed on the schematics for a NOT gate—that is, by moving the resistor and "output point" toward the supply voltage, thus reverting the output logic.*

We have now reached a point where we can combine transistors to implement one of the universal gates, but regardless of how many gates we can build, it is still quite far from real computing.

The preceding discussion is all well and good, but what makes Boolean logic more than a powerful tool for solving puzzles about Bob's diet?

From Logic Operators to Calculations

Combining trivial Boolean logic operations can lead to a number of surprising capabilities, such as the ability to perform arithmetic operations on binary representations of numbers. This is where things get interesting.

A set of XOR and AND gates, for example, can be used to increase an input number by 1, and this is the first step on our way toward addition. Figure 2-3 shows a design for a counter, based on this concept.

Ah, a new term! XOR is yet another "convenient" Boolean logic operator that is true only when one of its operands is true. In this regard, it is closer to the usual meaning of "or" in English. XOR is often used to simplify notation, but otherwise easy to implement by other means, by recombining AND, NOT, and OR. It is defined this way:

$$XOR(a, b) \Leftrightarrow AND(OR(a, b), NOT\ AND(a, b))$$

Back to the circuit of ours . . . what can it do? The device shown in Figure 2-3 is fed with a number written in binary. In this example, that number is limited to three bits, although this design could easily be extended to allow for a larger number of inputs.

Input number

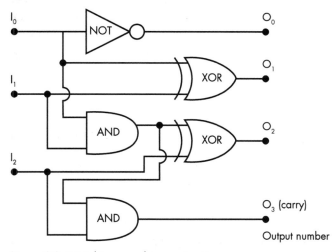

Figure 2-3: Trivial increase-by-one circuit

This simple computation device works the way humans add decimal numbers on a piece of paper—working from right to left, eventually carrying a value to the next column. The only real difference is that it uses binary.

Let's see how that would happen. We have a binary number written in a line. We want to increase it by one; we start at the rightmost digit, the way we would do with decimal addition.

We have a binary digit there; when increasing a binary digit by 1, only two outcomes are possible: if the input digit is 0, the output is 1 $(0 + 1 = 1)$; otherwise, the output is 0, and we need to carry 1 to the next column $(1 + 1 = 10)$. In other words, we do two things: we produce an output that is a negation of the input (1 for 0, 0 for 1), and, if the input digit is 1, we must keep that in mind and include it later.

The circuit does just that: for the first input, I_0. The topmost gate processes the input by negating it and supplying it on output O_0 and also feeds the input value itself to the gates that are responsible for handling the next column (O_1).

$$O_0 = NOT\ I_0$$
$$C_0 = I_0$$

Well, we have increased the number by one; there is nothing else for us to do in the remaining columns if there is no carry from the previous one. If there is no carry, O_1 should mirror I_1. If there is a carry value, however, we need to treat the case the same way we handled adding 1 to the previous column: negate the output and carry a value to the next column if applicable.

From now on, every subsequent output (O_n for $n > 0$) will be either copied directly from I_n if there is no bit carried over from the previous column or increased by 1 (which, again, boils down to negation) due to addition of a carry bit. And so, if I_n is 1, the carry from this column, C_n, will also be 1, and O_n will be 0 (because, in binary, $1 + 1$ is 10). As you might notice, the actual output at position n is simply a result of XOR of the input value at position n, and the carry bit from column $n-1$. Hence, the circuit generates O_n by XORing the bit carried from C_{n-1} with the value of I_n and then ANDing the carry from O_{n-1} with I_n to determine if there should be a carry to the next column:

$O_n = \text{XOR}(I_n, C_{n-1})$

$C_n = \text{AND } (I_n, C_{n-1})$

Consider the following example. We want to increase an input value, 3 (011 in binary), by 1. Inputs are as follows:

$I_0 = 1$

$I_1 = 1$

$I_2 = 0$

The circuit produces O_0 by negating I_0; hence $O_0 = 0$. Because I_0 was nonzero, there is also a carry passed to the next column. In the next column, the XOR gate sets O_1 to 0, because, even though I_1 was 1, there was a carry value from the previous column $(1 + 1 = 10)$. Again, there is a carry to the next column.

In yet another column, $I_2 = 0$, but the AND gate indicates a carry value from the previous row, because two previous inputs were both set to 1. Hence, the output is 1. There will be no carry to the last column. The output is:

$O_0 = 0$

$O_1 = 0$

$O_2 = 1$

$O_0 = 0$

. . . or 0100, which, quite incidentally, is 4 when converted to decimal numbers.

And voilà—that's +1, written in binary.

NOTE   *We have just expressed the first computing problem in terms of Boolean algebra. You might be tempted to extend the design to be able to sum two arbitrary numbers, rather than just one number and the number 1. Nonetheless, this basic circuitry is much where computing starts and ends.*

Digital arithmetic circuitry works by running certain input data through an array of cleverly arranged logic gates that, in turn, add, subtract, multiply, or perform other trivial modifications on an array of bits. Little magic is involved.

So far, I have explained the ability of silicon chips or crafted wood to perform certain fixed, basic operations such as integer arithmetics. Yet, something is missing from this picture: computers do not come with text editors, games, and peer-to-peer software hard-coded in a painstakingly complex array of gates inside the CPU. Where is the software kept?

From Electronic Egg Timer to Computer

The true value of a computer lies in its ability to be programmed to act in a specific way—to execute a sequence of software commands according to some plan.

Figure 2-4 illustrates the next step on our way toward developing a flexible machine that can do more than just a single, hard-wired task: data storage and memory. In this figure, we see a type of memory storage unit known as a *flip-flop design*. This memory cell has two control lines, "set" and "reset." When both are down, the gate maintains its current state, thanks to a feedback connection between its input and output to the OR gate. Previous output from OR is passed through an AND gate because its other line is set to 1 (negated "reset"), and through OR once again, because its other input is 0 ("set"). The state of the output is sustained for as long as the gates are powered.

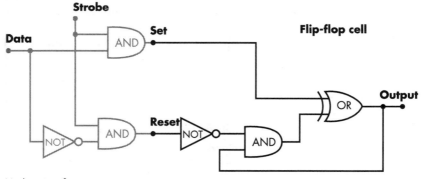

Figure 2-4: Flip-flop memory with a practical interface

When "set" goes high, the OR gate is forced to output 1 and will retain this value when "set" goes back down. When "reset" line goes high, the AND gate is forced to output 0 and break the feedback loop, thus forcing the circuit to output 0. Once "reset" goes down, the output remains 0. When both control lines are up, the circuit becomes unstable—something not quite pretty, especially when the computer in question is mechanical.

The truth table for this design is as follows (*V* denotes an arbitrary logic value):

Flip-Flop Truth Table			
Set	Reset	Q_{t-1}	Q_t
0	0	V	V
1	0	-	1
0	1	-	0
1	1	-	unstable

A more practical variant of a flip-flop circuit, which incorporates an "update interface" (see Figure 2-4), uses two AND gates and one NOT gate so that the state of an input line is captured (sampled and held) whenever an external "strobe" control signal occurs. This design eliminates unstable combinations of inputs and makes this sort of memory easier to use for storing information.

Improved Flip-Flop Truth Table			
Input	Strobe	Q_{t-1}	Q_t
-	0	V	V
S	1	-	S

This trivial gate configuration exhibits an important property: it can store data. A single cell can store only a single bit, but combining a number of flip-flops can extend the storage capacity. Although today's memory designs vary, the significance of this functionality remains the same: it allows programs to execute. But how?

In the basic design, the chip stores a special value, usually called the *instruction pointer*, in an internal on-chip memory latch (register) consisting of several flip-flops. Because popular computers work synchronously, with all processes timed by a clock signal generator working at a high frequency, the pointer selects a memory cell from the main memory on every clock cycle. The control data retrieved this way then selects and activates the appropriate arithmetic circuit to process the input data.

For some control data, our hypothetical chip performs addition; for others, it gets involved in an input-output operation. After fetching each piece of control data (every machine instruction), the chip has to advance its internal instruction pointer so that it will be prepared to read the next command in the next cycle. Thanks to this functionality, we can use the chip to execute a sequence of machine instructions, or a program.

It is now time to find out which operations the chip has to implement in order for it to be usable.

Turing and Instruction Set Complexity

As it turns out, the processor does not have to be complex. In fact, the set of instructions required for a chip to be able to execute just about any task is surprisingly small. The Church-Turing thesis states that every real-world computation can be carried out by a Turing machine, which is a primitive model of a computer. The Turing machine, named after its inventor, is a trivial device that operates on a potentially infinite tape consisting of single cells, a hypothetical, purely abstract storage medium. Each cell can store a single character from a machine "alphabet," which is simply a name for a finite ordered set of possible values. (This alphabet has absolutely nothing to do with human alphabets; it was named this way to promote a healthy dose of confusion among the laity.)

The device is also equipped with an internal register that can hold a finite number of equally internal states. A Turing machine starts at a certain position on the tape, in a given state, and then reads a character from a cell on the tape. Every automaton has an associated set of transition patterns that describe how to modify its internal state, what to store on the tape based on the situation after the read, and how to (optionally) move the tape either way by one cell. Such a set of transitions defines the rules for calculating the system's next state based on its current characteristics. These rules are often documented using a *state transition table* like this.

State Transition Table

Current State		New State/Action		
C_t	S_t	C_{t+1}	S_{t+1}	MOVE
0	S0	1	S1	-
1	S0	0	S0	LEFT

The table tells us that, if the current value of a cell under which the machine is currently positioned is 0, and the machine's internal state at that moment is S0, the device will alter the state of C to 1, will alter its internal state to S1, and will not move the reading head.

Figure 2-5 shows an example of a Turing machine positioned at cell C with internal state S.

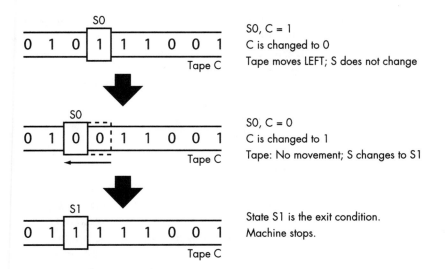

Figure 2-5: Sample Turing machine execution stages

Let's walk through this. As you can see in Figure 2-5, the machine uses an alphabet of two characters, 0 and 1, and has two internal states, S0 and S1. It starts with S0. (Starting conditions can be defined arbitrarily; I chose to start it there for no particular reason.) When positioned at the end (the least significant bit) of a binary number stored on the tape (C_0), the machine follows this logic:

- If the character under the machine head is 0, it is changed to 1, and the state of the machine is changed to S1, according to the first transition rule documented in the table preceding. Because there is no transition rule from S1, the machine stops in the next cycle.

- If the character read from beneath the head is 1, it changes to 0, and the state remains the same. The machine also moves the reading head on the tape to the left, per the second transition rule. The entire process then repeats, starting at the new location, because the machine remains in its current state, for which further transition rules are defined.

Functionality, at Last

Although this may come as a surprise, this particular machine is actually useful and implements a task that can be of more than theoretical value: it performs basic arithmetic. It does precisely the same thing as our increase-by-one circuit discussed earlier in this chapter. In fact, it implements the same algorithm: bits on the tape, starting at the rightmost position, are inverted until after 0 is encountered (and also inverted).

This is, naturally, just the tip of the iceberg. A proper Turing machine can implement any algorithm ever conceived. The only problem is that every algorithm requires the implementation of a separate set of transition rules and internal states; in other words, we need to build a new Turing machine for every new task, which is not quite practical in the long run.

Thankfully, a special type of such a machine, a Universal Turing Machine (UTM), has an instruction set that is advanced enough to implement all specific Turing machines and to execute any algorithm without the need to alter the transition table.

This über-machine is neither particularly abstract nor complex. Its existence is guaranteed because a specific Turing machine can be devised to perform any finite algorithm (according to the aforementioned Church-Turing thesis). Because the method for "running" a Turing machine is itself a finite algorithm, a machine can be devised to execute it.

As to the complexity of this machine, a one-bit, two-element alphabet machine (the smallest UTM devised) requires 22 internal states and instructions describing state transitions, in order to execute algorithms on a sequential infinite memory tape.[1] That's not that big a deal.

Holy Grail: The Programmable Computer

The Turing machine is also far more than just a hypothetical abstract device that mathematicians use to entertain themselves. It is a construct that begs to be implemented using a specially designed, Boolean, logic-based electronic (or mechanical) device and perhaps extended to make it far more useful, which brings us one step closer to useful computing. The only problem is that the prerequisite for an infinitely long input tape cannot be satisfied in the real world. Nevertheless, we can provide plenty of it, making such a hardware Turing machine quite usable for most of our everyday problems. Enter the universal computer.

Real computers, of course, go far beyond the sequential access single-bit memory, thus significantly reducing the set of instructions required to achieve Turing completeness. A UTM with an alphabet of 18 characters requires only two internal states in order to work. Real computers, on the other hand, usually operate on an "alphabet" of at least 4,294,967,296 characters (32 bits), and often far more, which allows for nonsequential memory access and for the use of a large number of registers with an astronomical number of possible internal states.

In the end, the UTM model proves and everyday practice confirms that it is possible to build a flexible, programmable processing unit using only a handful of features, composed of two or three internal registers (instruction pointer, data read/write pointer, and perhaps an accumulator) and a small set of instructions. It is perfectly feasible to assemble such a device with just hundreds of logic gates, even though today's designs may use many more.

As you can see, the notion of building a computer from scratch is not so absurd—even a wooden one.

Advancement through Simplicity

Coming up with such an unimpressive set of instructions is, of course, not going to make the device fast or easy to program. Universal Turing Machines can do just about everything (in many cases, by virtue of their simplicity), but they are painfully slow and difficult to program, to a degree that even implementing machine-assisted translation from more human-readable languages to machine code is difficult, at least without driving the programmer clinically insane.

Architectures or languages that come too close to implementing bare-bones Turing completeness are often referred to as *Turing tarpits*. This means that, while it is theoretically possible to carry out just about any task with their help, in practice, it is barely feasible, too time-consuming, and too burdensome to actually try. Even simpler tasks such as integer multiplication or moving the contents of memory can take forever to set up, and twice as long to execute. The less effort and time required to complete simple and repetitive tasks, and the fewer the tasks that have to be accomplished by software using a number of separate instructions, the better.

One popular way to improve the functionality and performance of a processing unit is to implement certain common tasks in the hardware that would be quite annoying to perform in software. These tasks are implemented using an array of specialized circuits (and include multiplication and home-loan-rejection processing), thus adding convenient extensions to the architecture and enabling the faster and saner deployment of programs, while still enabling the system to execute those functions in a programmed, flexible order.

Surprisingly, beyond the few initial steps, it is not always desirable when designing a processor to linearly increase the complexity of the circuitry in order to make processors achieve higher speeds, be more energy efficient, and provide a better feature set. You can, of course, build a large number of circuits to handle just about any frequently used complex operation imaginable. However, this won't be practical until the architecture is truly mature, and your budget allows you to invest additional effort and resources in making a chip. Although programs on such a platform indeed require less time to execute and are easier to write, the device itself is far more difficult to build, requires more power, and could become too bulky or expensive for routine use. Complex algorithms such as division or floating-point operations require an insanely large array of usually idle gates to complete such a task in a single step.

Split the Task

Rather than following this expensive and possibly naive path of building blocks to carry out entire instructions at once, it is best to abandon the single-cycle execution model until you have a working design and plenty of time to improve it. A better way to achieve complex functionality in hardware is to hack the job into tiny bits and execute advanced tasks in a number of cycles.

In such a multicycle design, the processor goes through a number of internal stages, much like the add-one Turing machine example. It runs the data through simple circuits in the right order, thus implementing a more complex functionality step by step, which relies on more basic components. Rather than use a complex device to do all the math at once, it might use a circuit to multiply subsequent bits of 32-bit integers and track carry values and then produce a final result in the 33rd cycle. Or, it could perform certain independent, preparation tasks that precede the actual operation. This would free us from having to design dozens of circuits for every variant of an opcode, depending on where it should get its operands or store results.

The added benefit of this approach is that it enables more efficient hardware resource management: for trivial operands; a variable-complexity algorithm can complete sooner, taking only as many cycles as absolutely necessary. For example, division by 1 is likely to require less time than division by 187,371.

A simple, cheap circuit, with maximum usage and a variable execution time could quite easily be more cost efficient than a complex and power-consuming one with a constant execution time. Although some of today's processors have attempted to use a fixed number of cycles to complete more and more tasks, virtually all began as multicycle architectures. Even for these big boys, the model seldom remains truly single cycle, as you'll see in a moment.

But first, let's take a look at how this very advantage of simplicity through multicycle execution can backfire.

Execution Stages

One of the variations of multicycle execution is a method that splits a task not into a number of repetitive steps, but rather into a number of distinct yet generic preparation and execution stages. This method, called *staging*, is used in today's processors to make them perform better without necessarily becoming linearly more complex. Execution staging has become one of a processor's more important features.

Today's processors can translate every instruction into a set of largely independent small steps. Certain steps can be achieved using generic circuits shared by all instructions, thus contributing to the overall simplicity. For example, the circuitry specific to a given task (our favorite multiplication comes to mind once more) can be made more universal and reusable as a part of various advanced instructions by separating it from any generic I/O handling tasks, and so on. The set of execution stages and transitions depends on the architecture, but it is usually similar to the scheme shown in Figure 2-6.

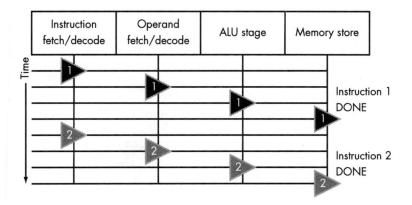

Figure 2-6: Baseline instruction execution stages

Figure 2-6 shows the following stages:

Instruction fetch/decode

> The processor retrieves an instruction from memory, translates it to a low-level sequence, and decides how to proceed and which data to pass to all subsequent stages. The circuit is shared for all operations.

Operand fetch/decode

> The processor uses a generic circuit to fetch operands from sources for this particular instruction (for example, from specified internal registers) so that the main circuit does not have to support all possible operand combinations and fetch strategies.

ALU

> An arithmetic logic unit (ALU) tailored to perform this particular operation, perhaps in a number of steps, is invoked to perform a specified arithmetic task. For nonarithmetic (memory transfer) instructions, generic or dedicated ALU circuits are sometimes used to calculate source and destination addresses.

Memory store

> The result is stored at its destination. For nonarithmetic operations, the memory is copied between calculated locations.

This, alone, may appear to be merely a variation of regular multicycle execution and a circuit reuse measure—one that is prevalent in most of today's CPU designs. But as you will see, it is also of utmost importance to execution speed.

The Lesser Memory

The simplicity of circuitry is not where this story ends. One additional advantage to the multicycle design is that the processor speed is no longer limited by the memory, the slowest component of the system. Consumer-grade external memory is considerably slower than today's processors and has a high access and write latency. A single-cycle processor can be no faster than it takes to reliably access memory, even though it is not accessing memory all the time. It needs to be slow simply because one of the single-cycle instructions it could encounter *might* require memory access; and hence, there must be enough time to accomplish this. Multicycle designs, on the other hand, allow the CPU to take its time and even idle for a couple of cycles as necessary (during memory I/O, for example), but run at full speed when performing internal computations. Too, when using multicycle designs, its easier to speed up memory-intensive operations without having to invest in faster main memory.

The flip-flop design, commonly referred to as SRAM (static RAM), offers low-access latency and consumes little power. Current designs require about 5 nanoseconds, which is comparable to the cycle interval of some processors. Unfortunately, the design also requires a considerable number of components per flip-flop, typically about six transistors per bit.

Unlike SRAM, DRAM, (dynamic RAM) the other memory design popular today, uses an array of capacitors to store the information. Capacitors, however, tend to discharge and need to be refreshed regularly. DRAM requires more power than SRAM and has a considerably higher access and modification latency, as high as 50 nanoseconds. On the upside, DRAM is much cheaper to manufacture than SRAM.

The use of SRAM for main memory is practically unheard of because its cost is prohibitive. Besides, we would have trouble using all that increase in performance, which would require us to run the memory at nearly the same speed as the CPU. Alas, because main memory is sizable and designed to be extensible, it must be placed outside the CPU. Although the CPU core can usually run at a speed much higher than the world around it, serious reliability issues (such as track capacitance on the motherboard, interference, costs of high-speed peripheral chips, and so on) arise when data must be transferred over longer distances.

Rather than take the cost-prohibitive routes of using faster external memory or integrating all memory with the CPU, manufacturers usually adopt a more reasonable approach. Advanced CPUs are equipped with fast but considerably smaller in-core memory, SRAM or some derivative, that caches the most frequently accessed memory regions and sometimes stores certain additional CPU-specific data. Thus, whenever a chunk of memory is found in cache *(cache hit)*, it can be accessed rapidly. Only when a chunk of memory has to be fetched from the main memory *(cache miss)* can there be a considerable delay, at which point the processor has to postpone some of its operations for some time. (Single-cycle processors cannot take full advantage of internal caching.)

Do More at Once: Pipelining

As I have mentioned, staging offers a considerable performance advantage that goes far beyond a traditional multicycle approach. There is one major difference between them, though: because many of the stages are shared by various instructions, there is no reason not to optimize execution a bit.

Figure 2-6 shows that, with separate stages executing separately, only a specific part of the device is used in every cycle. Even though the instruction currently executed has already passed the first stages, it blocks the entire CPU until it completes. For systems with a high number of execution stages (the count often reaches or exceeds 10 on today's chips, with the Pentium 4 exceeding 20) this proves to be a terrible waste of computing power.

One solution is to let the next instruction enter the execution pipeline as soon as the previous one moves to the following stage, as shown in Figure 2-7. As soon as a particular stage of the first instruction is finished, and the execution moves to the next stage, the previous stage is fed with a portion of the subsequent instruction, and so forth. By the time the first instruction completes, the next is only one stage from being completed, and the third instruction is two stages apart. Execution time is thus decreased rather dramatically, and chip usage becomes optimal, using this cascading method.

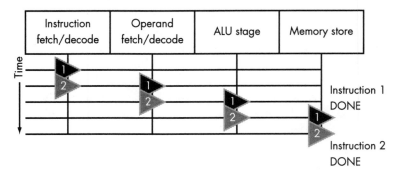

Figure 2-7: Pipeline execution model

Pipelining works fine as long as the instructions are not interdependent and neither operates on the output of its predecessor still in the pipeline. If the instructions do depend on each other, serious problems are bound to ensue. As such, a special circuit must be implemented to supervise the pipeline and to prevent such interlocking situations.

There are more challenges when it comes to pipelining. For example, on some processors, the set of stages may be different for distinct operations. Not all stages are always applicable, and it might be more optimal to skip some. Certain simple operations could conceivably be run through the pipeline much faster, because there are no operands to be fetched or stored. In addition, some stages can take a variable number of cycles, which contributes to the risk of collisions when two instructions reach the same execution stage at the same point. To prevent this, certain additional mechanisms such as pipeline "bubbles," no-op stages designed to introduce ephemeral delays when necessary, must be devised.

The Big Problem with Pipelines

Traditional pipelines are a great tool for achieving high performance with simple, multistaged chip design, by reducing the latency of subsequent instructions and ensuring optimal circuit usage, but they are not without concerns: it is not possible to pipeline instructions past a conditional branch instruction if those instructions could alter further program execution.

In fact, it often is possible, but the processor has no idea which execution path to follow, and if an incorrect decision is made, the entire pipeline has to be flushed down immediately after a branch instruction. (The CPU must also delay committing any changes made by these instructions that, after all, were not to be executed.) Dumping the pipeline introduces an additional delay.

And, unfortunately for this design, many CPU-intensive tasks, including plenty of video and audio algorithms, rely on small conditional-exit loops executed millions of times in sequence, thus inflicting a terrible performance impact on the pipelined architecture.

The answer to this problem is *branch prediction*. Branch predictors are usually fairly simple counter circuits that track the most recent code execution and maintain a small history buffer to make educated guesses about the most likely outcome of a conditional branch operation (although more complex designs are also often deployed[2]).

All branch predictors employ a strategy that is designed to offer the best pipelining performance for a given code: if a specific branch instruction is executed more often than it is skipped, it is better to fetch and pipeline instructions. Of course, the prediction can fail, in which case, the entire queue must be dropped. However, today's predictors achieve up to 90 percent success rates in typical code.

Implications: Subtle Differences

The advanced set of optimizations employed in today's processors results in an interesting set of consequences. We observe that execution times depend on the following characteristics, which can be divided into three groups:

Type of instruction and the complexity of the operation. Some operations execute much faster than others.

Operand values. Certain multiple cycle algorithms prove faster for trivial inputs. For example, multiplying a value by 0 is generally rather trivial and can be done quickly.

The memory location from which the data needed for the instruction must be retrieved. Cached memory is available sooner.

The importance, prevalence, and impact of each of these characteristics depends on the exact nature of the CPU architecture in question. The first characteristic—variable instruction execution times—is shared by all multicycle architectures, but might be absent on some basic chips. The second—dependence on operands—is increasingly extinct in top-of-the-line processors.

In top-end devices, ALU and Floating Point Unit (FPU) components sometimes work at a speed higher than the CPU itself. Hence, even if there are computation speed differences, they cannot be precisely measured because much of the arithmetic is done within one CPU clock tick.

The last group of timing patterns—memory location dependence—is, for a change, exclusive to today's, high-performance computers and is unheard of in low-end controllers and various embedded designs.

The first two timing pattern groups—operation complexity and operand value dependences—can also manifest themselves on a level slightly higher than the CPU itself, namely software. Processors feature arithmetic units that deal well with fairly small integers (usually from 8 to 128 bits) and some floating-point numbers, but today's cryptography and many other applications require the manipulation of large numbers (often hundreds or thousands of digits), high-precision floats, or various mathematic operations that are not implemented in hardware. Therefore, this functionality is commonly implemented in software libraries. Algorithms in those libraries are again likely to take variable time, depending on the specifics of the operation and operands.

Using Timing Patterns to Reconstruct Data

It can be argued that an attacker could deduce certain properties of the operands or of an operation performed by monitoring how long it takes for a program to process data. This poses a potential security risk because in several scenarios, at least one of the operands can be a secret value that is not supposed to be disclosed to a third party.

Although the concept of recovering data by watching someone with a stopwatch in your hand might sound surreal, today's CPUs offer precise counters that allow parties to determine exact time intervals. Too, some operations can be considerably more time-consuming, with certain advanced opcodes on the Intel platform taking as much as thousands of cycles to complete. With ever-increasing network throughput and ever-improving response times, it is not entirely impossible to deduce this information, even from a remote system.

The nature of information leaked as computation complexity measurements may not be immediately clear. If so, Paul Kocher from Cryptography Research demonstrated a great example of this attack last century (that is, back in the '90s[3]), using an example of the RSA algorithm we discussed in Chapter 1.

Bit by Bit . . .

Kocher observed that the process of decrypting data in the RSA algorithm is rather simple and is based on solving the following equation:

$$T = c^k \bmod M$$

in which T is the decrypted message, c is the encrypted message, k is the secret key, and M is a moduli, which are a part of the key pair.

A trivial integer modulo exponentiation algorithm used in a typical implementation has an important property: if a specific bit of the exponent is one, a portion of the result is calculated by performing modulo multiplication on a portion of the base (some bits of c). If the bit is 0, the step is skipped. Even when the step is not actually skipped, the time needed by software to carry out multiplication varies, as indicated earlier. Most trivial cases—such as multiplying by a power of 2—are solved more quickly than others.

Hence, on such a system, it would appear that we can determine plenty of information about the key (k) by repeatedly checking to see how long it takes to decrypt a piece of information. Even on platforms on which hardware multiplication takes a fixed amount of time, a timing pattern often results from the use of software multiplication algorithms (such as Karatsuba multiplication algorithm) that are needed for processing large numbers such as the ones used by public key cryptography. Subsequent bits of the exponent make the private key, whereas the base is a representation of the message supplied or visible to the curious bystander.

The attack is rather trivial. The villain sends the attacker two similar but slightly different portions of encrypted data. They differ in a section X, so that decrypting that section would presumably take a different amount of time to decrypt. One of the variants of X, as far as the villain's idea of victim's modulo multiplication implementation goes, is a trivial case that would hence make the task of decrypting X fast. The other variant is expected to take more time.

If it takes the same amount of time for the attacker to decode and respond to both sequences, the attacker can safely assume that the part of the key that was used to decode section X consisted of zeros. They can also assume that the multiplication algorithm took the early optimization path, that of not performing any multiplication at all.

If, on the other hand, one of the scenarios takes more time, it's obvious that in both cases, the multiplication was carried out, with one case being simpler to solve. The corresponding part of the secret key bit must have been set to a nonzero value.

By following this procedure, treating subsequent bits of the encrypted message as our "section X" and generating, or even (if one has more time) simply waiting for encrypted messages that will happen to work with this scenario, it is possible to reconstruct every bit of the key.

NOTE *Research suggests that this approach can be successfully extended to just about any algorithm that is carried out in a variable time and discusses some practical optimizations for the attack, such as the ability to deploy limited error detection and correction functionality.*

In Practice

The ability to deduce tangible properties of operands for arithmetic instructions based solely on timing information is the most obvious, effective, and interesting vector for performing computational complexity attacks. Other techniques, such as cache hit and miss timing, usually require considerably more detailed analysis and reveal less information in every cycle.

It is clear that this problem would, to a degree, affect many software algorithms, such as large-number arithmetic libraries commonly used in cryptographic applications. But software algorithms and theory aside, a couple of important questions remain: how real is the execution time dependency on the hardware level, and how can it be measured?

An example is well within reach. At least a portion of the Intel IA32 architecture exhibits this behavior. The *80386 Programmer's Reference Manual*[4] describes an integer-signed multiplication opcode, denoted by the mnemonic IMUL. The opcode, in its basic form, multiplies the value stored in the *accumulator* (a multipurpose working register going by the name [E]AX on this platform), by a value stored in another register. The result is then stored back in the accumulator.

The documentation further explains:

> The 80386 uses an early-out multiply algorithm. The actual number of clocks depends on the position of the most significant bit in the optimizing multiplier [...]. The optimization occurs for positive and negative values. Because of the early-out algorithm, clock counts given are minimum to maximum. To calculate the actual clocks, use the following formula:
>
> Actual clock = if m <> 0 then max(ceiling(log2(m)), 3) + 6 clocks
>
> Actual clock = if m = 0 then 9 clocks

Although this may look cryptic, its meaning is simple: The processor optimizes multiplication based on the value of the multiplier. Instead of multiplying the multiplicand until all bits of the multiplier are exhausted, it skips zeros at the beginning of the operand.

Early-Out Optimization

To understand the relevance of this tactic to integer multiplication, imagine a traditional iterative multiplication method taught in schools, except this time in binary. A hypothetical "dumb" implementation of this algorithm performs the following set of operations.

```
  00000000 00000000 11001010 11111110     Multiplicand (P)
* 00000000 00000000 00000000 00000110     Multiplier (R)
  -------------------------------------
```

```
00000000 00000000 00000000 00000000        P * R[0] = P * 0
00000000 00000001 10010101 1111110         P * R[1] = P * 1
00000000 00000011 00101011 111110          P * R[2] = P * 1
00000000 00000000 00000000 00000           P * R[3] = P * 0
00000000 00000000 00000000 0000            P * R[4] = P * 0
00000000 00000000 00000000 000             P * R[5] = P * 0
...
+ 0                                         P * R[31] = P * 0
---------------------------------------
00000000 00000100 11000001 11110100
```

It should be obvious that a large number of these operations are completely unnecessary and unwarranted and that continuing the operation once nothing but zeros remain at subsequent bits of the multiplier is simply pointless. A more reasonable approach is to skip them:

```
  00000000 00000000 11001010 11111110      Multiplicand (P)
* 00000000 00000000 00000000 00000110      Multiplier (R) - optimizing
  ---------------------------------------
  00000000 00000000 00000000 00000000      P * R[0] = P * 0
  00000000 00000001 10010101 1111110       P * R[1] = P * 1
+ 00000000 00000011 00101011 111110        P * R[2] = P * 1
  ...Bail out - ignore leading zeros of R!
  ---------------------------------------
  00000000 00000100 11000001 11110100
```

And this is, in essence, the nature of the *early-out optimization* that Intel deployed.

NOTE   *This optimization makes multiplication nonsymmetrical in time. 2*100 will compute more slowly than 100*2 (!), even though the result is obviously the same.*

With early-out optimization, Intel processors require a variable number of cycles to perform multiplication, and the length is directly proportional to the location of the oldest (most significant) bit set in the second operand. By applying the clock count algorithm provided in the documentation, it is possible to determine the correlation between the multiplier and IMUL time, as shown here:

Multiplier Value Range	Cycles to Complete
0 – 7	9
8 – 15	10
16 – 31	11
32 – 63	12
64 – 127	13
128 – 255	14
256 – 1,023	15
1,024 – 2,047	16
2,048 – 4,095	17

(continued)

Multiplier Value Range	Cycles to Complete
4,096 – 8,191	18
8,192 – 16,383	19
16,384 – 32,767	20
32,768 – 65,535	21
65,536 – 131,071	22
131,072 – 262,143	23
262,144 – 524,287	24
524,288 – 1,048,575	25
1,048,576 – 2,097,151	26
2,097,152 – 4,194,303	27
4,194,304 – 8,388,607	28
8,388,608 – 16,777,215	29
16,777,216 – 33,554,431	30
33,554,432 – 67,108,863	31
67,108,864 – 134,217,727	32
134,217,728 – 268,435,455	33
268,435,456 – 536,870,911	34
536,870,912 – 1,073,741,823	35
1,073,741,824 – 2,147,483,647	36

A similar dependency exists for negative multiplier values.

Working Code—Do It Yourself

The following code listing shows a practical implementation in C for Unix-type systems that can be used to confirm and measure differences in timing patterns. The program is invoked with two parameters: *multiplicand* (which should not affect performance in any way) and *multiplier* (presumably used in early-out optimizations and hence impacting the speed of the entire operation). The program performs 256 tests of 500 subsequent multiplications with the chosen parameters and returns the shortest measured time.

We run 256 tests and select the best result in order to compensate for cases in which execution is interrupted by the system for some period of time, a condition fairly common in multitasking environments. Although a single test can be affected by such an event, at least some of the test in a rapid sequence of short tests can be expected to complete without interruption.

The code uses the system clock to measure execution time in microseconds.

NOTE *Several of today's Intel chips feature a precise timing mechanism available through RDTSC opcode. This method for accessing the internal clock cycle counter is not available on older platforms, and so we will not rely on it.*

```c
#include <stdio.h>
#include <stdlib.h>
#include <unistd.h>
#include <sys/time.h>
#include <limits.h>

int main(int argc,char** argv) {

  int shortest = INT_MAX;
  int i,p,r;

  if (argc != 3) {
    printf("Usage: %s multiplicand multiplier\n",argv[0]);
    exit(1);
  }

  p=atoi(argv[1]);
  r=atoi(argv[2]);

  for (i=0;i<256;i++) {
    int ct;
    struct timeval s;
    struct timeval e;

    gettimeofday(&s,NULL);

    asm(

      "   movl $500,%%ecx    \n"/* Loop repetition counter (R) */
      "imul_loop:            \n"
      "   movl %%esi,%%eax   \n"
      "   movl %%edi,%%edx   \n"
      "   imul %%edx,%%eax   \n"/* Comment out for first run */
      "   loop imul_loop     \n"
      :
      : "S" (p), "D" (r)
      : "ax", "cx", "dx", "cc");

    gettimeofday(&e,NULL);

    ct = ( e.tv_usec - s.tv_usec ) +
         ( e.tv_sec - s.tv_sec ) * 1000000;

    if (ct < shortest) shortest = ct;

  }

  printf("T[%d,%d] = %d usec\n",p,r,shortest);
  return 0;

}
```

By compiling the code with the IMUL instruction initially commented out and invoking the program with arbitrary parameters, we can estimate the timing code overhead (T_{idle}). If the value falls outside the range of 10 to 100 microseconds—which is high enough to provide a fine-grained readout, but low enough to maximize the chance of not being interrupted by the operating system—readjust the loop repetition counter R, which is set to 500 by default.

After restoring the IMUL instruction and recompiling and running the program with a chosen multiplicand D and repetition counter R, it is possible to use the returned time approximation $T_{D,R}$ to estimate the number of CPU cycles spent on IMUL operation ($C_{D,R}$), as long as the operating frequency of the processor (F_{MHz}) is known:

$$C_{D,R} = (T_{D,R} - T_{idle}) \cdot F_{MHz}/R$$

As expected, pipelining and branch predictors on newer and more advanced chips will kick in and skew the result slightly, but a good estimate can be made.

NOTE *On newer Intel processors, the time needed to complete multiplication is already constant.*

Prevention

You can take a number of approaches to protect against computational effort analysis. The most obvious is to make all operations take the same amount of time to execute. However, this is difficult and often results in severe performance penalties because the time taken by all computations would have to be extended to match that of the slowest one.

Introducing random delays sometimes appears to be an acceptable defense tactic for applications if latency is not critical, in particular many noninteractive network services, and puts less stress on the processor itself. However, this random noise can be effectively filtered out if the attack can be carried out repeatedly.

Another approach, known as *blinding*, relies on introducing a certain amount of noise in the system by running random or otherwise bogus and unpredictable data combined with the actual input to the algorithm in order to make it impossible for the attacker to deduct meaningful properties of the input even if the encryption algorithm is vulnerable to timing attacks—then discarding the surplus information we did not intend to send out. Although the performance penalty is considerably lower in this scenario, it is difficult to perform blinding well.

Food for Thought

I've taken you on a long ride, but I hope it was worth it. As usual, I will leave you several possibly quite interesting problems to consider:

- First, although I have focused on the impact that computational complexity attacks have on cryptography-related application, the problem is not strictly limited to this area, and often manifests itself whenever private or confidential information is processed. Certainly, various basic information about HTTP requests or SMTP traffic can be deduced by carefully observing the appropriate service on a system; can you think of any more practical scenarios?

- Second, even if no secret data is being processed by a service, computational complexity information may be of some use. Consider applications such as network daemons that prevent disclosure of secrets by providing perhaps overly generic error or success messages, with the goal of, for example, making it difficult for an attacker to find out whether he is getting "login incorrect" because of a mistyped password or a non-existent user. However, depending on the time it takes to receive this message, a careful observer may determine which path in the code was indeed executed, and whether the error occurred earlier (when just checking for a valid username), or later on (when verifying the password). I encourage you to experiment with common network services such as SSH, POP3, and Telnet to see whether there is a measurable and consistent difference.

- As always, even the best defenses against information disclosure tend to fail unexpectedly. Too, computational complexity is not the only way to determine what's going on inside a silicon chip. Consider this example: Biham and Shamir[5] have devised a brilliant scheme for cracking "secure" chip designs used in smart cards. Smart cards are designed to securely store a piece of information such as personal identification data or cryptographic keys and to divulge it only to certain authentication services and trusted clients. As it turns out, you can deduce the properties of the guarded data or the protection mechanism by abusing the device and inducing faults due to mechanical stress, high-energy radiation, overheating, or similar external factors that cause the device to misbehave.

Just thought I'd share.

3

TEN HEADS OF THE HYDRA

*Where we explore several other tempting scenarios that occur
very early on in the process of communications*

In Chapters 1 and 2, I discussed two distinct information disclosure scenarios that occur as a result of brilliant, but in the end poorly thought out, attempts to make computers either more functional or easier to maintain. The passive snooping vectors these design decisions open are buried deep beneath the actual implementation and provide a fascinating insight into the earliest threats to processed information.

On the other hand, the exposure is naturally limited to the physical or logical proximity of the environment monitored. Although a nearly endless number of information disclosure possibilities arise early along the route of a portion of information, I've chosen to single out these two cases for their uniqueness, beauty, and the relative ease with which a potential attack can be carried out by a determined attacker. The other scenarios are also worth mentioning, though, and in this chapter, I touch on some of the more interesting possibilities that may not warrant a detailed discussion but that you might want to explore in more detail on your own.

Revealing Emissions: TEMPEST in the TV

In the 1950s, researchers concluded that electromagnetic radiation (EMR) can often be practically and easily used to recover or reconstruct information about the behavior of the device emitting it. EMR is undesirable noise caused by virtually all electronic, electromechanical, and electric devices, regardless of their design and intended purpose, and often propagated over considerable distances via power lines or by air.

Prior to their findings, the problem of EMR was believed to be relevant to engineering due to a risk of unexpected interference between separate devices or circuits, but not confirmed to be of any value to a person monitoring the radio frequencies polluted by the device. However, with the world on the brink of the era of information warfare, and with the development and increasing deployment of electronic data processing and telecommunications devices (some used to transfer or store classified or sensitive information), the conclusion that a remote observer can reconstruct some of the information processed by a system by merely listening to a specific frequency became quite worrisome for governments of the free (or not so free) world.

The term TEMPEST (Transient Electromagnetic Pulse Emanation Standard) originated from a classified EMR emissions study commissioned for the U.S. military in the 1960s and was originally used to denote a set of practices to prevent revealing emissions in electronic circuits processing sensitive data. It later became just a buzzword for describing a general class of problems and techniques related to intercepting and reconstructing radio frequency (RF) emissions.

Although this risk initially sounded more like bad science-fiction than an actual threat in the ears of skeptics, an important research paper released in 1985 by Wim van Eck,[1] demonstrated that it would be—and in fact is—quite easy to reconstruct the image displayed on a CRT monitor by intercepting radio frequency signals generated by high-voltage circuits inside such a device.

A typical CRT (see Figure 3-1) builds its display by illuminating every pixel of the image in sequence, line by line and then row by row, at very high speed, and modulating the strength of the signal depending on the location of the screen that is lit up at any moment. To achieve this, a narrow beam of electrons is emitted from a cathode gun in the back of the device. This electron beam hits the anode (a conductive layer of material on the display), which, in turn, emits photons of visible light that we see. The electron beam is modulated by a special circuit, but also positioned by a set of electromagnets that cause it to sweep the entire display area from left to right and top to bottom to produce and update the image on the screen. Wim noted that the oscillators controlling the electromagnets and the electron gun electronics emit several types of characteristic signals at standard frequencies. It is rather trivial to spot these signals in the radio spectrum,[*]

---

[*] For this reason, and because of power line interference, "nature radio" enthusiasts who want to listen to earth's ultra-low frequency signals must often travel with their recording equipment to distant, secluded areas.

and each of the signals is usually clear and strong enough to make it easy to build a fairly inexpensive device that can snoop on CRT displays, even from a considerable distance.

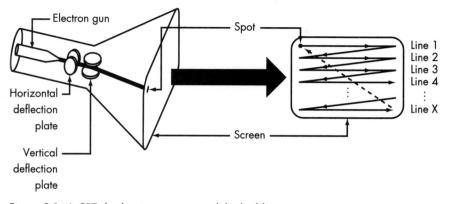

Figure 3-1: A CRT display image scan and the buildup process

NOTE *Emissions are, of course, not limited to CRT screens and are just as common in LCD (TFT, or thin film transistor) displays and any computer circuitry. They are also just as common on databuses, where the information between separate chips is carried over a large set of usually fairly long and sharply cornered conductive tracks laid out on the main board that, among other things, serve as a great antenna (although the ease of extracting and interpreting a specific signal, as well as the range of an emission, can vary rather significantly).*

Although there are no verifiable accounts of emission attacks being carried out in the wild, other than for military and intelligence applications (particularly during the Cold War[2]), some anecdotal accounts of industrial espionage can be found in the literature.[3]

Obviously, this kind of attack has its limitations: The attacker must be near the target. Too, except when snooping on analog CRT displays, the attacker must be armed with expensive and nontrivial equipment, especially when snooping on today's low-interference displays and higher CPU and bus speeds. Still, any such attack is difficult and costly to prevent.

Privacy, Limited

The exposure scenarios discussed so far can be classified as the undesired or unexpected results of the way a specific technology was designed and deployed, despite the identical goals or expectations of both the developer and the end user. In some cases, however, the exposure results in small differences in the goals and expectations of the two groups. Although software-level privacy problems resulting from the incompetence or malice of a programmer are notorious and usually pervasive, more subtle design problems that are not a flaw per se are also being seen. Some of the more interesting groups of problems in this area fall into the category of data disclosure in electronic documents.

We naturally assume when authoring a document that all information not related to the document's contents (and in particular, any information that uniquely identifies the originator) is hidden from other parties able to access the document, unless specifically disclosed by the author. But the days of plain-text editors are long gone. Today's document formats support extensive meta-information storage functionality, in an effort to make it easier to uniquely tag and later index, search, and track documents. What is worrisome, though, is that the designers of authoring tools often decide to fill in certain information automatically, frequently giving the author little or no control over the process and without making them immediately aware of this practice. Although the practice can be considered just another exercise in making the environment more user friendly and transparent to the user, the lack of widespread awareness of this process is appreciated only by a few.

Tracking the Source: "He Did It!"

One common problem with authoring software is that certain applications store unique identification tags that make it possible to correlate a document with its source. In particular, Microsoft Word long used the hardware address of a computer's network card (if the computer had one) to construct a Globally Unique Identifier (GUID) field in a document—be it a cookie recipe or a terrorist's handbook. Although the problem has been fixed in the most recent versions of Microsoft's Office suite of applications, the practice has had some interesting implications:

- Every device has a unique hardware card address. Because hardware addresses are used to locate a specific device on a local network, this uniqueness is necessary in order to prevent problems that would arise were two computers with the same hardware address to connect to the same network. As such, the number recorded in the GUID field of a Microsoft Word document can be used to uniquely identify the document's author, whether that person wrote the document anonymously or signed it. This can serve both as a valuable forensics investigation tool and as an effective way to suppress the freedom of speech in certain situations (by an employer hunting down whistle-blowers, for example).

- Hardware addresses are assigned in batches to a specific manufacturer. Furthermore, in many cases, network cards are manufactured with numbers in sequence and then sold in batches to computer manufacturers. Thus, a knowledgeable person can determine not only who made a specific card, but also who sold it and to whom. In many situations, it can be possible to actually track a specific hardware address to an individual machine and, effectively, to a private entity or a particular corporation. This might then make it possible for a determined investigator to figure out the origin of a specific document.

- Because hardware addresses are assigned in batches, it might also be possible to draw limited conclusions as to the hardware configuration of the system on which a document was authored. Although this poses a mild threat, it can be an interesting source of information for the easily amused or particularly curious.

Some functionality, although accessible to the user, is buried deep enough within the interface that a typical user is unaware of what is being saved and how to change these defaults. Productivity software such as Microsoft Word and OpenOffice.org are notorious for inserting "default author" information. This information is usually taken from the data provided with the software license or automatically stored after the first run, deep inside the metadata in the document where most users do not bother to look. Although this is a mildly useful feature that comes in handy when sharing documents, its privacy implications usually far outweigh any eventual benefit for an end user.

Another example is the "user-friendly" practice of automatically filling the "title" field in metaheaders of a document based on the first sentence in the document. This is a nice touch, but the selection is often permanent, meaning that even if the first paragraph is changed later (so that, for example, the new business offer is now addressed to a competitor), the original contents can be deduced by a careful observer. This "feature" once again exposes more than the author expected to be revealed to the recipient of a document.

Older versions of Microsoft Word also saved documents without properly clearing out all the data that had been edited out, effectively providing undo information, and recording all previous revisions of the text. This information could easily be recovered later by any sufficiently skilled attacker with software to parse object linking and embedding (OLE) containers, the format in which the editor stores all its data. The problem is particularly severe when a previous version of a document is reused as a template and sent to another party, perhaps a competitor. The ability to recover the previous version of an offer, a motivation letter, or an official response to a customer is definitely entertaining and enlightening, but not always desirable for the sender.

Of course, with the recent push for trusted computing and increased "accountability" for the purpose of reducing piracy, it is reasonable to expect that it will become commonplace to tag all documents so that they can be traced to their originator.

"Oops" Exposure: *_~1q'@@ . . . and the Password Is . . .

The last group of problems shared by a variety of text editors is that of leaking random memory. This type of disclosure is the result of sheer incompetence or insufficient testing, but it differs from other coding flaws in that it doesn't so much render the code vulnerable to an attack, as it divulges some useful hints to a careful observer. Whether this problem is limited to the program alone or is caused by systemwide leaks (the latter on systems with poor memory protection, such as Windows 3.x or 9x), this leaked data can include such sensitive information as other documents, browse history, email contents, or even passwords.

The problem occurs when an application allocates a chunk of memory (to an editing buffer, for example), perhaps used previously for some other task, and forgets to clear it before reusing it for a wholly different purpose. For performance reasons, the memory is not always zeroed before being granted to an application. The application can then operate on and overwrite only a small portion of the chunk of memory, but write the entire allocated block of data when saving the file, storing both the data it wanted to and some leftover contents from who knows how long ago. And, not surprisingly, older versions of Microsoft Word were once notorious for dumping sizable chunks of random memory within almost every document produced.

This problem has surfaced a number of times in Microsoft Windows, first in 1998 on all systems, and then on Mac OS only in 2001. Some anecdotal evidence suggests other sightings, but those are rather poorly documented.

4

WORKING FOR
THE COMMON GOOD

*Where a question of how the computer may determine the
intent of its user is raised and left unanswered*

The beauty of, but also one of the biggest problems
with, any sufficiently extensive and diverse computer
network is that you cannot blindly trust any connected
party to be who they claim to be, and it is impossible to
determine their intentions or the real driving force
behind their actions.

I'll discuss the issue of confirming the identity of a source in the third
part of this book, when I dissect the architecture of the network and explore
the risks that result from the way a network is built. However, the issue of the
originator's intentions is a separate and fascinating aspect of computer
security, with often serious and far-fetched social and judicial implications
that extend beyond the world of computing. As we make computers better
and better at predicting what their users want to do (itself a means of
achieving intuitiveness and ease of use) and give them more autonomy, it
becomes increasingly easy to trick machines into becoming a tool to be used
by someone else, instead of helping the user.

A long river of words has been written on the subject, followed by a number of heated disputes about where to put the blame and whom to sue when things go wrong. I believe it is important to tackle the problem but not appropriate to impose any particular viewpoint on you. As such, I will close this section of the book with a short and mostly technical paper that I originally published in 2001 in *Phrack* magazine, vol. 57. I've made some minor edits to it and will refrain from further commentary.

Let me dig it up . . . /me searches for paper . . . Ah, here it is:

```
                              ==Phrack Inc.==
                 Volume 0x0b, Issue 0x39, Phile #0x0a of 0x12
|=---------------=[ Against the System: Rise of the Robots ]=----------------=|
|=---------------------------------------------------------------------------=|
|=----=[ (C)Copyright 2001 by Michal Zalewski <lcamtuf@bos.bindview.com> ]=----=|


-- [1] Introduction -------------------------------------------------------

" . . . [the] big difference between the Web and traditional well-controlled
collections is that there is virtually no control over what people can put on
the Web. Couple this flexibility to publish anything with the enormous
influence of search engines to route traffic, and companies that deliberately
manipulate [sic] search engines for profit become a serious problem."

                                        -- Sergey Brin, Lawrence Page [A]

Consider a remote attacker who can compromise a remote system without sending
any traffic to his victim. Consider an attack that relies on simply creating a
file to compromise thousands of computers and that does not require any local
resources to carry it out. Welcome to the world of zero-effort exploit
techniques, automation, and anonymous as well as virtually unstoppable attacks
that result from the ever-increasing complexity of the Internet.

Zero-effort exploits create their wish list and leave it somewhere in
cyberspace where others can find it. The utility workers of the Internet [B] --
hundreds of tireless, never-sleeping robots, information browsers, search
engines, intelligent agents -- come to pick up the information and,
unknowingly, become a tool in the hands of the attacker. You can stop one of
them, but you cannot stop them all. You can find out what their orders are, but
you cannot guess what these orders will be tomorrow, lurking somewhere in the
abyss of not-yet-indexed cyberspace.

Your private army, close at hand, is picking up the orders you left for them on
their way. You exploit them without having to compromise them. They do what
they are designed to do the best they can. Welcome to the new reality, in which
our AI machines can rise against us.

Consider a worm. Consider a worm that does nothing. It is carried and injected
by others, but does not infect them. This worm creates a list of 10,000 random
addresses with specific orders. And waits. Intelligent agents pick up this
```

list, and with their united forces they try to attack the targets. Imagine that they are not too lucky and achieve a 0.1% success ratio. Ten new hosts are now infected. On every single one of them, the worm does exactly the same thing—prepares a list. Now the agents come back to infect 100 new hosts. And so the story goes (or crawls, if you wish).

Agents are virtually unnoticeable, as people are now accustomed to their presence and persistence. Agents just slowly move ahead in a never-ending loop. They work systematically. They do not choke connections with excessive data, and there are no network meltdowns, traffic spikes, or telltale signs of disease. Week after week they try new hosts, carefully, and their exploration never ends. Is it possible to notice that they carry a worm? Possibly . . .

-- [2] An example ---

When this idea came to mind, I tried to use the simplest test just to see if I was right. I targeted, if that is the correct word, several general-purpose web-indexing crawlers. I created a very short HTML document and put it somewhere on my home page and then waited for a couple of weeks. And they came -- AltaVista, Lycos, and dozens of others. They found new links, picked them up enthusiastically, and then disappeared for days.

```
bigip1-snat.sv.av.com:
  GET /indexme.html HTTP/1.0

sjc-fe5-1.sjc.lycos.com:
  GET /indexme.html HTTP/1.0
```

[...]

They came back later to see what I had given them to parse.

```
http://somehost/cgi-bin/script.pl?p1=../../../../attack
http://somehost/cgi-bin/script.pl?p1=;attack
http://somehost/cgi-bin/script.pl?p1=|attack
http://somehost/cgi-bin/script.pl?p1=`attack`
http://somehost/cgi-bin/script.pl?p1=$(attack)
http://somehost:54321/attack?`id`
http://somehost/AAAAAAAAAAAAAAAAAAAAAA...
```

The bots followed the links, each of the links simulating vulnerabilities. Although these exploits did not affect my server, they could easily compromise specific scripts or the entire web server on a remote system by causing the script to execute arbitrary commands, to write to arbitrary files, or, better yet, to suffer a buffer overflow problem:

```
sjc-fe6-1.sjc.lycos.com:
  GET /cgi-bin/script.pl?p1=;attack HTTP/1.0

212.135.14.10:
  GET /cgi-bin/script.pl?p1=$(attack) HTTP/1.0
```

```
bigip1-snat.sv.av.com:
    GET /cgi-bin/script.pl?p1=../../../../attack HTTP/1.0
```

[...]

Bots also happily connected to the non-HTTP ports I prepared for them and
started a conversation by sending the data I supplied in URLs, thus making it
possible to attack even services other than just web servers:

```
GET /attack?`id` HTTP/1.0
Host: somehost
Pragma: no-cache
Accept: text/*
User-Agent: Scooter/1.0
From: scooter@pa.dec.com

GET /attack?`id` HTTP/1.0
User-agent: Lycos_Spider_(T-Rex)
From: spider@lycos.com
Accept: */*
Connection: close
Host: somehost:54321

GET /attack?`id` HTTP/1.0
Host: somehost:54321
From: crawler@fast.no
Accept: */*
User-Agent: FAST-WebCrawler/2.2.6 (crawler@fast.no; [...])
Connection: close
```

[...]

Other than the well-known set of web search engines, a bunch of other, private,
crawl bots and agents run by specific organizations and companies also
responded. Bots from ecn.purdue.edu, visual.com, poly.edu, inria.fr,
powerinter.net, xyleme.com, and even more unidentified engines found this page
and enjoyed it. Although some robots did not pick all addresses (some crawlers
do not index CGI scripts at all, while others would not use nonstandard ports),
the majority of the most powerful bots did attack virtually all vectors I
supplied; and even those that were more careful always got tricked into
performing at least some.

The experiment could be modified to use a set of real vulnerabilities in the
form of thousands and thousands of web server overflows, Unicode problems in
servers such as Microsoft IIS, or script problems. Instead of pointing to my
own server, the bots could point to a list of randomly generated IP addresses
or a random selection of .com, .org, or .net servers. Or, you could point the
bots to a service that could be attacked by supplying a specific input string.

There is an army of robots encompassing a wide range of species, functions, and levels of intelligence. And these robots will do whatever you tell them to do.

-- [3] Social considerations --

Who is guilty if a "possessed" web crawler compromises your system? The most obvious answer is: the author of the original web page the crawler visited. But web page authors are hard to trace, and a web crawler indexing cycle takes weeks. It is hard to determine when a specific page was put on the Net because pages can be delivered in so many ways or even produced by other robots. There is no tracking mechanism for the Web that provides functionality similar to that implemented in the SMTP protocol. Moreover, many crawlers do not remember where they "learned" new URLs. Additional problems are caused by indexing flags, such as "noindex" without the "nofollow" option. In many cases, an author's identity and attack origin can never be fully determined.

By analogy to other cases, it is reasonable to expect that intelligent bot developers would be forced to implement specific filters or to pay enormous compensation to victims suffering from bot abuse, should this kind of attack become a reality. On the other hand, when you consider the number and wide variety of known vulnerabilities, it seems almost impossible to successfully filter contents to eliminate malicious code. And so the problem persists. (An additional issue is that not all crawler bots are under U.S. jurisdiction, which differs significantly from some of their counterparts when it comes to computer abuse regulations.)

-- [4] Defense --

As mentioned earlier, web crawlers themselves have limited defense and avoidance possibilities, due to a wide variety of web-based vulnerabilities. It is impossible to simply ban all malicious sequences, and heuristic investigation is risky: input that is valid and expected for one script may be enough to attack another. One reasonable defense tactic is for all potential victims to use secure and up-to-date software, but this concept is extremely unpopular for some reason. (A quick and nonscientific test: A search at http:// www.google.com with the unique documents filter enabled returns 62,100 matches for "CGI vulnerability" query [C].) Another line of defense against infected bots is to use the standard /robots.txt exclusion mechanism [D]. The price you pay, though, is the partial or complete exclusion of your site from search engines, which in most cases is undesirable and unacceptable. Also, some robots are broken or intentionally designed to ignore /robots.txt when following a direct link to new websites.

-- [5] References --

[A] "The Anatomy of a Large-Scale Hypertextual Web Search Engine"
    Googlebot concept, Sergey Brin, Lawrence Page, Stanford University
    URL: http://www7.scu.edu.au/programme/fullpapers/1921/com1921.htm

[B] "The Web Robots Database"
    URL: http://www.robotstxt.org/wc/active.html

[C] "Web Security FAQ", Lincoln D. Stein
    URL: http://www.w3.org/Security/Faq/www-security-faq.html

[D] "A Standard for Robot Exclusion", Martijn Koster
    URL: http://info.webcrawler.com/mak/projects/robots/norobots.html

|=[EOF]=---=|

It appears nearly impossible to fully prevent the automated abuse without the ability to anticipate and classify the actual intent behind a particular user action, which is not likely to happen any time soon. Meanwhile, the number of systems that rely on automated interaction with other entities increases every year, making this issue perhaps even more interesting than when I originally wrote this article, particularly with more and more sophisticated and populous worms hitting the Internet in the past several years.

Is there a moral to this story or a clear conclusion we should be drawing? Not really. It is, however, important to remember that machines do not always act on behalf of their operators, even when they are not clearly compromised or downright abused to become hostile. Determining the intent and the place where the desire to carry out a malicious action originated may be a tremendous challenge, as you'll see in later chapters.

PART II

SAFE HARBOR

*On the threats that lurk in between the computer
and the Internet*

5

BLINKENLIGHTS

Where we conclude that pretty can also be deadly,
and we learn to read from LEDs

The first part of this book focused on various problems
related to the design of the data entry point system.
Those problems were limited to deducing input by
observing seemingly unrelated behavioral patterns by a
user with local access to a system. But as information
moves farther down its path to the addressee and
leaves this system, its exposure broadens, and
problems become more tangible.

The second part of this book focuses on some of the problems that occur
while the data remains within reach, but just after it leaves the originating
system—moments before it enters the Internet. The exposure discussed
here is limited to roughly the physical footprint of a local area network with
its direct surroundings. An attack at this level requires an observation point
that is local to the origin, but it does not require system-level access.

The specific problem discussed in this chapter is somewhat different from
those discussed previously: the exposure now manifests at the hardware level,
much like in TEMPEST, but is different. The beauty of this phenomenon, and
the ease of observing it with no specialized equipment, more than justify giving
it a closer look.

The Art of Transmitting Data

The need for computers to communicate with other electronic devices has been apparent since the beginning of practical computing, as has the difficulty of achieving this task reliably and on a budget. We can control the machine's internal communication by providing generous and custom-fit interfaces among all major components with a desired capacity, maintaining precise signal characteristics, and using a common reference clock for all operations, so that the recipient always knows when to listen, and the sender always knows when to transmit data. But communication over longer distances or to devices equipped with nonspecialized, cheap interfaces is a different challenge: the computer is forced to communicate over a medium that usually does not allow for the degree of freedom we have grown accustomed to working with on the insides of a single machine.

In fact, the situation is quite the opposite. The customer expects simple, convenient, practical, and cheap solutions, and requiring computers to be connected through a $100, 3-inch, 100-wire cable didn't seem like a winning solution. Simplicity is a necessity. The core of any external communication channel almost always relies on the serial transmission of subsequent bits that only when reassembled and grouped together produce numeric values, text strings, or other pieces of data native to the machine environment of the sender or recipient. In the most seemingly trivial and obvious scenario, when two machines or devices connected only by a pair of wires need to exchange information, they do so by setting one of the wires to high or low voltage in relation to the other (reference) line—or by using any other differing signals or states, for that matter. They do so in order to send subsequent bits of data at a given frequency—a frequency that must be kept reasonably close and in sync on both devices.

Even in such a trivial design, a number of problems immediately arise. First, the devices do not share a reference clock. Although both have internal quartz-based clocks, no two affordable clocks are ever accurate enough to maintain reliable and fast communications over an extended period of time due to slight manufacturing imperfections, interference, and other physical conditions. And serial communications demand precise synchronization. The straightforward bit-encoding scheme, usually referred to as Non-Return to Zero (NRZ), simply outputs one signal (voltage) for 0 and another signal for 1. In such a system, it is easy to keep both endpoints synchronized when values change on a regular basis—the system simply needs to detect a falling or rising edge, use it as a rough reference, and adjust its own clock accordingly. But given a longer sequence of 1s or 0s, it becomes difficult for the receiving side to accurately determine how many bits are being sent. In fact, even a small clock drift can cause problems, and there is no way to compensate for this during the exchange of a constant sequence of bits.

The obvious solution, to simply interleave the data with a separate, distinguishable timing signal, is not always the most convenient and efficient method; increased complexity and reduced throughput is often perceived as a nuisance.

To effectively address this problem, many systems use a scheme called *Manchester encoding*, also known as *biphase code*. The algorithm for Manchester coding, shown along with NRZ in Figure 5-1, encodes data using signal edges, as opposed to signal levels. The original, aforementioned NRZ encoding uses an internal clock to measure voltage levels at a constant pace, interpreting low voltage as binary 0 and high voltage as 1. Manchester encoding, on the other hand, carries data in transitions from low to high voltage or vice versa. In such a design, the signal is switched to high to denote binary 1 and to low to indicate 0.[*]

Although such encoding does not require the clocks to be kept synchronized, it is also not quite enough as it is: there is no way to encode two binary 0s or 1s, because it is not possible to go from low to high voltage twice without returning to low halfway down the road (and vice versa). To allow this type of information to be encoded, transitions that occur shortly after a falling or rising signal edge are ignored, thus allowing the system to encode multiple occurrences of 0 and 1 by returning to the same voltage midcycle. To manage the "blackout" period after a transition, a simple one-shot interval clock is necessary.

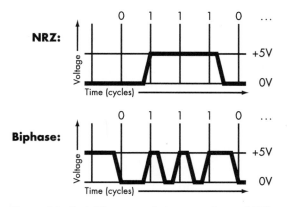

Figure 5-1: Serial line transmission encodings—NRZ and biphase (Manchester)

The design of a serial line based on the self-synchronizing scheme discussed above is often extended to provide full-duplex communications in which both parties can talk at once, either by using two separate lines (transmit and receive, Tx and Rx for short) or by using advanced echo detection and cancellation tricks to differentiate between its own signal and the data sent from the other side. Some mediums require or allow for more sophisticated signaling schemes, for example sending more than just one bit in every cycle;

[*] Or the other way around, depending on the transmitter design.

yet the principle of communications remains essentially the same, and Manchester encoding over the lowest possible number of wires—often two—is prevalent across the entire domain.

Equipped with a knowledge of the basics of "wire pair" serial communications, let's take a peak at two prominent examples of serial communications in the world of networking, see how they exchange data internally, and look at how this information can leak to third parties without the user noticing.

From Your Email to Loud Noises . . . Back and Forth

The most popular long-distance computer communications device is, hands down, a modem. Initially introduced in the 1950s for the maintenance and control of certain types of military equipment at remote locations, the modem brought the Internet to the masses. Although today often considered somewhat obsolete, the modem has given birth to many advanced technologies, such as affordable high-speed DSL (Digital Subscriber Line) systems or cable modems. These devices all use clever variations of the same set of techniques to communicate over phone lines or other nondedicated analog media using either audible or inaudible signals. The research invested in improving modems also contributed to our understanding of numerous large-scale design problems in electronics in general and computer and network design in particular. Thus, an understanding of how modems work is key to exploring other, perhaps more up-to-date, methods of long-distance data transmission.

The universality of the telephone line makes it a natural medium for computers to use for communication. Phone lines can be found almost anywhere, and phone systems provide excellent call-routing capabilities, making it possible to reach just about any location with little if any effort. There is a tiny caveat, though: phone lines were meant to carry the human voice, transmitted as a waveform, within narrow-frequency response range (usually not exceeding several kHz). Because these frequencies were recorded as voltage changes over a pair of wires and relayed through a number of analog repeaters and amplifiers, the standard of quality for the transmission wasn't particularly high. It had to be just good enough for people to hear and understand each other, and because the human brain is a superb signal filtering and processing system, occasional noise or sound-level fluctuations were not much of a concern—not until much later on, when customers grew a bit picky.

Computers, on the other hand, are generally engineered to exchange binary information, which is encoded using fairly precise voltage levels over well-designed, short lines with good signal characteristics and low capacitance—an exact opposite of long-distance, poorly shielded telephone lines with inadequate signal characteristics. Computers also need to talk much faster and much more than humans usually do. As such, modem designers had (huge understatement here) a difficult challenge to solve: They had to determine a way to encode bits of data not only in a manner that could be efficiently transmitted to a remote system over the wire (something that Manchester encoding made a bit easier), but also as audible signals that could be accurately distinguished at the other end of the line regardless of often entirely unpredictable voltage changes and other transmission artifacts. They had to employ robust error-correction algorithms and variable transmission speeds to compensate for poor line quality, occasional cross talk, trucks going over a buried phone line, birds building a nest on a pole, and so forth. The designers nodded, scratched their heads, and after perhaps just 40 years brought us an affordable and fairly fast method for computer-to-computer communication. Let's take an abbreviated look at how this developed and how the technology matured—yet essentially stayed the same—over the decades that followed.

The history of commercial modem development and standardization began in the 1960s when two standards, Bell 103/113 and V.21, were conceived. Both standards provided an amazing (for the time) 300-baud (bits per second) full-duplex connectivity using a technique called *frequency shift keying* (FSK). FSK is a mysterious-sounding term that happens to stand for a rather trivial signal-encoding scheme: it uses two different tones to denote different values, one frequency for "low," and another frequency for "high." The advantage of using audible frequencies over other types of signaling is rather significant: this is the only type of signal that can be relayed through the phone system fairly well—after all, this is what the system was designed for. All other signals are more or less destined to be trashed beyond recognition before reaching the other end of the wire, in the best-case scenario, or being immediately filtered out by bandpass filters somewhere down the line in the worst case.

In addition to FSK encoding, the aforementioned Bell 103/113 and V.21 standards split the frequency range that could be transmitted over phone lines in two: one of the modems, the caller, used a frequency of 980 Hz to encode low and 1,180 Hz to encode high. The other end, the answerer, used the higher part of the spectrum: 1,650 Hz and 1,850 Hz, respectively. Why split the frequency in this way? Because a phone line is essentially just a pair of wires, which can be used for transmission by two devices simultaneously (full duplex), but only if they are capable of dealing with the fact that their respective transmissions would superimpose on each other. In full-duplex communication, each device must be able to distinguish its own signal from the data it's receiving and filter it out. If it cannot do so successfully, each device would have to pause while the other end is talking (simplex mode), severely impairing the already sort of unimpressive throughput. By splitting the frequency, the phone line is essentially made to carry what it sees as two different "voices," thus ensuring that simultaneous communication can occur with no collisions.

It took 25 more years for modems to take another step in the right direction. The next major set of standards, Bell 212A and V.22, took a big leap forward and dropped frequency shift keying in favor of *differential phase shift keying* (DPSK). Rather than change the frequency of a wave, DPSK shifts its phase to signal different values.

The phase shift technique essentially introduces a minimal time shift, or delay, that causes the output audio signal to be slightly out of sync with the original reference wave, while maintaining exactly the same shape (see Figure 5-2).

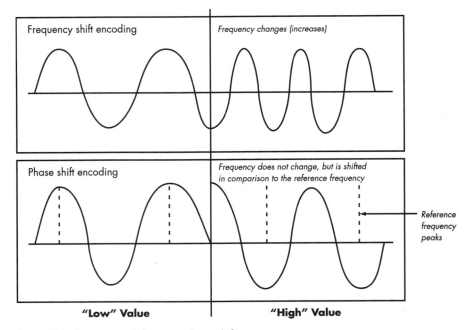

Figure 5-2: Frequency shift versus phase shift

The value of the phase shift, also called the *shift value*, is expressed in degrees (a reference to its effect on trigonometric functions: $y = \sin(x)$ shifted by 90° is exactly the same as $y = \sin(90° + x)$. A shift value of 360° denotes a shift by the entire wavelength, which simply puts the waves right back in sync and has no effect on the waveform. The correspondence of various phase shifts is shown in Figure 5-3, on the left.

Once both parties are synchronized and have a way to compare the signal received over the cable with the expected waveform, the actual encoded data can be easily retrieved. A differential circuit can compare two signals, subtract them, and easily determine the exact phase shift of the signal, by comparing it to a reference signal, as shown in Figure 5-3, on the right.

The new standard also took advantage of a more advanced data-encoding method. Instead of simply using two alternating signals to transmit 0s and 1s, as was the case previously, V.22 encodes whole *dibits*—slang for pairs of bits. Encoding two bits at once can be achieved using four phase shift values, with the amount of shift used to denote each of the possible values chosen so that values are uniformly and possibly farthest spaced through the entire 360° spectrum—and thus easily distinguishable from each other (see Table 5-1).

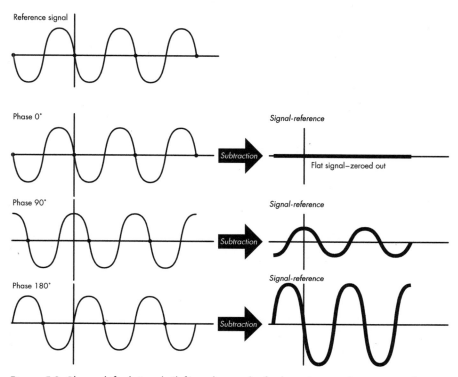

Figure 5-3: Phase shifted signals (left) and a result of subtracting a reference waveform to more easily distinguish between phases (right)

The use of dibits allowed for significantly faster transfer speed (1,200 baud) without the need to increase the physical rate with which the actual signal was modulated. Twice as much information—twice as many bits—was carried within every single beep.

Table 5-1: Using phase shifts to encode two bits of data (dibit)

Dibit	Phase Shift
00	90°
01	0°
10	180°
11	270°

NOTE *Although it is theoretically possible to use such an extended alphabet—that is, composite signal units similar to dibits (that have more than two states and thus encode more than one bit at once)—with FSK encoding as well, it is a bit more problematic to do so. FSK signals must avoid subharmonics and other frequencies that are particularly prone to distortion when sent through phone systems, thus severely limiting the set of possible states. The advantage of DPSK over FSK is that it uses a fixed frequency that is known to cause the fewest transmission problems and, hence, can be used more reliably at higher transmission rates.*

In the next few years, the pace of research accelerated a bit, and a number of new standards surfaced. The V.22bis standard took the concept of wide alphabet signaling a bit further, combining DPSK with signal amplitude (loudness) modulation to build a two-dimensional set of 16 possible values. The transition from a measured signal to binary values was expressed using a two-dimensional table. The value to which a signal corresponds is obtained by first looking up the column, based on the measured phase-shift value, and then the row is looked up based on the amplitude measurement. A simplified but analogous two-by-four example is shown in Table 5-2.

Table 5-2: Two-dimensional encoding of three bits using two distinct signal parameters

	Phase 0°	Phase 90°	Phase 180°	Phase 270°
Low amplitude	000 (0)	001 (1)	010 (2)	011 (3)
High amplitude	100 (4)	101 (5)	110 (6)	111 (7)

To add to the confusion, this new approach was called *quadrature amplitude modulation* (QAM). QAM once again made it possible to go from 1,200 to 2,400 bps without actually improving signal modulation speed, but by extending the number of meanings a single atom of signal can have.

The next major evolutionary step was V.32. V.32 was the first design to introduce a novel concept: instead of splitting frequencies, it used advanced echo cancellation circuitry[*] to detect and subtract the signal transmitted by the device itself from the data received over the wire. This technique allowed both devices (sender and receiver) to use the entire frequency spectrum, instead of just half of it, while still doing full-duplex.

Development continued, and the V.34 protocol soon appeared. Although the rate at which the signal could safely alternate before introducing excessive distortion did not noticeably change over the years, the standard was considerably faster than its predecessors. V.34 achieves a throughput of 28,800 baud, sometimes pushed a bit further by manufacturers to a unofficial speed of 33,600 baud (33.6 Kbps) by sending only about 2,500 to 3,500 signal samples (alphabet symbols) per second; however, it combines four different encoding schemes to build a four-dimensional structure with 1,664 possible states, making it possible to send as many as 41 bits at once. As it turns out, it's not about raw speed but how you use what you've got.

It is widely believed that the V.34 standard and its derivatives approach the theoretical limit for transmission of data via the voice-oriented telephone system. Although this may seem an odd statement given the prevalence of 56 Kbps modems, there is a catch: 56 Kbps devices achieve this transmission rate in a wholly different way than in analog solutions. Given that most phone systems have migrated from analog to digital since modems were first

---

[*] Echo cancellation circuits attempt to distinguish signals being sent by the device itself from those coming from the other party, and to eliminate or significantly reduce the former. Various types of such devices are commonly used not only in digital data transfer, but also to improve phone call quality, eliminate microphone feedback during public events, and solve many other everyday problems.

developed, and because most dial-up providers can now interface their systems directly with digital telecommunication systems, service providers can return to the most obvious but, until recently, impossible solution: changing line voltages instead of shifting frequencies when sending data to a subscriber. Because the signal is carried as digital data from the beginning—and can travel over buried copper lines only till the nearest telco facility—there are virtually no signal quality problems, and the only limit is the voice-carrying capacity designed into the phone system hardware. Working at 8,000 symbols per second, but operating with a considerably smaller alphabet (usually about 128 symbols, or voltage levels), it is possible to send data to a subscriber who is connected to a digital phone system with high-quality wire using a 56 Kbps modem at a higher speed than usual. The upstream transfer is still implemented the old-fashioned way, though, and is considerably slower; as such, the modem is only partly 56 Kbps, and only when conditions permit.

The Day Today

Not much has changed since the conception of modem technology. As transmission protocols advanced, so did the error-correction and fallback mechanisms needed to ensure reliable transmission when your favorite quadruped decides to chew the phone cable. A jungle of standards were spawned: V.42 provided a basic CRC (cyclic redundancy check) implementation, MNP-1 to MNP-4 provided proprietary error-correction algorithms, V.42bis and MNP-5 provided integrity checking combined with compression, and so on. But the real revolution is yet to come.

Or is it? You might argue that DSL and cable modems are a revolutionary technology that has changed the world. I am willing to argue: in fact, they are quite similar to their older cousins, modems. The only significant difference between the two is that the other endpoint—the server that handles all connections—has moved from a distant city where the service provider is located to the nearest local telco facility, and the connection to it can be made directly using the copper wire coming from the customer's residence or business. Because that direct connection again does not go through any other equipment, these devices can use high, inaudible frequencies and subtler signals that would otherwise be distorted or not relayed at all over the telephone network. In contrast, the good old modem was strictly limited to a narrow range of audible frequencies and signals that the phone system was intended to carry and that it could carry well. In many ways, DSL devices have it much easier than the old modem.

As we see, designing a modem is actually quite a complex and difficult task; that's why it took us decades to advance from bulky and expensive 300-baud devices to where we are now.[1] Surprisingly, all these devices can talk to one another, even to devices ten years older, even at the lowest speeds we long forgot about. Too, all are usually aware of the standards known to date, including the dozens of alternatives and forks of each. Doesn't that make modems even more a marvel of computer engineering?

But who pulls the strings?

Sometimes, a Modem Is Just a Modem

Modem-to-modem communications is, of course, not where the story starts or ends. The modem is just a piece of fairly inert middleware that's hardly even a good paperweight. For a modem to be of any use, it must be able to communicate with a computer to receive commands and exchange data, even when it's only being used for something as feeble as random web browsing. Internal modems have it easy: ISA (Integrated Systems Architecture), PCI (Peripheral Component Interconnect), PCMCIA (PC Memory Card International Association), and some other dedicated buses provide high-speed and fairly generous parallel interfaces that make the communication process almost trivial.

External modems (of the analog or DSL kind), however, have to do things the hard way, with a serial link. Most analog modems use the well-known serial protocol RS-232 (renamed in the '90s to the much more descriptive EIA/TIA-232-E[2]); many newer ones use USB (Universal Serial Bus). As we get close to the information disclosure scenarios in those devices, we want to get a glimpse of what happens to the data on its way between the modem and the computer, too, because that plays a crucial role in the attack.

Although external modems have to use inhumane means of communicating not only with a remote system, but also with the local machine itself, thanks to the proximity to the computer and the fact that interfaces such as RS-232 are digital and were designed for use by computers to start with, this stage is still much simpler than the phone line modulation and demodulation for which bit modems became famous.

RS-232 uses a fairly straightforward implementation of bipolar encoding for the data exchanged over two separate lines and backs this with a set of NRZ control lines. To make life a bit more interesting, RS-232 comes with a multitude of link or protocol features that make it fairly difficult to implement from scratch: its asynchronous nature, a wide array of possible settings and speeds, and unusual voltage levels. But with all this, RS-232 still does not even come close to a real challenge for an implementator who had dealt with signal modulation over phone lines.

USB, on the other hand, attempts to standardize and unify the serial interface. Although USB requires higher-end circuitry than RS-232 in order to interface a computer with a device (because of, among other things, a higher level of abstraction and higher supported transmission speeds), the USB is universal (hence its name) and has fewer oddities and legacy features.

Last but not least, a common method of communicating with local devices is the use of Ethernet, a mechanism somewhat similar to, but predating, USB. Let us look at Ethernet for a while now, and I am sure all those communication protocols will eventually meet in one place.

Collisions Under Control

Ethernet networks are, in essence, an advanced type of a multiparty serial link.[3] An Ethernet network is composed of a number of computers connected by a shared medium—nothing particularly complex, in its most basic form, just a pair of fairly regular wires. When a device on the network uses the medium, it applies a specific voltage to the wire, and all other connected systems can interpret the data by measuring the voltages. A set of checks ensures that devices do not try to use the link at the same time and that recovery is smooth if an accident happens. Still, even considering this possibility, the basic design is unbelievably trivial, compared with modems.

To work around the problem of two parties talking at once, a standard named Carrier Sense Multiple Access with Collision Detection (CSMA/CD) is used as the core mechanism controlling all communication via Ethernet. Before sending any data, every device connected to Ethernet follows a CSMA procedure to see if another device is using the cable by checking the modem's electrical properties. If no other transmission is occurring, the device enters the transmission phase and beams its data out to the masses.

In this phase, the data is sent on the wire as a sequence of bits using *bipolar encoding*; the traffic contains a header with all the necessary sender and recipient information and a proper checksum intended to protect the integrity of the data in case of external or internal interference, quadruped or not. A network interface that considers itself to be acting on behalf of a recipient, presumably by comparing the observed destination address provided in the packet with its unique MAC (hardware) address stored on the card, should accept this traffic and verify the checksum. At the same time, all other parties should ignore this frame; naturally, if they do not (and almost every card can be instructed not to), the user can view or react to traffic addressed to others. (You can see how Ethernet was designed in the spirit of far-fetched trust and altruism—a noble but risky approach.)

It is possible (and not very unlikely) for two devices on an Ethernet network to start sending at exactly the same moment, even though both checked just microseconds or nanoseconds ago for another party transmitting. And, if they do transmit at exactly the same moment, a disaster is bound to happen. Two transmissions are mixed up and mangled, and the sent data should fail the checksum test at the destination . . . or should it?

Although the use of a checksum implemented within the Ethernet frame specification is typically sufficient to verify data transmission accuracy, it may not be particularly effective if the link is saturated and hundreds or thousands of collisions occur in a short period of time; it is just small enough to accidentally come out correct from time to time. The law of probabilities tells us that some damaged packets will—just by chance—have the same checksum as an original packet. Furthermore, even if we ignore the problem of checksum deficiencies, we still want to stop collisions as soon as possible—by just letting collisions run rampant, you might find that you are no longer able to ensure the timely retransmissions of mangled and dropped frames in your network. After all, the sender sent it with no indication of a problem, and the recipient did not receive anything even remotely resembling a useful packet.

The solution comes with the latter part of the standard: collision detection (CD). The specification calls for the sender to monitor the network link while explaining their business to others. If another party is caught trying to talk at the same time, that should be detected (again, with a simple measurement of the electrical properties of the line), and the transmission should be immediately aborted. The device should also send a special jam code to ensure that both frames (the one being sent and the one that interfered with it) will be unconditionally dropped, without even getting to the checksum verification; the recipient should be able to spot the jam code and stop the reception of data being processed. The device then idles for a gradually increasing and preferably (initially) random period of time after every attempt (called retransmission backoff), to minimize the likelihood of a subsequent collision.

NOTE *A fun fact: The jam code mechanism imposes an unusual requirement on the protocol. All frames must have a minimum (!) length, with the value calculated such that it allows the jam code to be generated and propagated to all machines before the transmission is completed. With very short frames, there may not be enough time to achieve this. Hence, the sender is required to artificially pad all their outgoing transmissions.*

Figure 5-4 shows the exact sequence of events in a typical collision scenario. As you can see, Sender A hopes to send data to the recipient but notices another transmission occurring, at which point they decide to wait until that transmission stops. Sender A then prepares to send the data but, unfortunately, Sender B does the same, and both conclude that it is safe to send data at nearly the same time.

Both attempt to transmit, data gets mangled, and at that point both detect the other transmission and quickly send a jam code to instruct the recipient to disregard this frame. Finally, both senders back off for a random amount of time and hopefully manage not to start simultaneously the next time around.

Behind the Scenes: Wiring Soup and How We Dealt with It

Although not an example of a particularly scalable or elegant design, the Ethernet protocol is amazingly powerful and easy to deploy; it enabled the building of cheap peer-structure networks using coaxial cables just about anywhere. As such, it has become a de facto standard, replacing many other (and sometimes superior, but more expensive or proprietary) networking architectures.

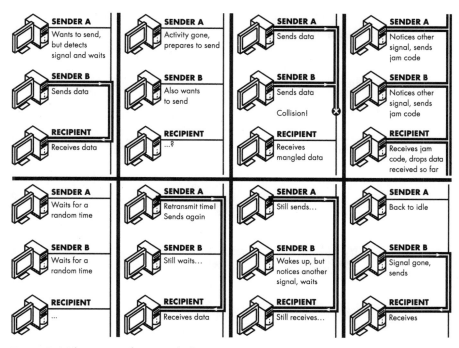

Figure 5-4: The stages of a typical Ethernet conversation

Naturally, simple Ethernet over coaxial cable had its limits and disadvantages; it was essentially based on a long piece of wire with devices hooked up to it at various locations, and with resistors on both ends, not something you'd want to be responsible for maintaining in a large office. A simple and difficult-to-debug mishap, such as a shorted terminal, could bring the entire infrastructure down. A more advanced—but only marginally more expensive—replacement was warmly welcomed.

Electronic multiport repeaters (hubs) made it possible to run wiring without much effort using twisted pair wiring (Cat-3 and Cat-5 cables with RJ-45 connectors). To use them, you simply plugged a piece of wire from your machine into a black box, and all other devices connected to this black box could communicate with it without much consideration of electrical problems or the risk that a single cable failure would bring down the entire network.

Hubs are, in essence, simple repeaters that broadcast all traffic received on one port to all other ports. They make it possible to build easily reconfigurable and more reliable star-type networks, but they do little else. As the network grows, the cost of broadcasting every bit of information to all locations, and the fact that only one party can talk at once across the entire network, makes it all too evident that the simplicity of this design is its major weakness.

Switches turned out to be the solution. Switches are the next generation of hubs. Equipped with a decent processor and some memory, they're a more expensive alternative to hubs that provide, under normal circumstances, additional high-level analysis of Ethernet frames. This analysis associates hardware addresses with specific ports and optimizes frame routing by delivering certain packets directly to the appropriate port (in unicast mode), instead of broadcasting them to all parties (see Figure 5-5). This greatly improves performance in more extensive networks.

NOTE *Another fun fact: Real hubs are almost extinct nowadays. Almost all 10/100 Mb devices marketed as hubs actually use basic switch chipsets; it is simply cheaper to repackage the chip than to develop and maintain several variants.*

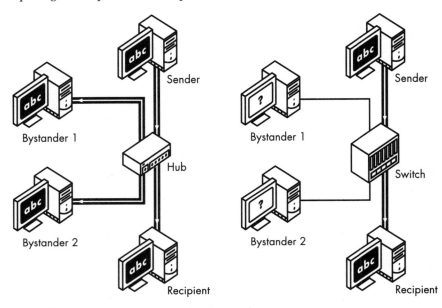

Figure 5-5: Hubs versus switches in local networks

I'm guessing that at this point you're asking yourself, Where the heck are you going with all this? What do modems have to do with information disclosure? What significance do serial links have in this context? How do Ethernet networks fit in? And what the heck are blinkenlights?

Glad you asked. I am about to get there—to the last question, that is.

Blinkenlights in Communications

Historically, almost all refrigerator-sized computers were equipped with numerous prominently exposed diagnostic interfaces. These included arrays of tiny lights that displayed, among other things, certain arcane properties of the internal state of a machine, such as internal registers or flags of the core processing unit or an indication of whether the cat living underneath had been fed today. As computers became more reliable and compact, and an average user no longer had to understand the machine's internals in order to use it efficiently, the lights started to disappear from many devices. Ever-increasing clock speeds also contributed to the decline—most of the time it was no longer possible for humans to get any meaningful information from such a visual signal that would change thousands or millions of times every second.

Yet, the lights prevailed in some applications; for example, almost all networking devices feature light-emitting diodes (LEDs) on their front or back panel. These provide link diagnostics, such as an indication of whether a particular module or socket is functioning properly, a party is connected, data is being transferred, and so on. The lights are not merely a diagnostic tool either; their hypnotic patterns have strange appeal, and their mystery plants seeds of uncertainty, fear, and respect in the hearts of lay people who enter the realm of the server room.

The term *blinkenlights* or *blinkenlichten* has been used to describe the much-adored institution of diagnostic LEDs on computer equipment ever since the dark ages of computing, bathing the computer geek in the soothing green light during those long, lonely nights spent at the terminal. It came from an amusing prank note in mock German (itself a spoof of another, noncomputer joke from WWII), displayed some time in the 1950s at IBM laboratories. The note later propagated into a majority of server rooms and computer science laboratories across the world and went like this (as quoted from Eric S. Raymond's *Hacker's Dictionary*):

```
ACHTUNG!

ALLES LOOKENSPEEPERS!

Alles touristen und non-technischen
looken peepers! Das computermachine
ist nicht fuer gefingerpoken und
mittengrabben. Ist easy schnappen
der springenwerk, blowenfusen und
poppencorken mit spitzensparken.
Ist nicht fuer gewerken bei das
dumpkopfen. Das rubbernecken
sichtseeren keepen das cotton-pickenen
hans in das pockets muss; relaxen und
watchen das blinkenlichten.
```

Communications equipment is one of the last domains in which blinkenlights prevail and prosper. But that's not all. Almost all these devices use serial lines for communications. And, for the sake of simplicity and aesthetics, "activity" LEDs are sometimes wired almost directly, through a simple driver circuit, to the transmit or receive line of the device. Curtain falls.

The Implications of Aesthetics

It took decades for the problem to be discovered, and once it happened (in 2002), it struck us all as so obvious and trivial we wanted to bang our heads on the keyboard a couple of times.

Joe Lughry and David A. Umphress, in a research paper titled "Information Leakage from Optical Emanations,"[4] discovered a new type of signal-disclosure scenario in certain types of network equipment, most often modems. They concluded that someone observing these lights could go beyond simply watching the magic lights with the naked eye.

LEDs, unlike incandescent bulbs, usually have short rise and fall times, meaning that they turn on and off almost instantly. That's not surprising; after all, high-end LEDs are used to control fiber-optic links and some other optoelectronic communication channels. As such, the blinking of an LED hooked up to a serial data transmission line can actually often mirror single bits of the transmission as it occurs on the wire. Given a way to record this activity at a sufficient speed, it should be possible to retrieve this information, from at least as far as you can see the tiny blinking light on a device with the naked eye (or with a telephoto lens).

This research caused some stir in the industry; it was eventually also both downplayed and overhyped, and hence a great deal of confusion ensued, and very little has changed. The paper resulted in many conflicting reports, but its basic premise is simple and truly beautiful. The beauty of this technique is that it is trivial to devise such a device to receive the signal: the equally cheap and popular counterparts of LEDs—photodiodes and phototransistors—are easy to acquire and equally easy to interface with the computer. And the exposure zone, unlike most of the TEMPEST activity we discussed in Chapter 3, is not merely the subject of urban legends and pure laboratory results, but can be directly observed and measured.

In the course of their research, the authors performed a set of experiments to verify that the signal could be successfully acquired from as far away as 20 meters (just under 100 feet) without the need for additional digital signal conditioning. And common sense suggests that this might actually be an understatement, especially when good optics are used. (The authors used a 100 mm focal length, f/2.0 lens for the test, but a much better telephoto lens is commonly available to many midrange SLR (single lens reflex) photography amateurs. Those who are willing to part with their money can buy a superb-quality lens with a focal length of as much as 1,200 mm.)

The paper takes a defensive stance in several cases, and a careful reader might be tempted to conclude that some of the devices classified are not vulnerable to the problem. In particular, some of the Ethernet devices may exhibit a more subtle variant of the vulnerability, as you'll see in the prevention section later in this chapter. But first let's peek at the problem with our own (computerized) eyes, shall we?

Building Your Own Spy Gear . . .

The simplicity of building a snooping device makes it quite tempting to do so. This section contains several suggestions and rough schematics on how to build and connect such a device to an ordinary computer. Although the circuit is not particularly complex and does not require a master's degree in soldering and a printed board circuit design software, a minimum level of proficiency in electronics is desirable, as is a dose of common sense. Although external interfaces of today's computers are fairly robust and foolproof, there is always the risk of damaging equipment when attaching home-brew devices in a really innovative way, in a brief moment of insanity. It's happened to the best of us.

The baseline design is extremely trivial. It calls for a single phototransistor (a component consisting of a transistor driven by a built-in photodiode), a regular low-power NPN (Negative-Positive-Negative) transistor to amplify the signal a bit further (not always necessary), and a set of potentiometers (perhaps in the range of 10 kΩ just to have enough flexibility) to experimentally pull down the voltage and control the circuit's sensitivity and threshold points. There are no particular requirements for the components, although your mileage will vary depending on which ones you use. Be sure to select a phototransistor that has a decent response in the visible light range, though all cheap ones should work. (For reference, a green LED emits a wavelength of approximately 520 nm.)

A sample circuit design is shown in Figure 5-6.

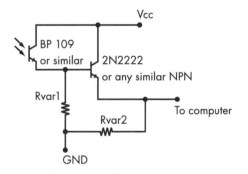

Figure 5-6: A simple receiver circuit

The circuit has an optimal running voltage of approximately 5V and a low maximum current: a power supply capable of delivering perhaps 10 to 50 mA is more than enough. A word of warning: If you use a supply capable of delivering a higher voltage, you will risk damaging the port or the computer; likewise, if you use a more powerful supply and do not prevent higher current from flowing through the circuit.

NOTE *Setting Rvar1 or Rvar2 to a very low resistance may short the circuit. If you want to fiddle with the knobs mindlessly, it might be a good idea to add a fixed resistor to limit the current drain.*

You must shield the phototransistor from external light sources—for example, by enclosing it in an opaque tube. Because the phototransistor has no focusing mechanism, it is not likely to pick up more distant signals (other than ambient light). Thus, for initial tests, it is a good idea to cover it entirely to simulate darkness and then put it by an LED to excite the circuit. You can also connect another LED temporarily between the GND and the output line to test the circuit. The test LED should light up when the sensor is directed at a light source, but otherwise be fairly dark.

. . . And Using It with a Computer

If the circuit with a test LED hookup works so far, well done; you have built a fancy TV remote tester. Because generic, cheap phototransistors are eager to pick up infrared light, your creation should "translate" IR (infrared) into visible light, but that's about all the fun stuff it will do. To make it a bit more useful, you need to interface the circuit with the computer. A good way to do so is through a line printer interface, LPT, if your computer has one. Unfortunately, this wonderful hardware hacker's tool is being dropped from some of the more compact and fancy designs.

Although initially designed to be unidirectional (for output only), the LPT interface provides a number of status feedback lines, such as "paper out," "busy," and "acknowledgment," that were intended to provide a means for the printer to complain about problems. You can easily read the data that issues through this interface by accessing port 0x379 (the LPT1 status register) on a PC-compatible system. By hooking the circuit to a parallel port, you can easily transmit information back to the computer. Although you might want to connect the circuit to a different interface, LPT is much faster than, say, RS-232, and you won't have to cope with any mundane protocols, signaling schemes, or unusual voltage levels. Too, unlike USB and some other current solutions, you do not need special controllers to implement a fairly complex protocol to even be able to talk to your PC.

NOTE *Although LPT also offers bi-directional operation modes (ECP or EPP), it is usually pointless to attempt to use this functionality for such a simple task. In the unidirectional mode, four bits are available for input, more than enough for this application; switching to bi-directional modes such as EPP or ESP provides an extra four bits.*

It is up to you to choose the status line to use. Table 5-3 shows a pin layout of the DB25 connector used for a printer port. The rows shaded gray can be used for input.

To interface the circuit with this port, you can simply connect the ground reference point on the connector with the one used in your circuit and then hook up the output line to any of the five pins. (Remember to disconnect the LED used for diagnostics first.) Next, monitor the status port as you first expose it to light and then cover the sensor. In either case, the value read depends on how you hooked up the circuit; the exact value does not matter, as long as the two values are different.

Table 5-3: LPT pinout

LPT Port: DB25 Pinout (Standard Mode)

Pin	Name	Function
1	Strobe	Control output bit 0
2	D0	Data output bit 0
3	D1	Data output bit 1
4	D2	Data output bit 2
5	D3	Data output bit 3
6	D4	Data output bit 4
7	D5	Data output bit 5
8	D6	Data output bit 6
9	D7	Data output bit 7
10	ACK	Status input bit 2
11	Busy	Status input bit 3
12	Paper Out	Status input bit 1
13	Select In	Status input bit 0
14	Autofeed	Control output bit 1
15	Error	Status input (unused)
16	Init	Control output bit 2
17	Select	Control output bit 3
18	GND	Ground (0V)
19	GND	Ground (0V)
20	GND	Ground (0V)
21	GND	Ground (0V)
22	GND	Ground (0V)
23	GND	Ground (0V)
24	GND	Ground (0V)
25	GND	Ground (0V)

Because chip logic requires somewhat different input levels than your test LED diode, you might have to tweak the Rvar2 until you get distinct readings from the port when you cover the sensor, and when you expose it to light. To accomplish this, it is best to be able to monitor the port in real time on the computer itself.

The way you can monitor the state of the port will depend on the operating system and the programming language you are using. If you're using C, the function used to read the value off a port is inb(port), so in this particular case you would issue inb(0x379) and check the return value. In other languages, it is likely to have a similar name. (Try looking for in, inport, readport, and so forth.) Also, Windows users may find the built-in "debug" utility and its "i" (port read) function quite handy.

NOTE *On some systems, such as Linux, you might need to request that the system give you permission to access a specific port first. Consult the documentation for* iopl(3) *or a similar call for more information.*

At this point, you are ready to go. You can choose to point your probe at any LED on a device, adjust the sensor based on its brightness, and start reading alternating patterns of light and dark signals, as you discover how they correspond to the exchanged information, if at all.

NOTE *If you're curious, you might try to examine the brightness of the indicator diode, not only a binary representation of its state. It might turn out that even though a specific LED is not intended to directly map a signal on the serial line to its blink patterns, there is some analog cross talk between circuits, and the serial line signal will have some influence on the brightness. A cheap analog-to-digital converter such as TLV571 from Texas Instruments is just asking to be used this way.*

You can use this approach to sample the frequency of less than 1 million bits per second, which should suffice for capturing transmission on many interfaces, but not necessarily on Ethernet ports (which transmit at least 10 million bits per second). Past this capture capacity, your LPT port will likely reach its physical throughput limits, but do not despair: as long as the sensor (phototransistor) can switch at the rate sufficient to capture communications in question, you still have an option. Remember that LPT is a parallel port. To reach faster capture speeds, such as the one needed for Ethernet, combine a trivial clock, a counter circuit, and a set of sample-and-hold latches (such as 74LS377) to sequentially store data between the port read attempts on the computer side. You can accumulate this information for a short period of time and then, by using more than just one status pin (or by switching the port to bi-directional mode), easily send several bits—samples—to the computer, in a single burst, in one read cycle, thus improving the read rate four- or eightfold.

I'll spare you a further, perhaps needless, excursion into the world of electronics. If you want to toy with the idea of high-speed or analog sampling, or perhaps just get your kicks from soldiering stuff together and hooking it to a computer, you might want to take a look at my fairly comprehensive introductory tutorial under the thin disguise of a computer-controlled robot design project. You should be able to find it at http://lcamtuf.coredump.cx/robot.txt.

And now, for those with interests that lean more toward practical security: a brief discussion of how to address the issue, short of covering all LEDs in the office with duct tape.

Preventing Blinkenlights Data Disclosure—and Why It Will Fail

The easiest solution to the problem, and one suggested by the original research, is *pulse stretching*—a practice intended to distort the blinks on an indicator by prolonging some of them, thus making any practical data recovery seemingly not feasible. *Pulse stretching circuits* are a group of fairly trivial devices that extend the duration of an encountered "high" input signal for an additional period of time. Most basic pulse stretcher design relies on a capacitor that charges in the presence of an input signal and then discharges slowly. This capacitor is connected to a *binary discriminator,* which is not a nickname for a vicious wrestling champion, but rather a device that converts analog data into binary output by applying a particular threshold (outputting a voltage for logical 1 for all input voltages above *n,* and 0 for all input voltages below). In this case, it uses a certain capacitor charge level as the discrimination point.

More advanced and reliable designs, including purely digital circuitry, are also common, and all can be used in hubs and switches to make LEDs nice to look at. Without them, the high-speed blinking at way more than 50 cycles per second (considered the limit on our ability to perceive flicker), would usually result in our seeing the lights as dim but seemingly constant. A discriminator causes the LED to be driven by 1 more often than by 0 by extending the duration of each 1 pulse. This makes the LED light brighter and blink less often. Figure 5-7 shows the behavior of such a pulse stretcher: a single spike (single 1) is stretched to last three times as long, whereas all 0s are left as they are.

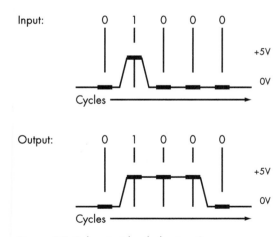

Figure 5-7: Pulse stretcher behavior, 3x

While their primary purpose is aesthetic, as I have mentioned, this also seems to be a good way to solve the problem of light emissions information disclosure, by letting the attacker deduce only certain general properties of the traffic. Thus, at best, the attacker can figure out only general properties of the traffic, such as when something is being sent and when it is not.[*]

What seems to be a good solution, however, is not always. Consider the following sample data and the corresponding serial line signal:

Data:
0 1 0 1 0 0 1 0 0 0 0 0 1 0 0 0 0 1 1 0 0 0 0 0 1 1 0 0 0 0 0 0

NRZ signal:

Assume the signal is processed using a 5x pulse stretcher that makes every 1 last for five additional cycles. (The original paper suggests a safe limit of 2x, but we'll exaggerate to make a point.)

Original signal:

Level activated stretcher (5x):

Data we can read out of LED after stretching:
0 1 1 1 1 1 1 1 1 1 1 0 1 1 1 1 1 1 1 1 1 1 1 0 1 1 1 1 1 1 0 0

Although it might appear that almost all important information has been lost when compared with the input signal we want to intercept, it is possible to recover much of it by making four important observations:

- Obviously, all areas where the stretcher output is zero must have been zero in the original signal.
- Each stretched run of 1s must have been triggered by 1 at the starting location in the original stream.
- Each run of L 1s must have originally contained at least one 1 for every N cycles, where N is the stretch factor for this circuit; otherwise, there would be gaps in the run. The count of 1s in a block of data represented under a single stretch of 1s in output is greater than or equal to L/N rounded up.
- Every run ends after exactly N-1 zeros in the original stream. We know that these zeros must have been preceded with 1; otherwise the run would have ended sooner.

---

[*] This, technically speaking, is still an attack venue, per the discussion in Chapter 1, yet it is considerably less effective and practical, for we only get a rough idea of what is going on, not a copy of the data.

By applying this knowledge to the previous example, we can reconstruct most of the original data, as follows:

Stretcher output:

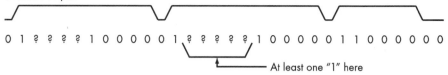

In the previous fairly realistic example, fewer than 9 out of 32 bits of data were lost due to pulse stretching and cannot be conclusively reconstructed (marked with question marks in the graphic). Thus, we recovered 99.999988% of the potential search space. We must guess at the remaining data, which (especially if the data snooped is regular English text, such as email) is rather trivial to reconstruct compared to the starting point. The authors of the research suggest that even $N = 1.5$ or $N = 2$ "on" time pulse stretching is sufficient to obfuscate the data, but this is not necessarily so.

The previous reconstruction scheme works with stretches of 0s or 1s. Some links use return-to-zero (RZ) encodings (such as the Manchester scheme mentioned earlier), and because the signal is constantly alternating there, the 2x stretching might indeed be sufficient to obfuscate all data. However, this is only true if the LED is driven by a signal prior to initial internal decoding to NRZ—which, in most situations, is not the case. In fact, applying pulse stretching to RZ-encoded signal is often a silly idea in that the LED would be on all the time; hence there seems to be no point in doing that in the first place.

As noted previously, an additional problem stems from the quality of the pulse stretcher and its susceptibility to interference from other internal circuits: LED voltage fluctuations that result in slight brightness changes during a "stretch" period might disclose some information. Capacitor-based solutions, in particular, can fall into this category.

Thus, some systems, particularly Ethernet devices known to deploy pulse stretching, can be partly vulnerable to attack, even though the original paper discussed earlier concluded that there is no direct correlation between the transmitted data and the behavior of an LED, based on the observation of a recorded blinking pattern using an oscilloscope.

The optimal solution, particularly with other types of encoding, or when pulse stretching is not desirable for some other reason (for example, if the designer wants to avoid making the LED light appear constantly for the time of a transmission) is to sample the line at a fairly low frequency (for example, 20 Hz) and latch it to a register that holds it until the next sample and that also controls the LED.

And, now, back to plain English.

Food for Thought

Other than network device LEDs, plenty of other, equally interesting light emissions leak scenarios can be found, although the amount of information disclosed can be significantly lower. For example, consider disk activity LEDs. Of course, disk communication is not using serial signaling; instead, portions of data, ranging from bytes to 32-bit words, are sent simultaneously using a set of signal lines. And, although the LED is usually attached to indicate only a state of a specific control line, it is still possible to deduce many aspects of system activity by measuring seek times or the amount of data stored and read. (Depending on what the LED is actually attached to, it may be possible to measure either or both.) Although it's unlikely that this information would give an attacker any immediate advantage, certain induced I/O activities can be combined with hard-disk drive LED observation to draw interesting conclusions, although I am unaware of any research in this area.

Other potential attack venues involve many USB devices and other proprietary interfaces. As mentioned earlier, USB is a serial bus, and some USB appliances do have activity indicators.

Various other unusual and arcane information-disclosure venues have also been proposed, partly researched or at least toyed with. These include measuring the acoustic effects of recharging capacitors as the CPU consumes various levels of power depending on the executed instruction[5] or measuring a black box device by analyzing its power consumption with the help of statistical analysis.[6] Once again, no truly comprehensive research has been done in the area of disclosure channels other than classic EMF (electromagnetic field) emanations—and it appears to be a good idea to investigate. Best of luck. :-)

ECHOES OF THE PAST

*Where, on the example of a curious Ethernet flaw, we learn
that it is good to speak precisely*

The previous chapter tackled the basics of Ethernet communications. This seemingly foolproof and amazingly trivial mechanism appears to be incapable of causing serious security issues, except for the possible abuse of the trust relationship caused by the regular broadcasting of data to all parties on the network. This is a well-known and well-understood property of Ethernet networks, for which good remedies include switches, bridges, and network segmentation, to name just a few.

Nonetheless, this issue manifests itself in ways wholly unforeseen, due largely to an unfortunate choice of words, or lack thereof, in the official implementation requirements for Ethernet drivers. A widespread implementation problem is the result, and it has reached a scale that has earned it a place as this chapter. It provides an interesting case study for this class of nobody-at-fault problems.

Building the Tower of Babel

The Ethernet protocol provides the basic means to distribute bytes over a piece of wire: a low-level data-encoding scheme, and a data format to contain a portion of the information. The Ethernet frame contains the information about the local disposition of the data it carries (that is, who is sending it and who should be the recipient) and a brief description of the type of information encapsulated. Additional methods for error detection are also provided, and then the entire frame is pushed out to a potential recipient and all other systems. In terms of functionality, Ethernet is similar to data portion encapsulation schemes used over different mediums or in different applications, such as frame relay, Asynchronous Transfer Mode (ATM), Point-to-Point Protocol (PPP), and so forth.

The question is, "What data should be carried by such an Ethernet frame?" Computers use hundreds of formats and application protocols and can run applications ranging from scientific simulations to network games and chat clients. As such, although it is possible to simply encapsulate the data for a remote recipient within an Ethernet frame as is, it is usually a bad idea because the recipient won't know how to handle it. Is it incoming email? A web picture? Or perhaps configuration data? You can't tell. Too, because a typical computer runs a variety of programs almost simultaneously, the distinction is even further blurred.

Ethernet poses yet another problem on a larger scale; specifically, how to reach the other end. Broadcasting data to all parties on a local network is easy; but what if the other system, the party one of the local users hopes to reach, is not local? What if it has to be reached over a wide area network (WAN) and uses a wholly different link-layer protocol? Even if a way can be found to route traffic to that remote destination, a more fundamental issue remains: how to address the package.

Ethernet uses its own unique, specialized addressing scheme. It calls hosts by their theoretically unique hardware card identification numbers (Media Access Control addresses, or MAC addresses) embedded by the manufacturer on every Ethernet adapter. These numbers are meaningful only to Ethernet; they are meaningless to any other type of network and are nearly impossible to use to track down a piece of hardware if you are not on the local setup. This raises a trust issue. For example, who bought a card with the address of 00:0D:56:E3:FB:E4, and where are they now? Can you trust them to really be the original purchaser and not an impostor?

Low-level host-addressing schemes, such as this one, usually are no help in relaying data to its destination unless the hardware with a particular MAC address is attached directly to the sender's physical network. There is no way to directly map a physical device identifier to a particular location on the globe and determine which path should be used to send it information.

The OSI Model

The link-level protocols were designed to support communication between local nodes or, in some extreme cases, between two fixed endpoints on a shared link. To make internetworking possible and some more practical uses of the networks feasible, a hierarchical structure of network protocols called Open System Interconnection (OSI) was devised.

The OSI model (see Figure 6-1) defines the physical connection level as the first layer and builds higher-level features on top of it. Link-level protocols constitute the second layer (data link layer) and are, as expected, defined as a way to communicate with other local nodes that use the same physical link. These protocols carry higher-level, link-independent protocol data, defined as the third layer (network layer) of the model. The Internet Protocol, IP for short, is the most prominent example of such a protocol.

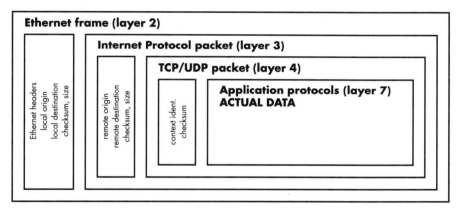

Figure 6-1: The physical data layout in the OSI model, an example

The third layer is designed to provide information about the general disposition of the traffic as well as universal identification of both the origin and final destination of data using network-specific addressing, thus making it easier to route the packet. Unlike the second-layer protocols, the third layer is not discarded or modified en route and is devoid of any link-specific features such as MAC addresses, CSMA/CD (Carrier Sense Multiple Access with Collision Detection) overhead, and so forth.

The fourth layer provides the means for establishing specific communication channels between endpoints starting and terminating on a given machine. This provides a way for simultaneous communication of multiple types and channels. None of the fourth-level protocols needs to be understood by intermediate systems to properly deliver the traffic to the destination. The packets are interpreted only by the final recipient to determine which application should be receiving the data and how this piece of information relates to adjacent packets.

The subsequent layers of the OSI model are perhaps less interesting and have a tendency to blend together. The fifth level is supposed to provide reliability features that are often incorporated either in fourth-level protocols, such as TCP/IP (Transmission Control Protocol/Internet Protocol), or on the application level. In some cases, they are not even implemented at all if there is no need to achieve reliable communications. The sixth level provides "library" functions, such as decompression and decoding of the data and, as with the fifth level, is usually perceived in terms of application-level functionality. Finally, the seventh layer is the application layer, the place where data is transferred in a specific format.

Notice that the higher layers in the OSI model are independent of the lower layers as they apply to the carried data. When the time is right, the lower layers can gradually be disposed of without losing the data or the ability to further process it. The second layer is discarded at every intermediate system; the third layer can be discarded once the data is delivered to its destination system. The fourth layer is dropped before delivering the data to the client application.

The third layer usually remains completely independent of the underlying link-level protocol by providing complete sender and addressee information, an integrity protection mechanism (checksumming), and information about the size of the carried payload. This is precisely what IP does.

One important consequence of this design is that any superfluous information appended to the packet on layer 2 while in transit will not affect the way the IP information is interpreted by the addressee.

The Missing Sentence

In the previous chapter's discussion of the design of the Ethernet, I mentioned an interesting requirement that arises out of a need to provide reliable jam code propagation for the purpose of collision notification: the *minimum* size limit for an Ethernet frame.

This requirement was carried over to the official IP-over-Ethernet encapsulation specifications, such as RFC 1042, "A Standard for the Transit of Internet Protocol Datagrams Over IEEE 802 Networks,"[1] by requiring frames that were shorter than this minimum length to be padded. The padding can be carried out at will and has no effect on the carried data on the IP layer, as the packet length specified in the IP headers does not change. Thus, the padding will not be interpreted by the recipient as a part of higher-level OSI model traffic.

There is, however, a slight problem. Although the RFC requires the padding to be initialized to zero, it does not specify who should provide and prepare the padding and at what software stage the padding should occur. The need for the padding to be of a particular value is also a requirement that in its nature is fairly arbitrary; hence, no attention is paid to it—setting it any other way would not impact how the protocol works, because the extraneous data is simply discarded upon receipt.

To add to the confusion, many network interface cards provide an autopadding feature if a packet the operating system sent to the hardware is too short—but, naturally, not to ensure the specific contents of a padding if frame size has been already taken care of in software. This led to widespread confusion among some developers who chose to obey the size requirement and extend the size of a packet in software by simply increasing its declared length. They often did not realize that the data between the end of the IP packet and the end of the padded frame was not prepared (initialized to zeros) by the driver, the operating system, or the hardware.

The problem went largely unnoticed for years, although it caused an awkward issue that regularly drove some network hackers insane. The packets they received from local systems often contained some extra garbage at the end—such as fragments of website contents or even chat conversations that were clearly irrelevant. They blamed the recipient (faulty equipment, the network traffic analysis application, libraries) but ultimately gave up looking for a cause because the issue was of marginal relevance. The issue never got the attention it deserved.

That is, not until Ofir Arkin and Josh Anderson of @Stake decided to give it a closer look in 2003. Their paper "EtherLeak—Ethernet Frame Padding Information Leaks"[2] examined the problem in more detail. The authors realized that a large number of mainstream systems, such as Linux, NetBSD, Microsoft Windows, and other platforms, fail to initialize the memory at the end of the newly prepared Ethernet frame after modifying its length. Some implementations even fail to change the size of a frame properly or to send a proper number of bytes to the hardware layer.

As a result, the IP packet is padded with data that happens to be stored in the portion of memory the system used previously for other purposes. The memory could contain part of a previously sent packet or some other kernel memory fragment, depending on the design of the driver or the operating system. This, of course, creates a fascinating information disclosure scenario: An attacker sends inconspicuous and legitimate traffic to the victim and, with some luck, obtains potentially sensitive information. The amount of information disclosed is typically sufficient to justify concern.

The exposure is limited to a single Ethernet network and, as such, is fairly localized and noncritical in a typical LAN environment. Still, it definitely remains a problem of some significance, and even though any local network is partly vulnerable to snooping, this particular problem suggests some conclusions that extend beyond the most obvious:

- On systems that use dynamic buffers for outgoing Ethernet frames (Linux, for example), the padding can expose not only the previous frame, but other memory contents, such as edited or viewed documents, URLs, passwords, or other sensitive resources. In this case, a careful observer might be able to gain access to information they could not otherwise intercept on the network.

- On systems that use static buffers only to prepare Ethernet frames, the problem can be exploited to defeat systems that protect against traffic sniffing, such as switches, enabling the attacker to intercept data from a different connection.

- In certain static buffer designs, information from another segment on a multihoned machine, with one network interface connected to a general LAN and the other interface hooked up to a restricted network, can be exposed, thus relaying portions of presumably secret data to the public infrastructure.

The authors of the paper extensively reviewed several open-source implementations and concluded that a variety of approaches and buffer layouts are commonly used and that there is no predominant buffer allocation and usage scheme. Their conclusion? A typical diverse network environment is likely to be affected by all three types of issues at some point.

Food for Thought

The issue discussed here is not unique to Ethernet or network design. These problems almost always arise when an otherwise detailed implementation guideline omits or only vaguely discusses a single necessary step, causing numerous developers to simply overlook the problem while implementing the standard. Had they been given more vague overall instructions, developers would probably be forced to think through the problem. Instead, they implement step-by-step instructions and are far more vulnerable to committing errors. "Foolproof" instructions that tell how to perform certain tasks, as opposed to what to achieve, often backfire.

We will return to the problems of protocol leak scenarios, albeit in a slightly different context, in Part III of this book.

7

SECURE IN SWITCHED NETWORKS

Or, why Ethernet LANs cannot be quite fixed,
no matter how hard we try

Ethernet networks do not provide a universal and easy way to ensure the integrity or confidentiality of the data they transmit, nor are they engineered to withstand malicious, intentionally injected traffic. Ethernet is merely a means for interfacing a number of local, presumably trusted systems.

Assuming this level of trust is convenient at the design stage and is theoretically sufficient for peer systems on the same network and often at roughly the same physical location. But, as the old saying goes, only in theory is there no difference between theory and practice. In practice, there is a difference.

As it turns out, local networks are difficult to fully control and must be protected from their own users as well as from external threats. Any expanding local network is bound to encounter a rogue user, whether from within the organization or from outside, exploiting a flaw in one of the systems. The occurrence of such an exploit is only a matter of time, as almost all network administrators learn at some point.

Practical network security is the art of detecting incidents, minimizing exposure, and assessing and understanding the risk on all levels, not only an exercise in building perimeter defenses. The problem? A bare-bones Ethernet infrastructure is prone to all types of data interception, hijacking, and impersonation scenarios; once an intruder or a malicious but legitimate user controls a single system on the network—breaking through a single line of defense—this person can wreak havoc on the infrastructure and gain access or take over certain resources and services with minimal effort.

Some Theory

Ethernet switches, a class of smart devices designed to route unicast traffic on the second OSI layer to the appropriate port instead of broadcasting it to all nodes (as is the case with hubs or direct connections), may appear to solve this problem. They are often thought to solve the security problems associated with the ability for one system to observe or hijack third-party traffic, but this is not so. The solution is not that simple, and the confusion caused by this presumption sometimes causes more harm than the switches could do good in the first place. But first things first. To understand the exposure, let's look at how Ethernet switches really work.

Address Resolution and Switching

All communication within a local network is based on the addressing scheme discussed in Chapter 5. Unique identifiers assigned by the hardware manufacturer to a specific endpoint device are used to address systems and deliver data frames. However, the Internet and most of today's private networks are built around a more flexible and universal suite of protocols and use an addressing scheme on the third OSI layer, commonly known as Internet Protocol (IP) addresses. The IP address is first used to direct the traffic across the world to an appropriate local network using a hierarchy of routing tables on middle systems all over the globe; not until the packet reaches the perimeter of the destination network must the final recipient be located the old-fashioned way, by a hardware address lookup.

Whenever a system on the local network decides to locate another local party with a specific IP address, it uses a special address resolution protocol (ARP) to determine the association between a physical card address—the basis for addressing systems on a local network—and the IP address, a universal internetworking system identifier.[1] The sender distributes an ARP query to a special broadcast address on the local network. This reserved address is guaranteed to be received and processed by all systems on the network, regardless of the actual hardware address assigned to specific nodes. In this scenario, the system that considers itself to have the right to use the IP address specified in the query is expected to send a response to the sender, thus disclosing its hardware address in answer to the query; all other folks are supposed to silently ignore the broadcast ARP packet. After this exchange, both parties now know each other's IP and media access control (MAC) addresses. They should cache the finding in a special buffer to eliminate the need to perform additional lookups every time a portion of data is exchanged and then proceed with the actual communications—but other than that, they are ready to swap some packets based on IP addressing. This design is a charming and delightful example of an old-time trust and courtesy. But what can be done to contain the exposure caused by a malicious bystander on the same network, who pretends to be someone else, and what can be done to prevent the more curious users or evil foes from reaching too far? Manufacturers of the Ethernet hardware most certainly did not help network administrators by making it possible and trivial to change MAC addresses on most of today's devices—presumably allowing the user to reprogram then in order not to end up in trouble should one day a batch of cards turn out to have duplicate addresses.

Again, switches appear to solve the problem. The basic design concept behind a smart switching device relies on duplicating the MAC address cache on the level of an interim network device. A switching device is equipped with numerous Ethernet ports, each of which connects to a single system (or, less often, a set of systems). But instead of serving as dumb repeaters, sending all traffic received on one port to all others (as Ethernet hubs do), switches attempt to memorize MAC addresses associated with a machine connected to each port, effectively creating MAC-to-port associations, as opposed to the MAC-to-IP mappings created by endpoint systems.

The data, stored in content addressable memory[*] (CAM), determines where to deliver incoming packets. Whenever a portion of traffic arrives, the switch attempts to determine which port the addressee is on. If this information is available, the packet is delivered directly (and only) to this particular port, keeping the information away from others and improving network performance.

Virtual Networks and Traffic Management

Some more advanced switch solutions provide additional features intended to make it easier to manage extensive networks and to lower deployment times and expenses. These features also appear to help with network security and may include the following:

Virtual LAN (VLAN)

A general name for a set of methods used to divide a pool of ports on a physical device into a set of separate logical networks, thus separating traffic on a group of ports from others and preventing any kind of traffic from crossing between those groups on the switch level. (This scheme is most commonly implemented using the IEEE 802.1Q standard, discussed in the next item in detail.) Implementing a VLAN is like splitting

---

[*] As its name suggests, this type of memory can be directly addressed by the parameter for which you are trying to determine the value, which saves time that would normally have to be spent on searching for the parameter. A library catalog is a trivial example of CAM—you do not need to go through all the books in the library just to find one; you determine where to look based on what you are looking for (a piece of information about the "content").

a single switch into several fully independent devices, except that the VLAN solution is far more flexible and cost-effective, because it is possible to reshape your network and reallocate physical resources at will. VLANs were met with a warm welcome by network staff everywhere because they promised to offer a simple yet powerful way to build a set of separate networks on a single device or, for example, separate servers from workstations, without the need to buy a dedicated switch for each group.

Trunking

A natural extension of the baseline VLAN design. Trunks use the IEEE 802.1Q frame-tagging scheme to tunnel multiple VLAN traffic over a single link, instead of forcing the user to run separate wire for every VLAN to be populated to another device, as shown in Figure 7-1. Packets from all or some VLANs on the source switch are tagged with enough information to determine their originating VLAN within the Ethernet frame header, tunneled to the other endpoint over a traditional link, decoded, and then pushed out into appropriate VLANs at the destination. Although this option usually results in lower performance than running a separate cable for every subnet, it is much more practical. Trunked systems often also feature DTP (Dynamic Trunking Protocol), a trunk autoconfiguration protocol that enables devices to automatically discover and exchange encapsulated frames other trunk-enabled devices with no special administrative actions required.

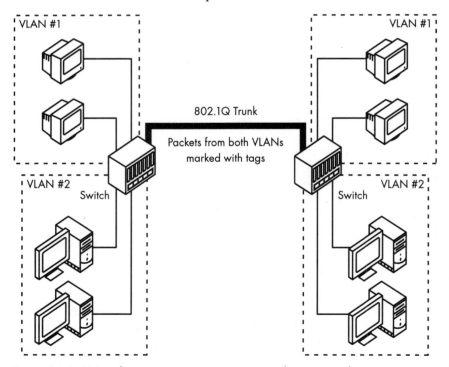

Figure 7-1: VLAN trunking in action. VLANs propagated across two devices. Devices on all instances of both VLAN #1 and VLAN #2 can talk with each other, but cross talk between VLAN #1 and VLAN #2 is not possible.

Spanning tree protocol (STP)

Lets you build redundant network structures in which switches are interconnected in more than one location, in order to maintain fault tolerance. Traditionally, such a design could cause broadcast traffic and some other packets to loop forever while also causing network performance to deteriorate significantly, because the data received on one interface and forwarded to another in effect bounces back to the originator (see Figure 7-2, left).

When designing a network, it is often difficult to avoid accidental broadcast loops. It is also sometimes desirable to design architectures with potential loops (in which one switch connects to two or more switches), because this type of design is much more fault tolerant and a single device or single link can be taken out without dividing the entire network into two separate islands.

To make it possible to build loops and other nontrivial architectures without causing serious performance problems, STP implements an election mechanism to select a "root" node switch. Based on the result of this election, a treelike traffic distribution hierarchy is built from this node down, and links that could cause a reverse propagation of broadcast traffic are temporarily disabled (see Figure 7-2, right). You can quickly change this simple self-organizing hierarchy when one of the nodes drops off and reactivate a link previously deemed unnecessary.

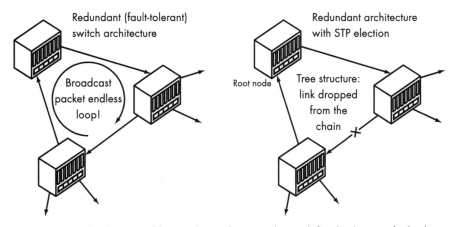

Figure 7-2: Packet storm problem and STP election scheme; left side shows a fault-tolerant network with no STP, where some packets are bound to loop (almost) forever between switches; right side is the same network where one of the devices was automatically elected a master node using STP, and for which the logical topology was adjusted to eliminate loops. When one of the links fails, the network would be reconfigured to ensure proper operations.

Attacking the Architecture

The mechanisms discussed so far were engineered to improve the bottom line while providing high performance, on top of a network design that provides no security features whatsoever.[2] Although certain common, well-understood, and easy-to-prevent attacks, such as *MAC spoofing* (the ability for any person to spoof an ARP message and impersonate a device with a particular IP) are widely recognized as a pitfall of local area networking and are easy to prevent with properly configured switches, some other serious design flaws are not so trivial and, in fact, not prevented so easily. It is not always obvious that solutions commonly perceived as designed to improve security in fact do nothing to help it.

CAM and Traffic Interception

One of the more spectacular reasons not to consider switches as a security feature is the *CAM overflow* scenario. The CAM that stores MAC-to-port associations has a fixed and limited size and is generally constructed in a nondiscriminatory manner. Whenever a system cannot be located in CAM, the switch has but one way to deliver the packet—it must fall back to the hub mode, broadcasting the packet to all systems, hoping the recipient will recognize this traffic as addressed to himself and that other systems will be nice enough to disregard it altogether. Thus, a careful attacker can employ a tactic to generate a large number of bogus ARP requests and responses, or some other packets, impersonating a vast number of separate network devices, just to fill up the switch's CAM. Once the CAM is full, the attack has effectively degraded the network security by disabling smart frame routing on the switch and forcing it to fall back to broadcasting all data. This, in turn, allows the attacker to snoop on all communications, as if the network was not switched at all. The attacker can do all this without impersonating the recipient or visibly affecting the operations of the network, so the victim might well remain completely unaware of this problem. This is a design issue; it is not a flaw in the intended purpose of these devices, but a serious misconception in the popular understanding of how switches work. And, rest assured, it is nearly impossible to fully address this problem in a typical environment. Some switches do implement port and time limits to prevent such attacks, but these are never 100 percent effective.

Other Attack Scenarios: DTP, STP, Trunks

Other problems are usually easier to prevent and remain more evident (can be often detected by the victim), but still illustrate Ethernet-level security issues. For example, an attack on the aforementioned DTP mechanism is one interesting possibility. DTP autonegotiation is often enabled for all ports on a device in order to provide easier setup. The problem is that a clever attacker can hence pretend to be a trunk-enabled switch, rather than a mere end-user workstation or a humble server; once recognized by the switch it is connected to as a friendly device, he would start receiving 802.1Q tagged frames, including traffic in other virtual LANs served by the switch it is connected to, being able to intercept or inject malicious traffic to networks with which he is not supposed to be able to communicate. In many networks where the same switch handles both protected, "demilitarized" networks and common corporate LAN infrastructure, such an attack may be yield very useful data by enabling members of one of the networks to snoop on or interact with the other.

You can resolve this DTP problem on some devices by changing the default configuration and clearly defining a set of dedicated trunk-enabled ports on the switch. However, the problem does not end here—our other friend, STP, can be abused in a similar manner, allowing an attacker to choose self as the "root" switch and receive a cut of the network traffic. Disabling STP discovery might be even more difficult in a typical corporate environment.

Still another problem arises when any trunk originates or terminates at a nondedicated VLAN. (That is, the port used for trunking is placed in a VLAN also used by workstations.) By injecting already tagged frames, it is possible to inject traffic to a trunk. This is arguably a configuration flaw, and the problem is often overlooked, since many engineers assume the method for implementing trunks is far more advanced and magical than it really is.

Prevention of Attacks

These problems are often difficult to solve, particularly in a network that was not firmly and closely supervised through all phases of its development and expansion. Although certain high-end devices provide extended security features to counter potential attack vectors and mitigate or eliminate some of the risks, Ethernet networks were not designed to provide security, nor were many of the smart devices created to manage these networks. The attacker can easily render some or all of their features useless and downgrade the network security model to the least desirable option.

Although there are methods and rigid practices to follow in order to secure a local Ethernet network, the complexity of this process and the additional financial cost and performance impact that doing so often carries, let alone the number of vectors to be addressed, all make it obvious that the technology was not engineered with any level of practical security in mind.

Food for Thought

When Ethernet was developed, it seemed reasonable to disregard any security considerations in the design decisions and to leave the burden of securing the network to higher-level architecture, encryption, and so on. Over time, however, this initial decision has begun to contribute to the overall maintenance costs of Ethernet networks and the difficulty of keeping them reasonably hack proof without sacrificing functionality in some ways.

The problem is hardly limited to the Ethernet, either. Many networks designed to be trusted based on physical-access or equipment-access criteria—including, for example, most of the world's phone systems—are inherently and uncontrollably exposed to internal threats with little or no way to efficiently contain the exposure and control the collateral damage resulting from a single-system compromise within the grid. As the size of the network grows, and the number of interchanges increases, the probability of one of the systems being operated by a malicious user or insufficiently protected either on physical or remote access steadily approaches 1. Although traditionally, access to the backbone, rather than access to an end-user station, would be required to compromise the system—thus making the situation somewhat different from Ethernet—nowadays, Voice-over-IP (VoIP) systems quickly make up for this inconvenience, frequently allowing easy spoofing and other trickery by putting too much trust on the user endpoint side.

US VERSUS THEM

What else can happen in the local perimeter of "our" network?
Quite a bit!

Local network designs, such as the Token Ring or now predominant Ethernet, were engineered under the assumption that there was no need to assure security on the level (or layer) of the technology used to transmit the data itself. When computers were first developed, users sharing a network were expected to play nice.

Although for this reason alone one might assume that the designers of Ethernet would have seen no need to incorporate full-fledged security functionality into their design, they are to be blamed for the unwarranted optimism and not foreseeing the inevitable. Ethernet simply did not leave space to easily implement integrity, confidentiality, and sender-verification mechanisms at higher-order OSI layers, devices, and applications. Subsequent protocols and communication schemes attempted to implement partial privacy and a level of undeniability of communications—but only to reach a point where we realized it is not possible to implement adequate security there without going back and reworking the link layer. The only other possibility we were left with was building computationally expensive and complex cryptographic hacks on top of the system, of which the sheer complexity contributes to a number of security problems discovered year after year.

This unfortunate and later quite intentional trend had effectively created a set of networking mechanisms that, although they perform well and are affordable, are not suitable for handling even moderately sensitive data in the presence of a hostile party (and almost all user-related data flow on a local network is sensitive). Solutions that try to address these problems—such as virtual private network (VPN) applications, encrypted encapsulation for the lucky few of the most popular web protocols, advanced switches, and so forth—are usually far more expensive and sophisticated than they could have been had security been a key factor when devising the initial concept for an Ethernet communications scheme.

Before we arrived there, we lived in partial denial for quite a while. When security became a real-world concern (with the expansion of the Internet and a sudden proliferation of system compromises), the first defenses to appear focused on the external world, while ignoring threats that could come from within the "trusted" network. But it wasn't too long before a couple of corporate and institutional entities learned some painful lessons. With time, it became obvious that external defenses such as firewalls and intrusion detection systems alone were not enough, even when properly configured across the enterprise. The network layer was still vulnerable, allowing an insider to compromise data exchanges without exploiting the security vulnerabilities of any single system in the company.

Although you can argue that the network could be secured by deploying appropriate encryption and cryptographic identity and integrity verification mechanisms on all interfaces, that is often impractical or impossible, particularly without impacting the performance and reliability of the network and incurring significant costs (not to mention the issues of compatibility with various operating systems and applications). Besides, as I have mentioned, cryptography is not always the answer: not only is it much easier to successfully attack when the data can be seen and intercepted (replay or timing attacks, for example), but certain types of information—such as the Ethernet frame-padding flaw discussed previously—can thwart all efforts to protect the user.

In Part II of this book, we are addressing some of the threats inherent in local networks that expose information without a traditional attack ever occurring. All these problems will remain with us as long as networks use the old and tested design that is rather ill-suited for networking today.

We are now ready to move forward, but before we dive into the wild and fascinating world beyond the local perimeter, let's glance at some other interesting (and more specific) exposure scenarios.

Logical Blinkenlights and Their Unusual Application

One such example relates to the abuse of logical indicators—that is, counters, flags, and other gizmos that have no physical representation but, rather, are maintained by a computer and made available in software, commonly implemented in local networks. Logical indicators are a helpful feature that, once again, assume that the local network is to be trusted.

The Simple Network Management Protocol[1] (SNMP) is the most popular method for monitoring and sometimes administrating network devices. SNMP is often implemented on endpoint systems (servers and workstations) as well as network devices, such as switches, routers, and printers.

SNMP provides a means for reading (or modifying) an abstract representation of many system and application internals, operational and configuration parameters, and statistics. Using SNMP, you can query a network printer about the number of network cards it has or its uptime and then use exactly the same method to query a mainframe for the same information, even though the information needs to be obtained internally by the device in a wholly different way on each system. Hence, SNMP makes it easy to monitor and manage heterogeneous environments without implementing a multitude of native access protocols and check procedures.

Naturally, SNMP itself has plenty of implementation and deployment security issues, but that is not my point here. Even when properly implemented, this functionality can lead to a security information disclosure, such as providing read-only access to the seemingly irrelevant statistics of a network interface. (This hole is eliminated if the protocol is carefully restricted, but that is often impossible on certain types of network equipment.) A careful attacker can observe frame or packet counters on a system running SNMP and use that information to derive profiling information needed for timing attacks, which can recover interactive session information or other interesting characteristics, in a manner similar to the approach discussed in Chapter 1.

Whoops. But really, can this much bad happen because of this?

Show Me Your Typing, and I Will Tell You Who You Are

Although I've mentioned this class of problems several times already, and they may seem abstract, their consequences are real, even when the keystroke reconstruction vector, on which I focused in Chapter 1, is disregarded. For example, in a fascinating development, a group of German researchers from Institut für Bankinnovation have created a commercial product, PSYLock, that provides typing-pattern-based biometrics[2]: Using PSYLock they have been able to uniquely identify (and hence possibly track) users by examining how they use the keyboard.

PSYLock relies primarily on measurements of interkeystroke timing, a trick I discussed previously. Given the ability to observe packet counters for a specific machine and calculate when, in an interactive session, a key is pressed by the user, you can identify a person regardless of which terminal they use. Some interesting applications, both malicious and supervisory in nature, can be suggested based on the application of this concept to the network layer. If the attacker knows that there is an interactive session of some remote access protocol between a station for which they can monitor SNMP switch port statistics, they can, by repeatedly polling the counter, determine when keys are pressed and, hence, draw conclusions as to what is being typed or who is typing.

A more lightweight variant of the attack, not requiring any of the advanced modeling that we had to cope with before, is also feasible. In their Bugtraq posting titled "Passive Analysis of SSH (Secure Shell) Traffic,"[3] Solar Designer and Dug Song, among other things suggest yet another possible attack, this time using the SSH protocol, a common method for connecting to a remote system. Although SSH is encrypted, in versions released prior to their research it is possible to measure the length of a password by carefully analyzing the size of an observed packet during login (the password is sent in a single chunk of data once entered by the user).

This technique could well be successfully applied to other cryptographic protocols that do not take active measures to hide the length of a password by padding it before sending. And, no suprise, the attack can be carried out simply by observing an SNMP byte counter, rather than by directly monitoring traffic.

The Unexpected Bits: Personal Data All Around

Yet another reason we should not be thrilled by the prospect of a hostile party peeking at our network (regardless of whether we believe the data they can see is sensitive) is that plenty of software violates the principle of least astonishment. The principle of least astonishment is a fundamental rule of software design that basically says that a program should respond to the user in ways that surprise them least—in a consistent, intuitive, predictable, or otherwise expected manner. As it turns out, many programs from several software publishers send an amazing amount of valuable information, far beyond what we might expect, often putting users in a situation they did not bargain for. As always, Microsoft Windows leads the pack of these astonishing programs and does a great job of releasing information in intentional, but often overlooked and nonobvious ways, but the friendly software giant is not alone.

Although few users know it, when Windows is working in a domain and is configured to use roaming profiles to enable the user to log in from a different workstation and access their personal data, large portions of the user's registry are sent to the domain controller each time they log in or out. Although the information contained in the profile may seem quite worthless at first, it includes various personal settings and history information that can be quite interesting, including last-executed commands, last-visited web pages, and last-opened documents.

Similarly, and perhaps even more astonishing, if a user's home directory within the domain resides on a network drive, Windows looks up all commands entered by the user in the Run box first on the remote server and then locally. Thus, the information about all commands issued by the user is disclosed via the Server Message Block (SMB) protocol to a careful observer.

These and many other examples make it painfully obvious that almost all network data should be assumed to be sensitive. As such, local networks at large are not particularly well suited to transport any commonly occurring data, except for specific, limited, or additionally protected setups. And we have no good way to protect this information without rolling out heavy artillery, such as cryptographic IP tunnels or similar software or by redesigning every aspect of networking from scratch.

Wi-Fi Vulnerabilities

It would be unfair to close this chapter and ignore the problems with the wireless replacement to Ethernet: wi-fi.

Wireless networks based on the IEEE 802.11 protocol are gaining momentum in the corporate world, as well as among ordinary home users. Unfortunately, even long before gaining widespread acceptance, and even though they were designed with the intent to maintain a level of additional security over wired hookups, wi-fi proved fairly difficult to deploy properly, perhaps because it attempted to follow in the footsteps of its older brother a bit too closely.

The 802.11 standard is, in its operating principles, not that much different from Ethernet. It uses a traditional "one can talk, others listen" media access control scheme, the only difference being that instead of a pair of wires, the carrier of the signal is now just a designated radio frequency. Which brings us to 802.11's first problem.

In May 2004, the Queensland University of Technology's Information Security Research Centre (ISRC) announced its findings that any 802.11 network in any enterprise could be brought to a grinding halt in a matter of seconds simply by transmitting a signal that inhibits other parties from trying to talk. Naturally, the same is true for Ethernet, except that you must be able to connect to a network plug first, which of course makes the attacker much easier to track and the problem easier to solve. You can simply check the switch then follow the cable. This attack is not exactly a surprise, but it's not what business adopters expected either.

That's not where the problems end. Where the 802.11 standard attempted to thwart carrier-level attacks, it actually failed miserably. The Wired Equivalent Privacy (WEP) mechanism was designed for wi-fi networks to provide a level of protection against eavesdropping on network sessions by external parties, thus providing security roughly comparable to traditional

LANs. However, a number of design flaws in the WEP scheme were found in 2001 by researchers from the University of California and Zero Knowledge Systems, which proved the scheme grossly inappropriate. Regrettably, even by that time wi-fi had been deployed widely enough to make necessary modifications difficult to implement.[4]

To add insult to injury, use of WEP is optional, and most wireless network devices have WEP turned off; they're ready to accept and relay any traffic they receive. Although this is generally acceptable with wired networks, where an additional layer of security is provided on the physical level, wireless networks are open to any random person within range.

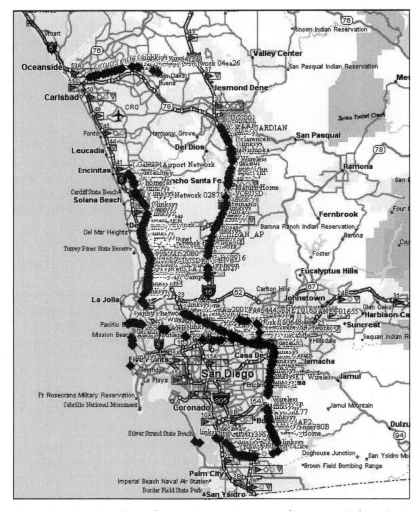

Figure 8-1: Tracy Reed's warflying adventure (courtesy of Tracy Reed of Copilot Consulting at treed@copilotconsulting.com)

The practice of wardriving—equipping a car with a wi-fi–capable laptop and going on urban network-finding expeditions—became extremely popular once it was discovered that a majority of large businesses—particularly in large shopping malls and commercial districts in every city—have partly or fully open wireless networks. The abuse is often quite trivial, ranging from networking for free to sending spam or conducting remote attacks through the victim's network, but the risk of a network being penetrated from inside by a skilled attacker is real.

What is the true scale of the problem? Suffice it to say that at some point wardriving became passé with the birth of warflying (wardriving, but with a plane rather than a ground vehicle). In 2002, Tracy Reed of Copilot Consulting decided to fly around San Diego and vicinity with a wireless scanner. Cruising at 1,500 feet, he managed to find nearly 400 access points with default configurations and likely free network access to the Internet or internal corporate networks for any person nearby (see Figures 8-1 and 8-2). Only 23 percent of the devices scanned were protected by WEP (which is, in general, easy to crack anyway) or better mechanisms.

Go figure.

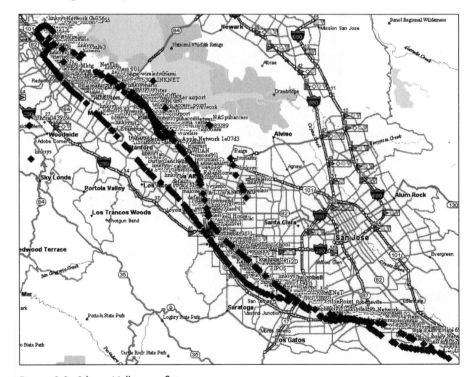

Figure 8-2: Silicon Valley warflying

PART III

OUT IN THE WILD

Once you are on the Internet, it gets dirty

9

FOREIGN ACCENT

*Passive fingerprinting: subtle differences in how we behave
can help others tell who we are*

On the Internet, the network of networks, information
sent to a remote party is beyond the sender's control
and supervision. Unlike on a local Ethernet, which is
usually a safe harbor for packets until a stranger wan-
ders in, once data is out in the wild it is no longer
possible to estimate and effectively manage threats that
it is likely to face, as no single person can control the
data's path or determine the intentions of all parties
involved in communications, let alone determine how they approach
security. On such a complex network, the likelihood of a middle party
becoming malicious is neither negligible nor easy to assess. In fact, even the
person with whom you are establishing legitimate communications may have
a hidden agenda or simply be a bit curious.

Unsolicited data acquisition attempts, so to speak, are also different
when carried out over the Internet for a couple other reasons. Most
important, they do not have to be targeted, and they are not limited to a
specific segment of physical infrastructure. Because they require so little
effort on the part of an attacker, they become a viable route for acquiring

potentially interesting data even prior to determining a precise way to profit or otherwise benefit from this knowledge. Too, the line between good and bad becomes even more fuzzy: the attacker can be your best friend. The profitability of general espionage and surveillance for the purposes of marketing reconnaissance and profiling is too tempting for many to resist; the world of service provisioning is not black and white, and flexible ethics is simply a viable business model for many people.

This part of the book focuses on the threats inherent in the open design of the Internet and on the ability of others to obtain way more information about you than you might expect—and more than would ever be needed in order for them to provide you a service such as an interesting website or an enjoyable network-based game. Once on the Internet, the enemy is no longer a lone madman sitting across the street, watching LEDs on the switch through a high-tech telezoom lens. The exposures covered here make it possible to carry out massive profiling, tracking, information gathering, industrial espionage, network reconnaissance, and preattack analysis—and are far more real than the scenarios described previously.

You need to understand the threats in order to maintain an informed level of privacy protection or perhaps to deploy effective monitoring whether of your users or of complete strangers, as they approach your systems. Understanding is also the key to maintaining sanity in a world where the line between being concerned about privacy and becoming clinically paranoid is fairly thin.

I'll begin with an examination of a set of core network protocols used over the Internet and their privacy implications. Shall we?

The Language of the Internet

The official language of the Internet is called the *Internet Protocol,* and the most popular dialect is labeled version 4. The protocol, specified in RFC793,[1] provides a way to implement a standardized method for transmitting data over vast distances and a variety of networks with as little effort as possible. IP packets constitute the third layer in the OSI model discussed previously and consist of a header that contains the information necessary to deliver a portion of data to its ultimate destination—the *remote endpoint*—and a payload constructed of higher-layer information that immediately follows the header data.

The routing information furnished by the sender within the IP packet prior to sending it out consists of the source and destination address and a set of parameters that simplifies the process of data transfer or improves its reliability and performance. When a machine on the local network wants to communicate with a remote party that is not directly reachable over the wire—at least not according to the host's knowledge—it forwards an IP packet with the ultimate recipient's destination address, encapsulated in a lower-layer frame addressed to a local machine that is believed to be a gateway to and of the network the sender resides at. The gateway machine is nothing more than a multihomed device—one that has a presence in more than one network, serving as a connection point between them. The gateway is expected to know how to route the packet to the outside world, what to do with the packet, and who should get the data next if there must be more parties involved before the data reaches the recipient.

Systems involved in routing traffic, from the local gateway through to the destination network, read the information provided on the IP layer to decide how to relay the data farther down its path, based on their knowledge of how to reach certain networks. (In this context, a network is defined as a pool of network addresses residing at a specific location.)

Naive Routing

In its basic form, a router uses a fixed routing table with which it distinguishes between a set of local networks (to which it can deliver traffic directly) and the outside world, which is unknown. Thus, all traffic destined for outside the local network must be relayed to a higher-order router that presumably has a better idea of where to deliver the data.

Figure 9-1 shows an example routing structure. The sender (shown at left) attempts to send a packet to a system whose address belongs to network C, a network that the sender knows nothing about. To facilitate delivery, the guy sends the traffic to the local gateway, hoping that it will know where to look for the recipient. However, this system, router 1, can only reach the sender's own network and network A, another network that has nothing to do with C. Because the target is not on their local network, the router decides it would be best to just send the packet to a higher-rank WAN router (router 2), which it happens to be able to reach locally.

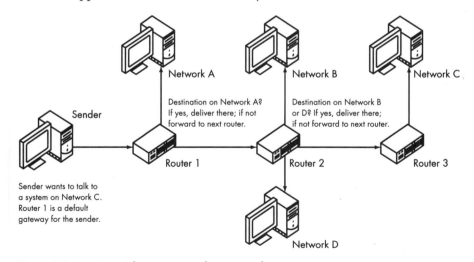

Figure 9-1: A naive wide area network routing scheme

This device also has no immediate connection with network C; it can only directly reach hosts on networks B and D. However, it knows that router 3 is serving the destination address and thus would surely know what to do.

Therefore, the packet is forwarded there, and router 3 can now deliver the traffic locally to the ultimate recipient, at which point all can rejoice and celebrate another success.

Routing in the Real World

In practice, networks are often highly redundant and do not have a strictly linear architecture. They have a complex treelike structure that makes selecting the optimal and most economical path difficult if we were to use a static configuration. (Never mind the challenge of staying up-to-date with all the infrastructure changes as the network grows.)

As such, a more reasonable routing strategy is implemented once the traffic reaches a *backbone router*. Run by a network operator, a backbone router is a dedicated WAN device that binds many networks controlled by a particular provider into a complex being called an *autonomous system*. Backbone routers are typically equipped with interfaces to other large routers and use an advanced path-discovery algorithm and a sizable "phone book" of network blocks and their whereabouts, controlled dynamically by a Boundary Gateway Protocol, to find the best way to route the data to the destination system, without blindly handing out the job of delivering the traffic to some system in hopes that it will be able to relay it properly.

The Address Space

This process would, of course, be quite impractical if destination networks consisted simply of a set of addresses arbitrarily assigned to devices around the world. A definition of an autonomous system would have to list all the addresses and might easily grow to enormous size. To solve this problem, continuous blocks of address space are assigned to backbone service providers instead; providers later lease smaller blocks to end users or lesser service providers. Routing to the provider's network is based on a lookup of the destination IP within the address ranges assigned to this entity and then within the network based on additional lookup in more detailed routing tables. An autonomous system can thus be defined as a range of IPv4 addresses (or a set of such ranges), using a netmask method.

The single IPv4 address used to uniquely identify an endpoint system in all Internet Protocol communications has a fairly simple structure, consisting of 32 bits, divided for convenience into 4 bytes, a total of 4,294,967,296 possible addresses. The address is traditionally written as four 8-bit values between 0 and 255, with each value separated by dots. For example, 195.117.3.59 corresponds to a 32-bit integer value of 3241036664.

Continuous IP address blocks are the basis for packet routing. They are defined on top of IPv4 addressing by defining the part of the IP address that is fixed and constant for all systems belonging to an autonomous system, as well as the part of the address that will be set to various values by the owner of a network in order to give computers unique identifiers.

When defining a network, a set of more significant bits of an IP—theoretically, anywhere from 1 to 31; practically, 8 to 24—is reserved as a *network address*. The fixed part of this address is shared by all addresses belonging to (and presumably routed to) this particular network. The less significant remainder bits can be set at will to assign addresses to systems within the network.

Historically (per RFC796[2]), the size of a network or the number of significant locked bits was a function of the address and could be determined from the network address itself. Based on the most important bits of each address alone, addresses were grouped to constitute class A networks (in which the 8 most significant bits are fixed, yielding more than 16 million possible user addresses), class B networks (in which 16 bits are fixed, yielding more than 65,000 hosts), or class C networks (with 24 bits fixed, and 256 possible hosts). Therefore, if your system has an IP address beginning with the number 1, you can tell that yours is a class A network and that all other systems with this prefix are next to your box.

Although this seemed handy at the time, the IPv4 address space shrank significantly once the initial implementers (the U.S. Army, Xerox, IBM, and other behemoths) were assigned a handful of class A network addresses in the early days of the Internet, and seemed not to be very keen on giving them up, despite not using even a fraction of the space they got for public infrastructure. Too, once the Internet became commercial, and IP addresses became a resource that users had to pay for, users demanded chunks of address space that would better fit their requirements; some folks only wanted four addresses, whereas others wanted a continuous space of 8,000. Users began to resell or otherwise partition their Internet space.

The result is that the current address space is partitioned in bizarre ways, often with tiny bits of address space excluded and rerouted from larger, otherwise continuous blocks, with general disregard for the original partitioning scheme. Each network address is now accompanied by a netmask specification, because it is no longer possible to tell which network a system is on based merely by the IP itself. The netmask has its bits set at positions that should be fixed in the network address and zeroed for positions that can be freely manipulated within a network.

As shown in Figure 9-2, by fixing 24 bits on 195.117.3.0 network, we end up with 8 trailing bits that can be changed. This allows us to create 256 addresses between 195.117.3.0 and 195.117.3.255 that belong to this network (albeit some implementations would force the first and the last address to be reserved for special purposes, leaving only 254 possible hosts). With such a relatively simple specification of a network of addresses, it is easy to determine which addresses belong to this network and thus which should be delivered to a system that is its gateway (and which should not).

Although this addressing scheme may appear confusing and needlessly complicated, it is successful: it lets us associate pools of addresses with specific systems and differentiate between systems with minimum computational effort. The Internet, in all its complexity, usually succeeds in finding a system in a really short period of time, without much maintenance.

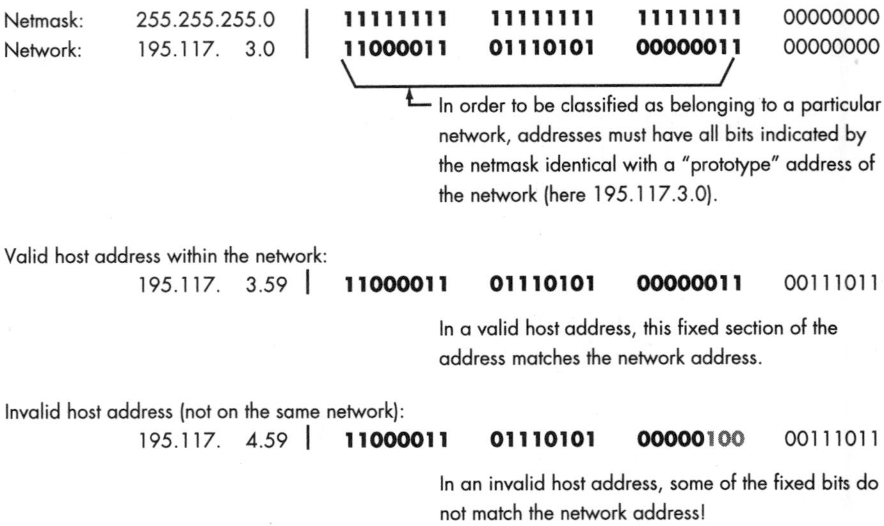

Netmask:	255.255.255.0	**11111111**	**11111111**	**11111111**	00000000
Network:	195.117. 3.0	**11000011**	**01110101**	**00000011**	00000000

— In order to be classified as belonging to a particular network, addresses must have all bits indicated by the netmask identical with a "prototype" address of the network (here 195.117.3.0).

Valid host address within the network:

	195.117. 3.59	**11000011**	**01110101**	**00000011**	00111011

In a valid host address, this fixed section of the address matches the network address.

Invalid host address (not on the same network):

	195.117. 4.59	**11000011**	**01110101**	**00000100**	00111011

In an invalid host address, some of the fixed bits do not match the network address!

Figure 9-2: Network addressing rules

Fingerprints on the Envelope

We know how the data makes it from point A to point B—but what happens on the way is more interesting than how the path is determined. Let's then look more closely at what is being exchanged between the routers and our endpoint systems. Although you might think that the actual data payload inside the packets sent over the Internet contains the most interesting information (considering all the private email and bizarre contents being exchanged around the world every second), there is more than meets the eye.

The format of IP packets used for routing the data, and the layer four information used to encapsulate the actual application-level data, is defined by the RFCs fairly strictly and with surprisingly little ambiguity. However, even with a competent TCP stack implementation, the underlying information can provide considerably and consistently more value to the recipient than the actual payload data it receives. The disclosure on this level is inadvertent and unexpected, but to learn more about it we need to take a closer look at the design of the underlying protocols.

Internet Protocol

First, the foundations. The Internet Protocol provides a universal long-distance delivery mechanism on the third layer of the OSI model. It contains a set of parameters that were meant to be interpreted and eventually modified by intermediate systems. The header is shown in Figure 9-3.

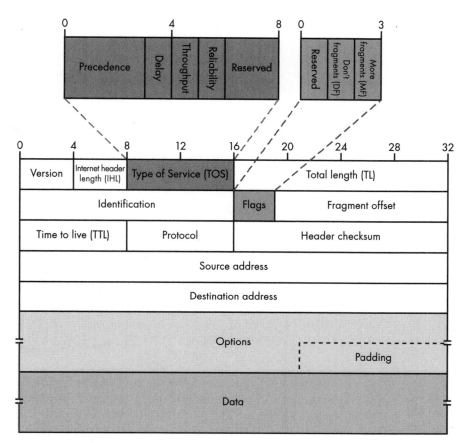

Figure 9-3: The IP header structure

Protocol Version

This is a four-bit value that is fixed to 4 (0100) in all IPv4 packets. IPv4 is the standard (and, in many cases, the only supported) layer three protocol over the Internet. Attempts to move toward a more advanced implementation, IPv6, have not been particularly successful so far—the author is willing to speculate this is perhaps because the new, extended IP address format is much more difficult for a typical system administrator to memorize.

The Header Length Field

This is a four-bit value that specifies the total length of the IP header itself, expressed as a count of 4-byte blocks (making it possible to express lengths from 0 to 60 bytes using the 16 values of field). This parameter tells the implementation where to stop parsing the IP header (which may have a variable length due to extra "options" that can be appended at the end of the header and immediately before any higher layer contents). It also makes it possible to skip some of the IP header without having to look at the options or understand them completely, and go directly to the data.

Because IP options aren't commonly used for anything other than diagnostics (they do things like make it possible to force a particular packet route and not much more), almost all IP packets seen in the wild are 20 bytes long (meaning this field is set to 5), which is the length of the fixed part of the header. Values less than 20 are, naturally, erroneous, and such a packet is not honored by a sane implementation. (Sanity, however, is not a rule of thumb.)

The Type of Service Field (Eight Bits)

The significance of this field is usually fairly marginal. It provides an honor-based routing priority description in which the sender is trusted to act in good faith and allowed to specify whether this traffic is of particular importance or otherwise requires special treatment. This value is sometimes used in local installations, where this level of trust can be exercised, but it is often ignored over the open Internet.

This field consists of three segments:

- The first three bits specify the priority.
- The next four denote the desired routing method (using abstract concepts such as "high reliability" or "low latency" and letting the router interpret this).
- The last part, a single bit, is reserved and shall be set to 0 (yeah, right).

The Total Packet Length (16 Bits)

This 2-byte field specifies the total length of this IP packet, including its payload. Although the highest possible value is 65,535, the maximum size of a packet is often limited to a much smaller value by the restraints of the lower-level protocol. For example, Ethernet has a maximum transmission unit (MTU) of 1,500 bytes; as such, a system connected to Ethernet will not send packets larger than this limit. MTUs greater than approximately 16 to 18 kilobytes are practically unheard of; values between 576 and 1,500 bytes are the most common.

NOTE   *Fun fact: The size limit of an IP packet, N bytes (resulting of the MTU parameter), also imposes the minimum bandwidth overhead limit for any IP traffic: there will always be at least 20 bytes of header added per N-20 bytes to be sent on a higher level.*

The Source Address

This 32-bit value—an IP address in the format discussed in the previous section—should represent the originating endpoint of the communications. Because the IP packet is prepared by the sender, and there is very little incentive for anyone to check the correctness of this parameter at the perimeter of the originating network, this value alone cannot really be trusted. It does provide a good hint as to who to talk back to, though— and if we have a reason to trust this hint, we can use it to talk back to the sender. The act of forging this value intentionally is commonly referred to as *IP spoofing*.

The Destination Address

This 32-bit value specifies the ultimate destination of the traffic. Like all other IP parameters, it is chosen at the sender's discretion and used by intermediate systems to direct the packet appropriately.

The Fourth Layer Protocol Identifier

This is an eight-bit value that specifies what is carried as a payload of the IP packet—TCP, UDP, ICMP, or more exotic options we will talk about in more detail in a moment.

Time to Live (TTL)

TTL is an eight-bit "kill counter" for IP traffic. To avoid endless loops when something goes horribly awry with routing tables, the counter is decreased by one every time it passes an interim system, or stays in the transmit queue for a period of time. When the counter reaches zero, the packet is discarded, and the sender may be mercifully notified via an ICMP packet. The TTL value, like all others, is chosen at the sender's discretion, but, by virtue of its bit width, cannot be more than 255.

An interesting side effect of the TTL counter is that it can be used to map the route to a remote system: A message with a TTL of 1 expires on the first router it encounters on its way to the specified destination (and the sender receives an ICMP message from the router); a message with TTL set to 2 expires on the next hop, and so on. By sending packets with gradually increasing TTLs and monitoring the origin of ICMP "time-to-live exceeded" responses, it is possible to map the set of routers and other IP-enabled devices en route to the destination. The technique is called *traceroute* and is a common method for diagnosing routing problems and performing preattack analysis.

The usefulness to the attacker lies in the fact that some effects can be achieved without actually compromising the intended victim: to compromise www.microsoft.com you might instead target the router of the network that hosts this server, or routers of their ISPs, hoping to intercept all its traffic and return forged responses. This would effectively cut off the actual server and, by impersonating it, make it appear to the outside world as if the site at www.microsoft.com had been changed. Naturally, this is just an example.

Flags and Offset Parameters

These 16-bit values control an interesting—and perhaps most flawed—aspect of IP packet routing. These parameters are used whenever a large packet must be forwarded by an intermediate system over a link with an MTU lower than the size of the packet. In such a case, the packet does not "fit" into the medium as is.

As an arbitrary example, a sender connected to Ethernet can send a packet up to 1,500 bytes in size and often will do so. However, if the first router the packet hits bridges the local LAN with a DSL modem, a problem arises: A common MTU for a DSL link (itself usually a bizarre combination of encapsulations over other protocols) is 1,492. As such, a 1,500-byte packet will simply not fit.

Given the large variety of links that make the Internet work, this is a serious problem. It is dealt with by splitting *(fragmenting)* the IP packet or, more precisely, its payload into several separate IP packets and adding information that makes it possible for the recipient to reassemble the payload before passing it to higher layers. The result is a new set of packets that fit over this particular link. An offset specified on each fragment indicates how each part of the payload should be inserted when the ultimate recipient attempts to reassemble the original packet.

All fragments but the last also have a special more fragments (MF) flag set in their headers. When the destination system receives a packet with an MF flag, or a packet with chunk offset set but no MF flag (which indicates the last chunk of a split packet), the destination system knows to allocate a scratch memory area to facilitate the reassembly of the original packet and to wait for all other remaining chunks before processing the packet any further.

Figure 9-4 shows the process of fragmentation and reassembly, in which an oversized packet is first split into two chunks and then completely reassembled by the recipient, despite chunks arriving out of order.

Although this process works, it is somewhat inefficient. It takes time for the systems to fragment and reassemble the traffic, and the trailing chunks often carry little payload—only the few bytes that do not fit over a different type of a link. It is better, of course, for the sender to be able to determine the lowest MTU between their location and the destination (also called path MTU, or PMTU for short) and construct their packets accordingly. Unfortunately, IP does not offer a flexible and clean way to implement this, but this has not stopped researchers from coming up with a clever hack.

According to this hack, a system that implements PMTU discovery sets a special flag, DF (don't fragment), on all outgoing traffic. If a router cannot forward a DF packet without fragmenting it, it should drop it instead and send an appropriate ICMP message that reads "fragmentation required, but DF set." The sender, upon receipt of such a message, can adjust their expectations accordingly, cache the finding, and continue with more appropriate packet sizes.

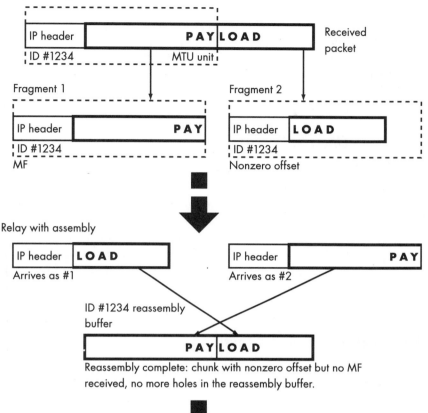

Figure 9-4: The packet fragmentation and reassembly process

NOTE *This practice, specified in RFC1191,[3] assumes that the single expense of resending the dropped packet is better than the constant performance loss caused by the need for fragmentation. The technique, however, is also quite controversial, because not all devices send proper ICMP notifications and, historically, there was no such requirement. Hence, enabling PMTUD (PMTU discovery) can result in a sender being unable to talk to some sites or in stalled file transfers that are extremely difficult to diagnose.*

Identification Number

The identification number (ID) is a 16-bit value that differentiates IP packets when fragmentation occurs. Without IP IDs, if two packets are fragmented at once, reassembly would severely mangle, interchange, or otherwise damage fragments of two packets that were fragmented simultaneously.

IP IDs uniquely identify several reassembly buffers for different packets. The value used for this purpose is often chosen simply by incrementing a counter with every packet sent; the first packet sent by a system has an IP ID of 0, the second an Internet Protocol of ID 1, and so on.

NOTE *On systems with PMTUD enabled, unique IPIDs are not needed, because in theory fragmentation does not occur, and the value is often set to 0 (although, arguably, not particularly wisely, because some fairly popular devices tend to ignore the DF flag).*

Checksum

The checksum is a 16-bit number that provides a trivial error detection method. The checksum must be recomputed on every hop (because parameters such as TTL change) and is thus designed to use a fast algorithm, which is not particularly reliable. Although in today's world, "checksum" is a sum only by name (using algorithms such as CRC32 or cryptographically safe shortcut functions), the IP checksum is in fact a sum, or a variant thereof, with a couple of bitwise negations[*] thrown in to confuse opponents (and, on a more serious note, to make it less likely for checksum to remain correct when common transmission errors occur).

Beyond Internet Protocol

One consequence of many of the design decisions made when devising IPv4 is the lack of a reasonable reliability guarantee, even if the network itself is behaving reliably. Although IP ID numbers are intended to minimize the risk of reassembly collisions, their relatively small 16-bit size (which allows for 65,536 possible values) permits problems to arise occasionally when two packets with identical IP IDs are reassembled at the same time. Also, IP header checksums are simply insufficient to provide reliable integrity protection; although unlikely, a random change in a packet could still give an identical checksum. Too, if the network actually failed, there is no way to find out what data has gone missing, even if the failure is due to something as straightforward as a brief overload of a single network component.

Finally, the Internet Protocol does not provide any way to verify the sender of a message, simply trusting that the real sender is the one listed in the IP header. It is left to higher-level protocols to provide some of the integrity and reliability assurance functionality as necessary—and more often than not, this is necessary. As such, higher-level protocols on top of IP are needed.

TCP, and to a lesser extent, UDP, not only provide much-needed protection for traffic, but also enable the user to specify the recipient (or sender) on a level beyond pointing at a certain system.

---

[*] Technically speaking, although it bears no particular importance for the discussion, IP checksum is based on 16-bit 1's complement of a sum of 1's complements of the checksummed data.

Whereas the IP header simply contains enough information to route traffic between two systems, and not enough to decide to which application the information should be delivered, UDP and TCP take things a step further: they move in the realm of the endpoint system, telling the recipient to which application they should direct incoming data.

User Datagram Protocol

As defined in RFC768,[4] UDP provides a minimal superset of IP functionality. UDP adds a mechanism for the local delivery of data, but keeps close to the level of unreliability of the underlying layer (as well as its low overhead). The use of UDP for communications can be likened to a phone service in which words sometimes get swapped or are dropped out of sentences, and there is no reliable caller ID—but the cost of a call is low, and your calls are answered quickly.

The UDP header (Figure 9-5) has a minimal set of features and is relatively simple. It introduces a small set of parameters that can be interpreted by the destination system and used to route a packet to a specific application or to verify that packet payload was not mangled down the road.

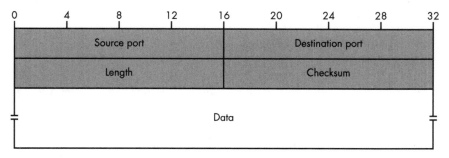

Figure 9-5: The UDP header structure

UDP is used for single queries, in other situations in which maintaining state information is unnecessary, and when performance and low overhead are more important than reliability. For example, UDP is commonly used for domain name system (DNS) name resolution, trivial network boot and autoconfiguration protocols (BOOTP), streaming media technologies, network file system sharing, and so on.

Introduction to Port Addressing

UDP introduces the notion of source and destination ports in addition to source and destination addresses, a concept that it shares with TCP (a more advanced layer four protocol that I will cover next). A *port* is a certain 16-bit number, either chosen by an endpoint application willing to send or receive data or assigned to it by the operating system (called an *ephemeral port*).

A port serves as a means to route data to a specific application or service on a multitasking system so that simultaneous communications can occur between programs. For example, a name server process can decide to listen on port 53 for incoming queries, whereas a system logger facility can listen to traffic addressed to port 514. Ports make it possible for clients to talk to these processes at the same time. Too, when the implementation supports a proper separation of source and destination port pairs, it is possible for two clients using different ephemeral source ports to talk to the same service (say, port 514) at once, without causing major confusion as to which client application should get which response from the remote service.

In order for the destination system to differentiate between communications addressed to a particular application and deliver them as expected, the sender must specify the destination port number in all their traffic. The sender specifies a different source port for every client application so that once the server replies, the answer is delivered to the correct component.

In this port addressing scheme, a quadruplet of values—source host, source port, destination host, and destination port—is used to ensure proper traffic separation and session management for simultaneous connections originating or terminating at a specific system. The design means that as many as 65,535[*] clients from a single IP address can connect to the outside world and that no more than 65,535 services can listen on a single IP address at any one time; that is, without some clever hacks. (We are not likely to suffer terrible consequences of this limitation any time soon.)

UDP Header Summary

The UDP header shown in Figure 9-5 earlier follows the IP header and precedes the actual user-space data in UDP packets. It consists of few fields: source and destination ports (16 bits each), packet length, and a 16-bit checksum for the purpose of additional integrity verification.

And now, for something completely different, it's . . .

Transmission Control Protocol Packets

TCP (RFC793[5]), the header of which is shown in Figure 9-6, aims to provide a reliable, stream-based method for establishing a meaningful conversation between two systems. TCP is more suitable than UDP for use with all applications except those that must exchange more than simple, short messages and single shouts.

Although technically implemented using separate IP datagrams traversing the network, the established TCP connection—a virtual channel, from an application's perspective—allows for a communications mode much like a regular phone conversation. Unlike with UDP traffic, when using TCP you can be sure that the recipient always receives the data as sent (or that, if error recovery is not possible, the conversation is dropped entirely). Under normal conditions, you can also be sure of the caller's identity, but this convenience comes at a higher price and with lower performance.

---

[*] Technically, that's 65,536; port number 0 should not be used, however. The operating system and its applications may allow this, naturally, and be in violation of the standard.

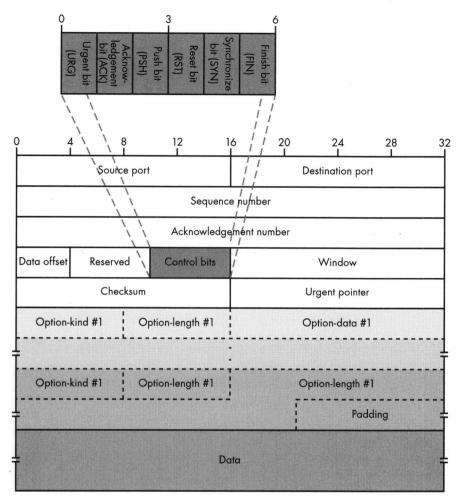

Figure 9-6: The TCP header structure

In TCP, two endpoints first initiate a connection using a so-called three-way handshake algorithm. Using special, as a general rule, empty packets (ones with only headers and no actual data payload), the parties agree on the intent, confirm each other's identity, and agree on initial sequence and acknowledgment numbers. These numbers (a set of 32-bit values) ensure reliable and seamless transmission because they are increased as the data is sent. This, in turn, allows the recipient to queue incoming packets in the correct order and to determine whether any portion of the data is missing.

Control Flags: The TCP Handshake

A TCP session begins when a remote system expresses a desire to connect to a specific port on a destination machine. The remote system sends the destination an empty packet with a SYN flag (meaning a designated bit is set in the header) and an initial sequence number set in the headers. Following receipt of this packet, any response to a packet must quote the sequence number in order to be honored. If the destination machine does not send the correct response in a reasonable time frame, the packet is sent again, until either the delivery succeeds or the sender concludes that enough time has passed and drops the connection.

The sequence number ensures that the response to the packet is from the actual recipient, not from an outsider who knows that a communication will be occurring and who intends to capture it. The sequence number also ensures that the response is not a lost, misguided packet from a previous session that finally made its way home, but a response to this particular request from the sender. (With 32-bit numbers and 4,294,967,296 possible values, the likelihood of a collision is considerably less than with 16 bits used in IP IDs, making both an accidental mishap and a successful guess by an outsider quite unlikely.)

The recipient is expected to respond to a SYN request with a similar packet addressed to the sender and source port they used. This packet should have an RST flag set (again, another bit in the headers) to indicate that they are not willing to establish a session. (No program is ready to answer connections on this endpoint.) This packet must also quote the original sequence number along with the response. Alternatively, in the unusual case that the recipient is actually willing to establish a connection and chat with the stranger, they should reply with a similarly constructed response, but with both SYN and ACK flags set, indicating acceptance of the request. They should also include the sequence number they expect from now on in all responses pertaining to this session.

As the last part of the handshake, the sender exchanges a single ACK packet just to make sure that both parties know each other's sequence and acknowledgment numbers exchanged earlier, and that they are on the same page in regard to the transaction. Assuming that their communication has reached this point, both endpoints can assume, with reasonable certainty, that both sender and receiver are who they claim to be. Why? Because each can observe the traffic addressed to their address. Otherwise, if one endpoint were just spoofing its IP address to establish a bogus connection in the name of somebody else, it would have no idea what number to include in its response to the other party. (And the other party would be quite surprised to find someone attempting to send them unsolicited SYN+ACK or ACK packets.)

This handshake protocol eliminates the chance of an outsider simply spoofing the traffic, but does not eliminate the possibility of a hostile privileged party on a legitimate path between the systems (though such an incident is unlikely, compared with the blind spoofing scenario).

NOTE *Needless to say, although the problem of using initial sequence numbers that are difficult to predict was not considered a problem, and many systems used designs such as a simple incremental generator, the possibility of either blindly establishing a session by* *spoofing a TCP handshake from a particular source or injecting data into already established connections by an outsider has become a bit problematic with time.* Careful selection of TCP initial sequence numbers so that a bystander cannot predict what your system is going to reply with in response to a forthcoming packet is now considered a necessity, and several approaches have been devised to address this issue.[6]*

Once a handshake is completed, the parties can exchange data, mutually acknowledging their sequence numbers each time; packets on which a mismatch of sequence numbers larger than an allowed "window" occurs are simply ignored. These numbers are from now on also steadily increased to reflect the amount of data sent up to that point, which makes it possible to process packets in the correct order at the destination, even if they arrive out of order. To ensure reliability, if a portion of data is not acknowledged within a reasonable time frame, a retransmission of the packet (or packets) must occur.

The termination of a session occurs when a FIN packet with a proper acknowledgment number is received by any of the parties. If, at any point, one of the systems gets quite agitated and wants to abruptly terminate the session (perhaps because, from their perspective, there is nothing to talk about, the session timed out, or their party severely violated the convention), an RST packet is sent.

A successful legitimate TCP handshake is shown in Figure 9-7 (on the left). A failure of a typical IP spoofing attack intended to create a session in the name of an innocent bystander who does not intend to exchange any data with the target is shown on the right. The attacker cannot see or predict the response sent to the system it tries to act on behalf of and thus cannot complete the handshake, let alone perform any actual data exchange within the TCP session.

As suggested, TCP provides reasonable protection against network reliability problems and is more suitable for ordered session-based communications. But the price is extra overhead that comes from the need to complete a handshake, as well as for both endpoints to maintain control information for the connection. Maintenance of this state exacts a heavy toll because it becomes necessary for every connection to track sequence numbers and current status of the stream (handshake stages, data exchange stage, closing stages), keep a copy of all sent but not yet acknowledged data in case it needs to be re-sent, and so on.

Because of their memory and performance costs, TCP stack implementations are a common denial-of-service attack vector.

---

* Kevin Mitnick, one of the most famous and controversial black hat hackers, compromised Tsutomu Shimomura's computer by impersonating one of their trusted workstations using TCP spoofing—an act that quite upset Mr. Tsutomu and, according to most accounts, did not really help Kevin in the long run.

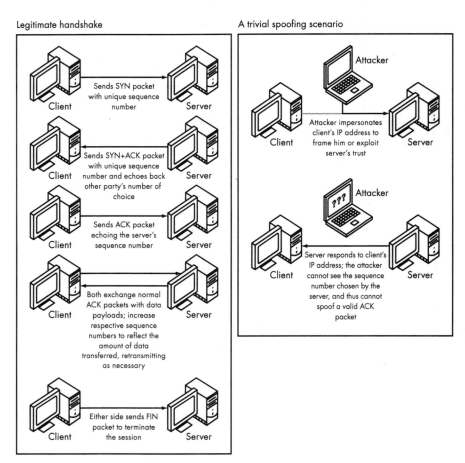

Legitimate handshake

Client — Server: Sends SYN packet with unique sequence number

Client — Server: Sends SYN+ACK packet with unique sequence number and echoes back other party's number of choice

Client — Server: Sends ACK packet echoing the server's sequence number

Client — Server: Both exchange normal ACK packets with data payloads; increase respective sequence numbers to reflect the amount of data transferred, retransmitting as necessary

Client — Server: Either side sends FIN packet to terminate the session

A trivial spoofing scenario

Attacker: Attacker impersonates client's IP address to frame him or exploit server's trust

Attacker ???: Server responds to client's IP address; the attacker cannot see the sequence number chosen by the server, and thus cannot spoof a valid ACK packet

Figure 9-7: A complete TCP handshake and a failure of a common spoofing attempt

Other TCP Header Parameters

Other TCP header parameters also control important aspects of packet interpretation and delivery. These will come in handy later when we attempt to gain information about the sender by just looking at the packet data they provide. Figure 9-6, shown earlier in this chapter, provides a complete listing of the TCP fields.

Source and destination ports

These 16-bit values identify the logical origin and endpoint on source and destination machines. They are similar to the source and destination port parameters used in UDP, although the UDP and TCP port space is kept separate on the system level—meaning one application can listen on UDP port 1234, and another application can listen on the same port number in the TCP space. The traffic is directed according to the proto-col specification in the IP headers.

Sequence and acknowledgment numbers

These 32-bit values ensure session integrity. A sequence number is the value the sender expects to have echoed back. An acknowledgment number is the value echoed back to the sender and will only be meaningful if the ACK flag is set.

Data offset (not to be confused with IP fragment offset parameter)

The information in this field indicates where in the packet the header ends and the payload starts. As with IP headers, the length of the TCP header can vary if certain variable-length settings were appended at its end. This information makes it easy to just skip to the actual data, without having to go through all the header information.

Flags

These eight-bit values define special properties of a packet. Each of the designated bits of this field represents a unique flag and can be turned on or off independently; as such, TCP flags can be recombined arbitrarily. *Primary flags* (SYN, ACK, RST, and FIN) define the way the packet should be interpreted in terms of a TCP session, as discussed earlier; *secondary flags* control certain aspects of payload delivery and other extended features, such as congestion notification, but are not used to change the state of a connection itself.

NOTE *Although flags can be combined as you please, many possible combinations are simply illegal or bogus. (For example, SYN+RST has no meaning and is, formally speaking, not allowed.) Only some combinations are meaningful for the handshake and normal data processing. Various systems respond in different ways to illegal flag combinations, and so sending bogus packets with unusual flags is a popular active operating system detection mechanism.*

Window size

This 16-bit value controls the maximum amount of data that can be sent without waiting for an acknowledgment packet. A higher value allows more data to be sent at once, without having to wait for an acknowledgment receipt, but can penalize performance if a portion of the data is lost in transfer or is not acknowledged and has to be re-sent.

Checksum

This trivial 16-bit method protects the integrity of the layer four data, similar to the packet checksumming mechanism used in UDP and IP headers.

Urgent pointer

This field is interpreted only by the recipient when one of the secondary flags, URG, is set in a packet. If URG is not set, the value specified in this region of the header is simply disregarded. This flag indicates that the sender is asking the recipient to relay a certain message to the application processing the traffic, presumably due to an "urgent" situation, so that the packet is inserted in the logical stream at a position earlier than it would otherwise belong to; the exact offset is controlled by the urgent pointer value. This mechanism is seldom used in normal communications.

TCP Options

The variable-length options block at the end of the header can specify additional settings or parameters for the packet. In some cases, it will be empty (zero length), but it is more commonly used to implement additional extensions for the protocol that were designed later on, without disrupting old implementations that cannot understand them. The options block is designed so that systems that do not recognize a specific option can safely ignore it. The most popular options include the following.

Maximum Segment Size (MSS)

This 16-bit value equals the maximum transfer unit on the sender's network, minus the size of lower-layer headers. It represents the maximum packet length that can be sent back to the recipient without causing fragmentation en route. The sender uses the MSS setting to ensure optimal performance whenever the recipient returns large portions of data that would otherwise require fragmentation and associated bandwidth overhead. Unfortunately, the MSS option is set by the endpoint system according to its best knowledge of the size of the packets their immediate network neighborhood can handle; it does nothing to avoid a common problem of midway fragmentation that occurs on intermediate systems (and hence the need to implement PMTU discovery on IP level, as discussed previously).

Window scaling

This eight-bit value described in RFC1232[7] extends the range of the window size field originally specified in the TCP header. With experience we have seen that acknowledging every 64 kilobytes of data (the maximum value expressed by the 16-bit window size parameter) can create a performance bottleneck when transferring large amounts of data, such as multimedia files, over high-bandwidth but high-latency links. Window scaling is a method to extend window size to allow more data to be sent without waiting for an acknowledgment. This speeds up data transfer but can also require more data to be retransmitted when a single packet is missing.

Selective acknowledgment options (RFC2018[8])

When using larger window sizes, losing a single packet requires retransmitting the entire group of data not yet acknowledged, a terrible waste of bandwidth. To prevent this, a mechanism for selective acknowledgment of chunks of data was devised. Endpoints first declare their ability and willingness to implement this functionality by specifying a Selective ACK Permitted option and then, eventually, acknowledge noncontinuous blocks of data using the actual Selective Acknowledgment option in the headers. Implementing this technique can significantly boost performance, but at the cost of certain memory and data processing overhead.

The time-stamp option (two 32-bit values)

This is another high-performance extension suggested in RFC1232. This mechanism for sending and echoing back time stamps (which are typically chosen to correspond to system time or uptime in one way or another) provides a method for each endpoint to estimate round-trip times for the traffic. The main advantage of this option is that the sender can measure the typical time a packet needs to reach its destination and proceed with a TCP retransmission sooner if there is no response. An additional application of the time-stamp option is preventing sequence number collisions (PAWS, Protection Against Wrapped Sequence [Numbers]), for example, when a long-gone packet makes its way to the destination after several gigabytes of data have been exchanged and after the sequence number counter has wrapped around.

EOL

This option should be interpreted as the end of options; it tells the recipient not to process any trailing data as a part of the header. Because the TCP header size is defined in units longer than a single byte, some unused space can remain after placing all relevant options before the beginning of the data, but before the payload data begins (which is only possible on a full four-byte boundary). The EOL option can be used to prevent the recipient from attempting to analyze this data.

The NOP option

This option means "do nothing," and is quite simply ignored by the recipient. The sender may and should use NOPs in a packet to pad it to ensure proper alignment of some multibyte options (which must be aligned due to performance and architecture constraints on some processors[*]).

T/TCP (Transactional TCP)

This esoteric extension provides support for separate virtual sessions (transactions) within an established TCP session. This makes it possible to avoid the overhead caused by the need to complete a handshake every time you want to perform a specific operation with one-shot services—an approach that is more common if an application wants to process a number of separate transactions with a server. This extension is rarely used, and it is most useful for certain database systems (see RFC1644[9]).

---

[*] "Must" as in "are required to be in order to ensure proper handling." Some processors have significant performance penalties when accessing multibyte data structures that are not aligned to 32 or 64 bits; others simply require them to be aligned this way or else cause a fatal exception (execution trap) and refuse to perform an operation. Naturally, a naughty sender can purposefully place misaligned data in the buffer and hope that recipient's system will go down in flames upon receiving such a packet. Of course, a sane operating system checks for this first or attempts to copy the option data to a properly aligned region before processing it. The sanity of a system need not to be taken for granted, though.

Internet Control Message Protocol Packets

ICMP packets (see RFC792[10]) are used to send diagnostic information and notifications for other protocol types. Logically considered part of layer three, ICMP packets are carried as a payload of IP packets and, as such, are no different from the layer four payload. ICMP does not carry any new user-space data between endpoints and provides a trivial signaling method for IP instead. Figure 9-8 shows the ICMP header structure.

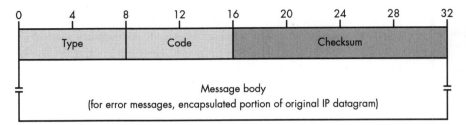

Figure 9-8: The ICMP header structure

A variety of messages are sent using ICMP in response to TCP or UDP traffic, usually indicating that a particular packet cannot be delivered, expired in transfer, or was rejected for some reason. Several types of ICMP can be sent spontaneously, such as router advertisements, echo requests (ping), and so on.

As with UDP packets, the ICMP header is simple. It consists of the following fields.

Message type

This eight-bit field lists a general category of the event that caused this packet to be sent (such as "destination unreachable"). This field can also carry a stand-alone message, though that use is infrequent.

Message code

This eight-bit value describes the exact problem, if applicable. It depends on the message type and might describe the condition in more detail ("network unreachable," "host unreachable," "port unreachable," "communication administratively prohibited"). The distinction between the level of detail that should be included in the message type field versus what should be left to the message code is unclear.

A checksum of the packet

This field verifies that the packet was not damaged (as with UDP and TCP).

The header of an ICMP packet is fairly simple and itself does not provide enough information to successfully troubleshoot the issue it attempts to report on or to identify what kind of traffic generated this message. This information is conveyed in the packet payload instead and immediately follows the header of a packet.

Although the payload of an ICMP packet depends on the message, it typically quotes the beginning of the packet that triggered the response. This makes it possible for the recipient to determine the communications to which the message applies and which application should be notified of the problem. It can also be used to ensure that the sender of the ICMP packet is actually somewhere on the legitimate network route between the two machines, rather than outside them. Otherwise, the sender would not be able to see the actual data being exchanged. (In particular, they would not be able to determine the exact sequence number in TCP packets.) This prevents malicious bystanders from sending bogus messages announcing connectivity problems and forcing one of the endpoints to drop a connection—or at least in theory. Naturally, it can be quite difficult to tell the good from the bad since some systems are notorious for mangling or misquoting the original data.

Enter Passive Fingerprinting

How does the design of this protocol relate to user privacy? The answer is a bit bizarre: although the design of IP, TCP, UDP, and ICMP packets is generally fairly strict, and the information transmitted in these headers is not particularly verbose, differences in the way various operating systems add information to these packets makes it possible to tell not only the type of operating system in use but even the specific version of an instance of a machine. The differences are particularly evident when dealing with traffic that is not clearly and appropriately discussed in the specification or that is not analyzed during normal quality assurance routines (say, an incoming packets with an illegal combination of flags such as SYN+RST).

Intensive research into differentiating systems by stress-testing their implementations has shown that it is safe to conclude that no two IP suite implementations in operating systems are the same. It is often possible to use sophisticated analysis to distinguish between the same system running on slightly different platforms or between slightly different versions of a system. Active analysis tools such as Fyodor's NMAP, a TCP/UDP fingerprinter and port scanner, and Ofir Arkin's Xprobe, an ICMP fingerprinter, exploit the flaws or oddities in every system and identify operating system genre and version by sending various types of malformed or unusual packets and then measuring and analyzing the responses they trigger.

Examining IP Packets: The Early Days

But the techniques of system fingerprinting do not stop here. In fact, poking the remote system by sending suspicious and easily detectable data is perhaps the least subtle way to approach this problem.

In early 2000, two folks at Subterrain Security Group, identified only by the nicknames *bind* and *aempirei*, demonstrated that it is often possible to get information about a distant entity on a network without conducting any intrusive communications with the remote party or, for that matter, without initiating any communications at all. (Their code and findings were first presented at DefCON 8, a slightly overrated hacker trade show of sorts, back in 2000.) Their technique, today called *passive fingerprinting*, involves passively (duh) observing casual legitimate traffic originating from a remote system. Although the metrics this technique uses are much more subtle and limited than those deployed by Fyodor and his predecessors, a good dose of research (to which I am proud to have made several contributions) has provided enough observations to achieve a fairly amazing level of precision.

To better understand what can be told from a single packet received over the network, let's take a look at the metrics upon which we can base passive fingerprinting and examine what they can tell us about the other party. This exploration is based on dissecting the most popular type of traffic on the Internet—a legitimate TCP packet in IP wrapping.

Initial Time to Live (IP Layer)

Recall that the TTL field controls the number of systems through which a packet can pass before being discarded as undeliverable. The packet's TTL value is decreased each time it passes a router, until TTL reaches zero, at which point the packet is discarded.

Because there is no strict requirement as to how this field should be set by the sender, many IP stack developers just roll the dice when determining the default for their pet system. Although a passive bystander cannot determine the packet's exact initial value without additional tests (because the packet would have surely crossed several routers before being observed), they know that its initial value must have been higher than the actual observed state. Too, the average distance to a remote computer on the Internet usually does not exceed 15 hops, and it is unusual for two systems to be more than 30 hops apart. As such, you can safely assume that the original value lies somewhere between the observed TTL and the observed TTL + 30 (but is less than 256, of course).

Because we know the initial values used by popular operating systems, we can hone in on the operating system genre the sender is likely running. (Linux and BSD-derived systems usually stick with 64; Windows developers use 128, and some true Unix descendants use 255.) Then, once we determine the operating system that sent the packet, based on this and other factors, we might also be able to determine how far the sender is from the observation point by subtracting the observed TTL from the value known to be used initially. By correlating this value with the actual previously observed or otherwise known distance to his network, we might then be able to draw some conclusions about the organization of the sender's internal network.

The Don't Fragment Flag (IP Layer)

The DF flag says, "If this packet does not fit over a specific network link, don't fragment it; just discard it." By observing whether this flag is set, we can determine whether the system uses the PMTUD mechanism described previously, which gives us yet another hint as to the operating system in use.

This also distinguishes between two sizable groups of systems: only newer IP implementations use this technique, and all others have no interest in enabling this flag in packets they send out.

The IP ID Number (IP Layer)

As mentioned earlier (in the discussion of the shortcomings of packet fragmentation), certain PMTUD-enabled systems set the IP ID number to zero on some (or all) outgoing traffic, because they assume that the traffic will not be fragmented and because of security concerns about displaying IP ID numbers (as you'll see in Chapter 13). Consequently, we can identify those systems by examining whether incoming packets have the IP ID number set to zero.

However, there is a catch. Although some PMTUD-enabled operating systems always set the IP ID to zero, some other systems can also set IP IDs to zero at some point, simply because there aren't that many IP ID possibilities to choose from. In other words, if you see a packet with an IP ID that is nonzero, it is safe to assume this is not a system that uses zero values for all outgoing communications. However, if you see a zero value in a packet, you might be seeing a particular species of PMTUD-enabled system, but you could also be seeing a "regular" system that has simply chosen zero for this packet, by chance.

Although the probability of this occurring is low, it is not quite negligible either. You might either want to take zero IP ID cases with a grain of salt (and only use nonzero IP ID observations to narrow down the set of possible operating systems) or to conduct several observations for the same source to confirm that zero values are always used.

Type of Service (IP Layer)

By design, this field should be chosen to correspond to the priority and type of the traffic in order to give interim systems a hint as to how to handle the packet, but it almost never is. Most operating systems set this field to an arbitrary fixed value because developers can set the value as they want without, in practice, affecting the operations of TCP networking. Depending on the developer's ego, they may merely default this parameter to zero or consider it appropriate to tag all communications originating from their system as "low latency," "high reliability," or some other setting using a combination of bits in this field.[*]

This should give us an advantage—by knowing the default values for particular systems, we can once again narrow down the number of possible systems the sender might be using. To add to the confusion, however, the value of this field is sometimes changed for all outgoing traffic by certain

---

[*] Some developers even choose to set the Must Be Zero bit of this parameter—which should never be set in a legitimate application—presumably just to make a style statement.

naughty DSL operators and other ISPs. Their hope is that some remote routers on the other side of the globe will fall for the trick, trust that their traffic, tagged as "high priority," deserves expedited handling, and prioritize it over other connections, thus providing this ISP's clients with faster browsing (doubtfully so).

As is the case with operating systems, the ISP's choice of Type of Service parameters is rather arbitrary. (For example, one Swedish provider uses a fairly unique and interesting combination of priority bits set to a value of 3 and uses Type of Service bits set to "high throughput.") This practice, in turn, makes it quite easy to detect traffic originating from particular ISPs by spotting their unique selection of Type of Service bits, without the need to perform active analysis such as WHOIS Registry lookups for the source IP.

Nonzero Unused and Must Be Zero Fields (IP and TCP Layers)

The specification for IP and TCP calls for a number of fields to be reserved for future use. All current systems should set these fields to zero so that a special meaning can be assigned to nonzero values at these positions in a packet in the future.

Needless to say, these are not zeroed in some implementations prior to sending, as they ought to be. This problem is not likely to be caught in the quality assurance stage because it causes no noticeable problems—other systems assume it is better safe than sorry and do not reject packets just because of this nuisance—and as such, this flaw can persist for ages (perhaps until those bits are actually used as a part of some TCP extension, causing it to fail spectacularly while talking to those broken systems). Once again, the ability to examine those values is a precious source of information that can lead us to a more accurate identification of the sender operating system.

Source Port (TCP Layer)

The source port identifies the party to a connection on the sender's side. Each system has a different policy for assigning so-called ephemeral (originating) ports for outgoing connections, and by examining the observed port number, it is often possible to determine the source operating system. Moreover, systems that perform masquerading commonly use a fairly specific range of ports for this purpose. (Masquerading, or many-to-one network address translation, involves rewriting outgoing traffic from a private network so that all connections appear to originate from the masquerading system and all responses are translated back and delivered to the actual sender when received by the system.)

Masquerading is commonly used by both corporate and home networks in order to preserve address space. The internal network can use a large pool of addresses that, technically speaking, are not assigned to them and that are not routed there (or anywhere else) from the Internet. However, systems using those addresses can still access the Internet by forwarding their outgoing connections through an agent box that uses its own, legitimate public address to reach the remote system in the name of the initiator. This approach also protects internal systems, making it impossible for an outsider to initiate a direct unsolicited connection to the system, while allowing only insiders to connect to the outside.

Examining the range of source ports chosen by the other party makes it possible to both make a better guess at the operating system the sender is using and (once the range is correlated with other observations) determine whether the sender is in a private network using address translation (in which case, source port ranges expected for the system and actually observed would most likely not match). If the sender's network is using address translation, it is also possible to draw certain conclusions as to the type of the address translation device, because various products use distinct ranges.

Window Size (TCP Layer)

Recall that the window size setting determines the amount of data that can be sent without acknowledgment. The specific setting is often chosen according to the developer's personal voodoo rules and other religious beliefs. The two most popular approaches say the value should be either a multiple of the MTU minus protocol headers (a value referred to as Maximum Segment Size, or MSS) or simply something sufficiently high and "round." Older versions of Linux (2.0) used values that were powers of 2 (for example, 16,384). Linux 2.2 switched to a multiple of MSS (11 or 22 times MSS, for some reason), and newer versions of Linux commonly use 2 to 4 times MSS. The Sega Dreamcast, a network-enabled console, uses a value of 4,096, and Windows often uses 64,512.

An application can sometimes change the window size value set by the operating system in order to boost performance, but it seldom is. (The presence of a value that does not match the default value that we would expect for an operating system is a good way to detect a specific application; one of the few examples of such applications is Opera, a moderately popular web browser.)

Urgent Pointer and Acknowledgment Number Values (TCP Layer)

The values specified in the urgent pointer (16 bits) and acknowledgment number (32 bits) fields are used only when a corresponding TCP flag—URG or ACK—is set in the packet. If these flags are not set, the values should be zeroed, but they often are not. Some systems simply initialize them to something nonzero, which causes no real problem: because the values will not be interpreted if an appropriate flag is not set, they simply serve to identify a particular system.

In some cases, however, these values are not initialized at all and are simply copied from whatever is found in the buffer being used to construct the TCP packet at the moment. I observed this behavior with Windows 2000 and XP stack implementations while working on passive operating system fingerprinting: whenever two TCP sessions occurred at once, these values leaked some of the information from a previous session to the current one (a case we will return to in Chapter 11). This tells you that the person is doing something else in the background and discloses some of the information transferred to another party. Hallelujah!

Options Order and Settings (TCP Layer)

The exact ordering and selection of options in a packet is unique to each system. Because there are no rules governing how options should be ordered in a packet, there are certain "signature" combinations. For example, Windows uses a characteristic sequence of "MSS, NOP, NOP, Selective ACK Permitted" options on SYN packets; Linux usually sticks with "MSS, Selective ACK Permitted, Timestamp, NOP, Window scale." Naturally, this once again serves as an excellent way of telling systems apart.

Window Scale (TCP Layer, Option)

A scaling factor for the window size is usually set to zero. However, some systems either default to a higher value or permanently increase the parameter for a specific type of traffic when they conclude that it is reasonable to do so, for example, if the user just fetched a pirated movie from a P2P network or completed an extensive download of a different kind (the latter is naturally a bit less likely).

Maximum Segment Size (TCP Layer, Option)

This field is fixed to a specific value on some systems; on others, it indicates the type of direct network hookup of the device. Different network types have different MTUs, making it possible to tell whether a person uses a high-speed DSL link or a puny modem line.

Time-Stamp Data (TCP Layer, Option)

Since this value often corresponds to system uptime, it is often possible to determine it by observing the time-stamp option. Furthermore, given a set of operating systems, it is possible to differentiate them and track each one by checking time-stamp variations in incoming traffic: different systems will have different uptimes (and are quite unlikely to have identical boot-up times), whereas the same computer would maintain a continuously increasing time-stamp parameter value.

This comes in quite handy in two situations. The first is when a set of systems acts under a single IP, as with masquerading. In such a case, a curious webmaster can determine how many unique users from corporation X visited their page and the whereabouts of each visitor to the websites they operate, even if all requests originate from one address and appear to be indistinguishable at first.

The other application is for tracking a single user who, for whatever reason, hops IP addresses. Why would one bother, and why would the other party want to determine if the user is doing it? For example, they might be switching between a pool of dynamic IP addresses assigned to a dial-up line (by disconnecting and connecting again), in hopes that their attack attempts will appear to be a set of meaningless, uncorrelated activities, rather than a well-planned, extensive probe. Or they might want to bypass interaction restrictions on a web forum, in an online poll or voting contest (with some old-fashioned ballot stuffing), and so on. All are common pastimes of the new generation.

The time-stamp option's measurement of time is usually precise, because it is based on a clock that most commonly ticks at 100 or 1,000 Hz (although some systems use 64 or 1,024 Hz, and values in between). This precision is enough to differentiate even similar boxes that were all booted up nearly at once after a power failure, and thus it provides extreme accuracy.

Other Passive Fingerprinting Venues

In this chapter, we have looked at the most common metrics used to determine the operating system of a remote host (and to track its users) without their ever knowing. But many exciting, yet lesser explored aspects of communications beyond these basics can be used to achieve the same ends, and more.

For example, an interesting variant of fingerprinting is related not to examining the packets themselves, but to measuring the timing and response rates for certain ICMP messages, TCP retransmissions, and similar features. The values used for all the time-out and retransmission count settings provide a good way to precisely and uniquely fingerprint a system. A CRONOS project, based on the research by Franck Veysset, Olivier Courtay, and Olivier Heen of the Intranode Research Team, aims at providing an active fingerprinting tool based on this set of metrics, but passive fingerprinting applications are just as tempting.

Another promising lead is the effort to combine and measure many other anomalies or uncommon settings, such as a sender's use of specific time-stamp values, sequence numbers identical to acknowledgment numbers, or unusual flags, as well as data payload in control packets, the use of the EOL option, and so on. These characteristics can also be used to differentiate between operating systems, although these characteristics are often specific to a small set of implementations. (The algorithm used for choosing initial sequence numbers is often a valuable source of information, as you will see in the next chapter.)

Passive Fingerprinting in Practice

These metrics make it possible to precisely identify operating systems and their configuration as well as network parameters and to track users efficiently and silently. Although it may seem difficult to believe that this is possible, a tool I have authored, p0f, implements most of the techniques to gather and analyze the information based on the analysis of SYN, SYN+ACK, and RST packets in a completely passive manner, with a high rate of success.

Let's look at an example packet to see the effectiveness of this approach. Following is a set of important parameters extracted from an actual TCP packet captured on the network. What can this tell us about the sender's operating system?

Internet Protocol (Version 4)	
Source host	nimue (10.3.0.1)
Destination host	nightside (10.3.0.3)
Flags	DF
Time to live	57
Identification number	4428
No IP options (packet size = 20)	
Transmission Control Protocol	
Source port	3803
Destination port	80 (HTTP)
Flags	SYN
Sequence number	1418000073
Acknowledgment number	0
Window size	32120
TCP Options	
#1 Maximum Segment Size	1460
#2 Selective ACK Permitted	
#3 Timestamp	170330930
#4 Window scale	0

A lot. Here's what we can infer from these observations:

- Because the DF flag in IP headers is set, the system must use path MTU discovery. Matching systems that use path MTU discovery are newer versions of Linux, FreeBSD, OpenBSD, Solaris, and Windows. We can rule out IRIX, AIX, many commercial firewalls,[*] and other systems that do not implement PMTUD for reliability reasons.

- The time to live of the packet is 57. We know that the initial TTL value could not have been lower because it might only be decreased in transit,

---

[*] A firewall is essentially a filtering router, often also capable of understanding and making decisions based on higher-layer traffic characteristics.

and it is unlikely that the value exceeds 87 (that would be a system really far away). We can match this with many Unixes (all of which use an initial TTL of 64) but we rule out Windows (with an initial TTL 128), versions of Solaris prior to 8 (255), and several network appliances (32).

- The identification number of the packet is nonzero. This rules out Linux 2.4 and newer versions, as well as several recent releases of other popular operating systems.

- The source port falls in the most commonly used range (1,024 to 4,095). Although this alone doesn't help us to exclude any systems, we can safely assume that the system had established more than 2,700 connections before this one and is unlikely to be behind a masquerade.

- The option selection and ordering (MSS, Selective ACK, Timestamp, Window scaling) is specific to Linux 2.2 and newer.

- The window size is a multiple of MSS, that is MSS*22. The only system that matches this is Linux 2.2.

- There are no observed anomalies, RFC violations, or other quirks in the packet, which confirms the hypothesis that Linux is the system being run.

- The Maximum Segment Size indicates an Ethernet or modem PPP connection (MTU of 1,500).

- The system's uptime is approximately 19 days, and it is located 7 systems away.

Certainly, single metrics can be modified by applications or user tweaks. (For example, users tend to modify TTL or enable or disable certain settings after reading network optimization guides or running "system doctor" applications.) However, by drawing a series of conclusions based on our observations we come up with a reliable way to determine the machine's operating system by identifying the system that appears to be the best match in most categories.

In this case, we have good reasons to believe that the system in question is Linux 2.2 and that the sender is connected to the Internet via Ethernet or dial-up modem. Based on this assumption, we can also conclude that the system is 7 hops away (64–57, where 64 is the initial TTL for Linux systems) and that its uptime is close to 20 days. If more users are hiding behind this particular IP, we can easily count them and differentiate their sessions based on their system characteristics and time-stamp data, if available.

Exploring Passive-Fingerprinting Applications

When observed by either the recipient or a bystander (such as an ISP between the sender and the recipient), network traffic can provide information beyond the actual data exchanged, including certain parameters of the sender's system. As suggested previously, the exposure is important and quite interesting because, unlike the data transmitted by applications, it is not necessarily obvious, and the disclosure is often beyond any user's control. Although users can change their browser settings and those of other applications in order to prevent being monitored, identified, and tracked, the disclosure that occurs on the lower IP or TCP layer can easily undermine this effort by revealing to the observer just as much about the victim as the victim is trying to hide. It can also carry data of more fundamental significance to the security of the infrastructure, including some useful hints about how the victim's network is constructed and protected.

That said, short of privacy invasion, passive fingerprinting can also be useful for quite legitimate reconnaissance tasks. The set of practical (and commonly deployed) applications of passive fingerprinting extends through the entire ethical spectrum, from malice to rightful defense.

Collecting Statistical Data and Incident Logging

One of the more legitimate uses for passive fingerprinting is that of monitoring the network to perform noninvasive and objective analysis of the platforms and network environments used, to ensure that users receive service that is optimized for their software, and to guarantee that no sizable group of users is neglected in some way. Too, gathering data about potential attackers or other unauthorized activity can be greatly enhanced by the use of passive fingerprinting. Indeed, passive fingerprinting is particularly popular in the field of honeypot research.

NOTE   *Honeypots are a concept aggressively promoted and researched by Lance Spitzner of Sun Microsystems.[11] The goal is to let the owner learn about their opponents and their goals, using devices (honeypots) whose value lies in their unauthorized and illicit use and that have no actual significance for the infrastructure, although they are designed to appear as if they do.*

Content Optimization

One active application for passive fingerprinting relies on providing services optimized for a specific recipient based on an immediate analysis of the setup they are using to access the server. I consider it my duty to include a shameless plug here for one of my aforementioned tools, p0f. p0f offers a method for querying it about the parameters of recent incoming connections from other applications, which makes the task of content optimization much easier: a web script does not have to know a lot about TCP and IP, can simply ask p0f, "Hey, who is that guy I am talking with?" and then get a useful response.

Policy Enforcement

The detection and eventual blocking of obsolete or noncompliant systems (say, devices that violate a corporate policy or pose a security risk) or infestations of unauthorized network hookups is another interesting application for passive fingerprinting. Since version 3.4, OpenBSD has provided a method for routing and redirecting traffic based on the operating system detection results, hence making policy enforcement based on remote operating system characteristics quite viable. The same functionality is now provided as a part of Linux netfilter patch-o-matic code. Both implementations are closely inspired by or based on p0f.

Poor Man's Security

Passive fingerprinting can also be used to minimize certain types of exposure. Although with some effort it is possible to fool the fingerprinting technique, fingerprinting might be used to prevent certain types of clients (such as Windows systems, a platform most commonly infested with spyware, backdoors, and worms and often used for unsolicited mass email distribution or attack hops) from using certain underlying services on the network, while allowing "less suspect" entities to access them.

Security Testing and Preattack Assessment

Active fingerprinting is often stopped in its tracks by firewalls and other solutions that carefully filter and analyze IP traffic. Passive fingerprinting, however, can examine even aggressively protected systems and can map networks without triggering any alerts.

The approach to security testing and assessment using passive fingerprinting is twofold. First, it can be used to analyze incoming traffic. Although the observer must wait for the remote party to connect to their systems, such a connection can be quite easily induced without triggering suspicion. In fact, it is often sufficient to send a specific email or a link to a website to the victim behind even the most sophisticated packet-filtering solution. Second, passive fingerprinting can be used to analyze the responses to legitimate traffic to an available service in order to determine the remote party's parameters. If a black-hat hacker knows how to compromise an internal network, but wants to know more about its internals in order to minimize the risk of being detected prematurely, passive fingerprinting can come in handy. The same can be said about legitimate security testing for which one is paid by the entity that undergoes the test.

Customer Profiling and Privacy Invasion

Many companies go to great lengths to gather and sell valuable information about people's habits, preferences, and behavior. Although this information is usually used for marketing purposes, it could—in theory—be used against a specific person. The ability to track users by correlating fingerprinting results from several locations that they have visited, whether to map internal networks and software used, track individuals, or gather other valuable statistical data, can be a source of information that might either have considerable value by itself or be used to enhance the attractiveness of other not-quite-ethical offerings.

Espionage and Covert Reconnaissance

The ability to gather additional information about a competitor's network architecture and user behavior and preferences is often quite tempting. Though this may sound like bad science-fiction, it is simply a more targeted type of the profiling discussed above.

Prevention of Fingerprinting

Given the complexity of a typical IP stack, it is extremely difficult to prevent fingerprinting in general, but it is possible to address specific issues and disable specific types of known fingerprinting software by determining what parameter it relies on most and then changing it. For example, certain packet-filtering solutions, such as pf in OpenBSD, provide a packet normalization service that ensures that all outgoing traffic "looks the same." Although this might prevent some aspects of fingerprinting to some degree or might simply make finger-printing more difficult by rendering some popular programs less accurate, it does not solve the problem completely.

Although the thorough and seemingly exhaustive manual or automated modification of certain operating system settings or TCP parameters can make system identification more difficult, certain behaviors are buried deep in the kernel and are not customizable. For example, it is fairly difficult to change the option ordering in a packet. Moreover, when users make manual modifica-tions, they risk introducing unique characteristics into packets originating from their system, which only further affects their privacy and anonymity.

Fortunately, certain solutions do address specific types of testing. For example, IP Personality by Gael Roualland and Jean-Marc Saffroy alters the TCP stack so that it appears to specific tools as if it comes from a different operating system. If you fancy, you can use IP Personality to make NMAP think that your system is a Hewlett-Packard laser printer. However, some problems arise. For one, it is easy to actually weaken a system's TCP stack by attempting to impersonate a device that uses a weak stack to begin with. For example, if, in order to comply with a printer's particular characteristics, you use trivial sequence numbers on all connections, someone will sooner or later take advantage of this to easily disrupt or tamper with your traffic. Too, software such as IP Personality will only work against the most popular, well-known, and well-documented tools, but it offers no guarantee of success against the rest, because the characteristics examined by each tool and the way these characteristics are interpreted are different from place to place. You can only hope to fool the least determined, most naive, "mainstream" attackers who use tools you know about.

NOTE   *Unlike masquerading agents, proxy-type firewalls and other proxy devices do not forward packets, but intercept connections instead and initiate new ones using their own IP stack. These are the only complete solution to third and fourth OSI layer fingerprinting, but they have a serious impact on performance and are more prone to problems due to introducing vastly increased complexity. Besides, a higher-level fingerprinting of the application itself is still possible.*

Food for Thought: The Fatal Flaw of IP Fragmentation

While discussing the defining features of the Internet Protocol, I casually mentioned that the process of packet fragmentation and reassembly is fatally flawed. This notion comes primarily from a fairly interesting observation I had while writing this book. Although the concept is related to an active and noticeable attack performed by an openly rogue entity (although it is not easily traceable back to that entity), it is a unique and interesting flaw inherent in the design of the Internet Protocol. It is not the result of a clearly defined mistake, but more a collision of paradigms on different design layers, both, curiously, specified by Jon Postel, one of the fathers of IP suite. I have decided to include it here to close this chapter, as food for thought for those interested in the pathology of computer flaws.

First, let's look at the state of affairs today, or perhaps yesterday, as we are dusting off a fairly old attack technique, mentioned previously in the TCP discussion. The technique in question, *blind spoofing*, was first described by Robert T. Morris in the mid '80s.[12] It had its golden age a decade later, but its significance has decreased ever since. We'll focus on a specific example of blind spoofing, that of injecting certain data into an existing session, to disrupt it, to convince the server that its user has issued a specific command, or to convince the user that they are getting a specific response from the server. This technique is often referred to as *connection hijacking*.

Under normal circumstances, a malicious bystander, wanting to insert data into an existing TCP stream, first needs to determine the sequence numbers used by at least one of the parties. Even though such an attack is highly time sensitive and must be targeted against a specific, existing connection, it can be (and has been, many times) performed successfully when the sequence numbers are predictable. In fact, in the late 1990s, many tools were used to disrupt Windows TCP sessions to Internet Relay Chat (IRC) networks (for amusement or other), exploiting the Windows weak initial sequence number (ISN) selection algorithm; it was trivial to inject a single RST packet here and there, kicking a person off the chat server. This is what we called fun back then.

Today, the situation is a bit different. Thanks to the efforts of many researchers (including the most humble author of these words), developers have worked hard to make initial sequence numbers in TCP connections more difficult to predict. Many attempts to improve the quality and strength of sequence number generators in popular operating systems have, in the end, rendered ISN prediction attacks harder, with few rather unnoteworthy exceptions. Systems that use sequential ISN numbers are largely extinct; an attacker, unable to determine the numbers used in a conversation with another party, is forced to search the entire 32-bit space of possible values in order to perform a precise data insertion attack (fewer if they only want to abort or irrecoverably mangle the session). That's some 4,294,967,296 combinations, and an attack like this requires the attacker to send an average of about 80 GB of data in order for it to succeed. Needless to say, this is not considered particularly feasible.

However, as to the actual benefits you can gain from a successful data injection attack, little has changed. Even though an increasing amount of communication is exchanged over channels that support encryption, the relevance of this type of attack has not decreased significantly; plenty of fruitful attack scenarios persist. Here are some examples.

- Data can be inserted into unencrypted server-to-server or router-to-router traffic, such as an email exchange, DNS zone transfers, BGP communications, and so on. Much of the server-to-server traffic can be generated by the attacker and yet contain sensitive or trusted information, which makes a targeted and timed attack more feasible.

- Data can be inserted into unencrypted client-to-server traffic, such as File Transfer Protocol (FTP) file downloads or HyperText Transfer Protocol (HTTP) responses. This attack can be used allow malicious, incriminating, or derogatory content to be provided to a visitor to a high-profile server or to make it appear as if a compromise attempt originates from an innocent visitor.

- Data can be inserted into an existing session to exploit a vulnerability in the service at a stage that is not available to a nonauthenticated user. This applies both to encrypted and unencrypted traffic. For example, a service such as POP3 (point of presence, a remote mailbox access protocol) can accept various commands only if the user previously successfully logged in. Prior to logging in, the only commands available are those that directly pertain to the authentication process (USER and PASS directives). Without a valid password, the attacker cannot exploit a flaw in one of the commands available later (such as RETR, a command used to fetch a specific message from a mailbox). However, if the attacker manages to inject a malicious RETR request into an existing session of an already authenticated user, they win.

- Even a secure and encrypted, integrity-protected stream is susceptible to a denial of service attack when a session is disrupted or terminated by a single, carefully crafted packet.

As such, it is tempting to be able to inject data with little effort, without having to go through the entire spectrum of possible sequence numbers. And this is where fragmentation comes in quite handy.

Breaking TCP into Fragments

When an IP packet carrying a TCP payload is fragmented (arguably, a common occurrence during file transfers, and one that is not always prevented simply by setting the DF flag as some systems do), the data is traveling the network in multiple chunks and is reassembled only when it arrives at the recipient. A clever attacker, in anticipation of this fragmentation, can send a specially crafted, illegitimate IP fragment, masquerading as one from the expected sender. Upon receiving this fragment, the recipient might, with some luck (a matter of precise timing), end up using it instead of the real fragment in the reassembly of the original packet.

In this attack scenario, the first fragment (containing the full TCP headers, including exact ports, sequence numbers, and so on) is merged with a malicious payload spoofed by the attacker. As a result, the attacker need not know sequence numbers or other session parameters to insert their data into the frame, thus effectively undermining the entire ISN-generation effort. Once the attack is complete, the final packet processed by the recipient consists of valid header data copied from a legitimate fragment and a malicious payload injected by the attacker.

NOTE *The attacker can replace any part of the payload in the first fragment by specifying a slight overlap between the fragments; many systems honor overlaps between fragments and overwrite previously received data with a newer copy. In an extreme case, the attacker can successfully replace all the data within a TCP packet except for the sequence number.*

Naturally, some pieces of the puzzle are still missing. But, other than the need for precise timing and a knowledge of when the transmission is occurring,[*] the attacker in this scenario must overcome only two obstacles:

- The fragment must have a correct IP ID number in order for it to be merged in. Thankfully, on many systems, this is not a problem, because IP identifiers are chosen sequentially. As such, the number likely to be used at the moment can be deduced simply by attempting a test connection. Some systems, most notably OpenBSD, FreeBSD, and Solaris, offer randomized ID numbers, which might make the attack more difficult but will still not prevent it. The attacker simply has to check thousands (not billions) of combinations, because the IP ID field is fairly small (only two bytes).

- The TCP header contains a checksum that is verified after reassembly, and the checksum of the data modified by the attacker must be the same as that of the original payload. However, because the design of a TCP checksum is trivial (simply a variation of a straight 16-bit sum), you can craft a payload that does not alter the packet's checksum, as long as the original section to be replaced is known to the attacker. (This is most often the case, particularly during file transfers when the attacker wants to insert malicious code or contents in a publicly available portion of data.)

---

[*] Timing itself is not as much of a problem as it might appear at first. The attacker can choose to send their malicious second fragment slightly in advance; the recipient then creates a reassembly buffer and waits for the remaining parts to arrive within a certain period of time. Once the first legitimate fragment arrives, the buffer contents are considered fully reconstructed, without waiting for the real second chunk to arrive.

The following simplified checksum of a packet that consists of header words H1 and H2 and of payload words P1, P2, and P3 illustrates:

C = H1 + H2 ... + P1 + P2 + P3 ...

H1, H2, and C are not known to the attacker. (Headers contain sequence numbers, and the checksum is affected by this data.) The attacker has no way to actually examine this packet, but knows that the victim performs a specific (predictable) transaction on the application level (for example, checks their mail, downloads a web page, chats with friends, and so on). The attacker can deduce the payload data P1, P2, and P3 and wants to replace it with their own malicious words N1 and N2, using a third word for checksum compensation (CC) so that the packet still validates.

C = H1 + H2 ... + N1 + N2 + CC ...

Solving these equations for CC, we conclude that the checksum must be compensated with CC = (P1 + P2 + P3 − N1 − N2). The attacker can then modify the packet so that the checksum remains the same without knowing the entire packet; they simply need the replaced bit. This is enough to calculate the compensation bit correctly and to preserve the checksum.

10

ADVANCED SHEEP-COUNTING STRATEGIES

Where we dissect the ancient art of determining network architecture and computer's whereabouts

Network reconnaissance and mapping is the art of exploiting a set of information disclosure vectors inherent in the Internet's core communications protocols in order to recognize systems and networks or to identify and track potential offenders, users, customers, or competitors. It is perhaps the most developed, most widely deployed, and most significant and immediately useful application of passive data analysis to date, but it has its share of problems that affect both its accuracy and usability in certain scenarios. This is particularly true for known and tested TCP/IP passive fingerprinting techniques.

Benefits and Liabilities of Traditional Passive Fingerprinting

Use of the passive fingerprinting metrics discussed in the previous chapter will let you easily identify some characteristics of an originating system and network. Too, in some cases, these techniques will make it possible to trace individuals as they change their address or share it with other users of a single network. You can employ these techniques without interacting with the remote party as long as you can persuade the observed earthling to interact with a specific network or for as long as their network communications passes through a specific set of systems controlled by a sufficiently curious person. Thus, passive fingerprinting, among other uses, enables a server owner or a specific ISP to acquire massive and completely stealthy information rather easily.

Passive fingerprinting provides such a remote party with a two-edged sword. You can deploy it to obtain useful data about the internal structure of a network, in order to make an attack easier or to learn more about the networking technologies used (even in a fairly complex environment, as shown in Figure 10-1). You can also use it (quite rightfully) to monitor your own network for policy violations (such as illegal connections or access points that connect an internal network with the outside world) or to track attackers.

The resulting privacy loss for a single user is generally negligible, unless the ability to link casual activities performed by a user with the additional data acquired by fingerprinting, or the ability to track a single user across domains, is a particular problem (this is most likely true only when the user's behavior is questionable to begin with). But the cumulative loss of privacy for all users could be quite worrisome, and the information gathered through fingerprinting or fingerprinting-assisted tracking can pose a noticeable market value. (Your personal data can be sold for much more to advertisers if it is combined with information about your preferences and interests, for example.) Too, the exposure of the technical inner workings of a network can indeed be undesirable for corporations and other portions of sensitive infrastructure.

Nevertheless, not all is lost just yet. As indicated previously, there are some problems with using passive fingerprinting to obtain accurate results. The reliability problem with traditional passive operating system fingerprinting technique stems from how easy it is to fool the observer by carefully tweaking some or all the network settings used by a system that is subject to observation. Even if completely altering all settings is not particularly easy, a partial modification might be enough to thwart certain automated analysis attempts (hooray!) or mislead a researcher investigating a malicious incident (oops). Although not a large-scale problem, and thus not a concern for statistical analysis, the reliability issue can cause concern in individual cases.

Moreover, the user tracking and counting capabilities of the fingerprinting approach we painfully dissected in Chapter 9 rely almost entirely on the availability of parameters such as the time-stamp information in TCP/IP packets. All other characteristics are either standardized or have too few possible options to provide a unique positive identification of a single computer, except in the most unusual cases. If such data is unavailable because this particular performance extension is disabled (as with most Windows systems, for example), the precise identification of a system is not possible.

This lowers the potential value of the data both to members of an overzealous, evil conspiracy cabal (that, as we all know, is after our most precious secrets), as well as to security testers or incident analysts (computer forensics experts). Without this time stamp–based identification capability, it can be impossible to differentiate several identical systems running behind a masquerade or to identify an individual whose IP was changed once they reconnected their modem.

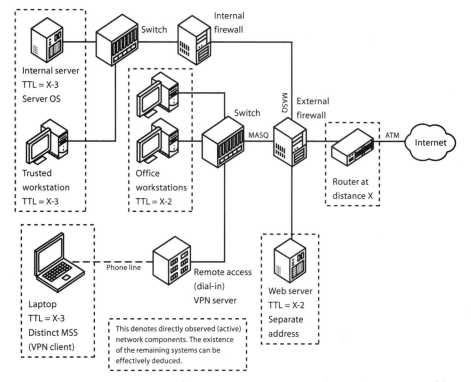

Figure 10-1: You can use passive fingerprinting to map a complex and even inaccessible network simply by observing traffic from some of the nodes (the most important being measuring operating system characteristics, TTL, and MSS values on packets) and then deducing the presence of other components to match the observed characteristics variances. It is left to the reader to determine how this network could be conclusively mapped out by merely observing traffic on the outside.

Another, perhaps more interesting, promising, and challenging passive fingerprinting method, however, easily addresses the shortcomings of passive fingerprinting. This new approach makes it extremely difficult to mislead a remote observer and is almost universally suitable for tracking systems. Perhaps more interestingly, the technique makes it possible to differentiate between instances of exactly the same system in exactly the same configuration, taking masquerade detection to a whole new level. This technique uses the properties of sequence number generation mechanism within TCP/IP, and it can produce some pretty pictures, too.

A Brief History of Sequence Numbers

Recall from the previous chapter that initial sequence numbers are a mechanism used within TCP to ensure session integrity, and—de facto—to guarantee its most basic security resilience.

The only truly universal way to protect a plain-text TCP/IP session against data injection, hijacking, or fakery by a complete stranger is to ensure that the initial sequence numbers are selected in a manner that is unpredictable to the attacker. This reduces their chances of making a correct blind guess (and spoofing a packet that will be accepted as a legitimate part of someone else's session) to a point where this risk is of little concern in the real world, even if the attacker takes the system by storm, sending thousands of packets in hopes that at least one will have a roughly matching sequence number.

In the early '80s, the security aspects of TCP-based communications did not seem to be a problem worth worrying about: the Internet was a fairly small, self-contained, and perhaps a bit elitist environment used by scientists and the like. As such, the RFC specification of the TCP protocol did not specify a requirement for initial sequence number selection, and almost all early (and some not quite so early) TCP/IP stack implementations used trivial, time-, or counter-based algorithms that returned subsequent numbers for subsequent connections. At the time, the idea of randomizing these numbers seemed a needless waste of precious computing power. Too, in doing so, the likelihood of a sequence number collision would be needlessly increased. (Collision is a situation in which two ISNs chosen for subsequent connections to a host are too similar, thus creating the possibility that old packets arriving in an untimely manner could be interpreted in the context of a wrong connection. Naturally, picking numbers randomly is more likely in the short run to produce collisions than picking sequentially increasing numbers.)

The Internet has advanced a lot since the 1980s, of course, with its increased availability and rapidly changing and growing user base; as more and more important data was sent over the wires, the security issues became more relevant. Unfortunately, popular and reliable integrity and privacy protection mechanisms have yet to catch up with the Internet's expansion: not all services support encryption, not all users know when to use it, and, more important, most users do not know how to properly validate cryptographic certificates provided by remote parties.

Over time, and particularly with the widespread practical abuse of the weak ISN-generation mechanism in the mid '90s (although mostly limited to online chat services and so forth), it became obvious that it was necessary to provide rudimentary integrity protection for TCP/IP streams. This was even important for the marginal fraction of all traffic that is actually cryptographically protected, because a disruption of the carrier layer by injecting junk data or RST packets is just as undesirable, even if the impact is only limited to disconnection (denial of service), as opposed to data injection.

Because the only way to fix things (without a major overhaul of just about every TCP-based communication scheme known to man) was to keep the protocol difficult to attack by itself, many developers undertook efforts to move away from the obsolete and dangerous trivial one-increment ISN-generation mechanisms. Although these efforts did indeed help to improve connection resilience to blind spoofing, they also opened several interesting information-gathering vectors that allow for more advanced fingerprinting of systems and networks, be it for security assessment or a planned attack.

Getting More Out of Sequence Numbers

Naturally, it is important to be able to tell the good ISN-generator implementations from the bad, both for quality assurance and for security testing. Until recently, the usual approach to assessing the quality of generated initial sequence numbers relied either on source-code analysis or on certain one-dimensional tests of the bit stream of subsequent ISNs to estimate the entropy carried by each bit of the output. The former is often complex and costly, is prone to errors, and is not always possible (in the absence of publicly available source code for a specific system). The latter lacked the ability to capture more subtle sequence dependencies and other characteristics of a generator in a reliable and readable way, focusing instead on more statistical imperfections than on the correlation between values returned for subsequent connections. Obviously, proving that an implementation is secure by observing only its output is just about impossible, but it is easy to check for certain common problems and to ensure that the underlying algorithm is reasonably robust. And yet, even there, the methods we used to check for this were rather weak at best.

Both the original, insecure ISN-generator designs and some of today's solutions are based on additive, iterative arithmetic systems that calculate new values based on their previous output; only the complexity of the recalculation algorithm and the amount of practical unpredictability introduced in the process seem to vary. The only secure designs that are not based on traditional arithmetic are some newer ones that use relatively slower but cryptographically secure shortcut functions to implement iterative systems. In all cases, though, it would be interesting to look for a nontrivial correlation between subsequent results produced by the generator for new connections to detect possible flaws in the algorithm design.

Clearly, if an apparent dependency between ISN-generator output at time t and one at $t+x$ can be observed, the attacker can choose to connect in advance of the connection they hope to interfere with or fake altogether, just to obtain the ISN output at t. Based on their observation of the returned sequence number, they can then determine the response that will be generated by the other party in the future ($t+x$). Hence, the attacker can spoof a valid packet for that new connection despite not being able to directly observe the ISN being used.

With this in mind, in 2001 I performed some research that would provide a unified method of examining less obvious time dependencies in sequences of ISNs acquired from remote systems. My work resulted in a paper that examined some of the ISN-generation algorithms in more detail, providing a way to detect subtleties that go beyond the detection of the most obvious patterns and flaws we had been aware of. The paper, titled "Strange Attractors and TCP/IP Sequence Number Analysis,"[1] used an approach well known in the world of applied mathematics, but quite novel for networking.

Delayed Coordinates: Taking Pictures of Time Sequences

When dealing with a black-box ISN generator in one of today's closed-source systems, you see only its output, a sequence of 32-bit values carried by TCP/IP packets, not the underlying algorithm. For many operating systems, the code is proprietary and well guarded, quite beyond the reach of mere mortals. Even in an open-source system, the sources can be tricky and misleading, and you can end up following the same mistakes as the original developer.

The typical input we would have to evaluate would likely look similar to this:

$$S_0 = 244782$$
$$S_1 = 245581$$
$$S_2 = 246380$$
$$S_3 = 247176$$
$$S_4 = 247975$$
$$S_5 = 248771$$
$$\ldots$$

Is the dependency in these numbers immediately obvious? And if so, is there is a relatively universal method for the computer to follow this and more complex schemes?

An elegant solution seemed far off. I hoped to develop a method to identify some universal properties of the ISN's underlying algorithm based on the observation of output alone. But before doing that, and in order to make the analysis easier, it was desirable and quite convenient to assume that, because many implementations are based on reiterating certain arithmetic operations, it is better to observe the changes between subsequent results than to observe absolute values. Watching changes is advantageous for such algorithms, and would not do much harm to the rest of the possible generators. To achieve this, we must calculate a discrete derivative of the input sequence: the increments between elements of S. The resulting sequence of deltas, D, obviously starting at $t = 1$, is given by the following equation:

$$D_t = S_t - S_{t-1}$$

In this example, the resulting sequence of deltas is:

D_1 = 799
D_2 = 796
D_3 = 799
D_4 = 796
D_5 = 799
. . .

By disregarding the actual values and looking only at the dynamics of ISNs, the underlying dependency becomes more apparent and will generally remain so for all implementations that rely on this type of arithmetics. (For systems not based on trivial iterative arithmetics, this has virtually no relevance whatsoever and will not significantly affect the quality of the data for the purpose of this analysis.)

NOTE *A particularly pedantic researcher would also compensate for timing irregularities during sample acquisition; here, we assume that a fixed amount of time, a base unit of 1, always occurs between acquisitions. In high-speed acquisition, however, network performance and other events may significantly impact timings. To ensure that these timing differences will not influence the algorithms that use clock input as a part of the ISN-generation process, it might be safer to use the following equation instead (in which T_t expresses the delay between acquiring S_{t-1} and S_t): $D_t = (S_t - S_{t-1})/T_t$.*

The advantage of this approach as applied to iterative arithmetics systems is fairly obvious. Trivial cases aside, however, this method alone is hardly sufficient: we simply move from one flat sequence of data that is fairly difficult to analyze to another.

The next thing I chose to do was to convert the sequence of deltas into a form that could be easily examined by a human or a machine for types of correlation perhaps less obvious than the previous example. Nothing works better than a three-dimensional model of the system dynamics for the first group of the intended audience of the data. Unfortunately, with ISNs we only have enough information to draw pictures in one dimension, on a single axis. So how do we turn our information into a neat three-dimensional shape?

The solution is to extend the data set by applying a coordinate reconstruction strategy called *time-delayed coordinates*. We use a method that extends every sample by constructing virtual coordinates based on the previous samples in sequence. If the existing sample is considered the x coordinate value, we can use this technique to assign y and z values to every existing sample, thus constructing a triplet of coordinates—x, y, and z—sufficient to map every sample to a single point (here, pixel) in a three-dimensional space. (The technique is not limited to three dimensions. However, for the dual purposes of visualization and data analysis, it seemed impractical to choose a higher number. At any rate, most human beings do not cope with more dimensions too well, at least when sober.)

Time-delayed coordinates are calculated so that the second coordinate is constructed using the value sampled at $t-1$, the third coordinate corresponds to the value observed $t-2$, and so on. In this particular application, coordinates for data at time t are given by the following set of equations:

$$x_t = D_t = S_t - S_{t-1}$$

$$y_t = D_{t-1} = S_{t-1} - S_{t-2}$$

$$z_t = D_{t-2} = S_{t-2} - S_{t-3}$$

Given a sequence of newly constructed (x,y,z) triplets for a system that is being tested for time dependencies, it is possible to plot the behavior of an ISN-generation system in three-dimensional space. Because the location of a pixel representing a given sample depends both on the "current" value and on a number of previous results, many even fairly complex dependencies result in abstract but noticeable, irregular density patterns in the phase space, thus creating a unique portrait of the underlying algorithm. (When used in reference to such portraits, the term *attractor* denotes a shape that maps out the dynamics of a system. The shape (set, space) represents a "trail" of states through which the system cycles or evolves when left on its own.)

Figure 10-2 is a rendition of a set of data that originally looked as follows:

4293832719
3994503850
4294386178
134819
4294768138
191541
4294445483
4294608504
4288751770
88040492
. . .

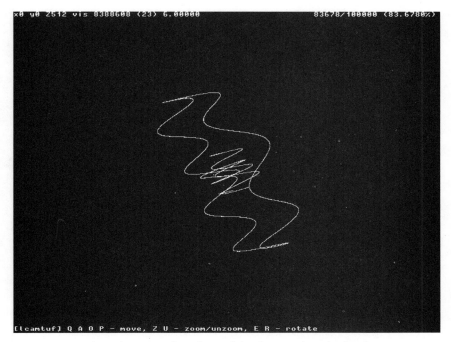

[lcamtuf] Q A O P - move, Z U - zoom/unzoom, E R - rotate

Figure 10-2: A three-dimensional rendition of the data set described in the text

Figures 10-3 through 10-5 illustrate several other common yet not necessarily obvious dependency patterns.

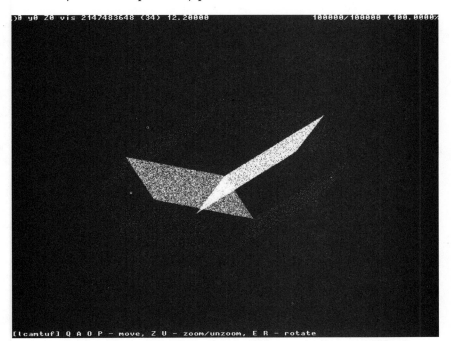

)0 y0 20 vis 2147483648 (34) 12.20000   100000/100000 (100.0000%)

[lcamtuf] Q A O P - move, Z U - zoom/unzoom, E R - rotate

Figure 10-3: A three-dimensional rendition of a data set acquired from a complex but insecure random number generator function

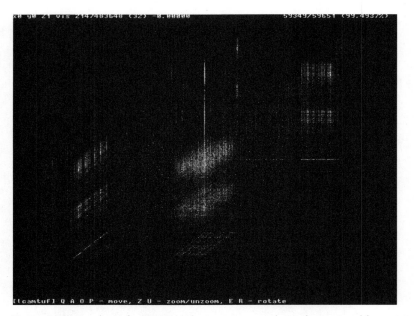

Figure 10-4: Rendition for PRNG with no strong correlation but noticeable statistical biases

Pretty Pictures: TCP/IP Stack Gallery

The visualization method seemed to work like a charm, producing unique and often instinctively worrying, charming patterns for many implementations that had been believed to be reasonably secure; many of these pictures can be found scattered on the next pages. But can these pictures do more than give us a visual representation of hard-to-quantify parameters and characteristics of a generator? Could an attacker use these mysterious three-dimensional shapes in meaningful ways, or could a computer examine them somehow to give us a clear answer about what is wrong and what is right? Is a sunflower-shaped generator easier to crack than a brick-shaped one?

Before answering this question, allow me to interrupt myself and include a short gallery of some of the more interesting results acquired in the process of writing the original paper. This should help to demonstrate the wide variety and beauty of some of the observed patterns, following the ancient rule that a three-dimensional plot is worth a thousand words. Figures 10-6 through 10-14 show PRNG portraits for several operating systems.

Not all plots are drawn to the same scale; some shapes are considerably smaller than others. The scale and other parameters can be read from the top line of every plot, as shown in Figure 10-6.

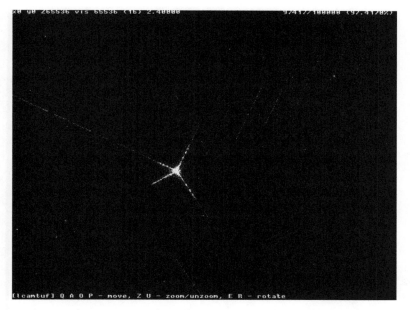

Figure 10-5: A common time dependency pattern, as observed in imperfect testing conditions

Current X position   Zoom factor   Currently visible plot points (percentage)

Current Y position   Bit size of the viewport   Currently visible and total plot points

Visible range   Viewport rotation factor

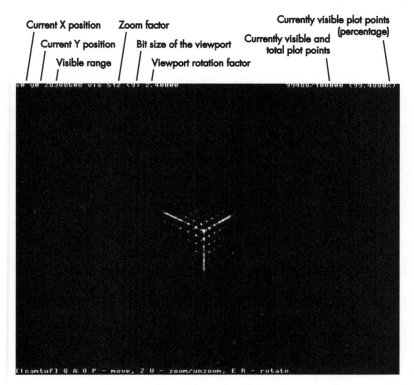

Figure 10-6: Windows 98. The set shown here has a diameter of approximately 128, which indicates that subsequent ISNs are increased by a number carrying about 7 bits of "randomness." Within the set, there is a strong frequency pattern similar to one of the examples discussed in the previous section, perhaps suggesting a trivial time dependency in all results. The size of the attractor is worryingly small.

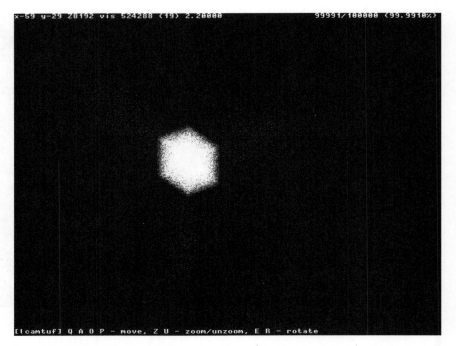

Figure 10-7: FreeBSD 4.2. A 16-bit-wide uniform cube, likely a sign of small but truly random increments in every step

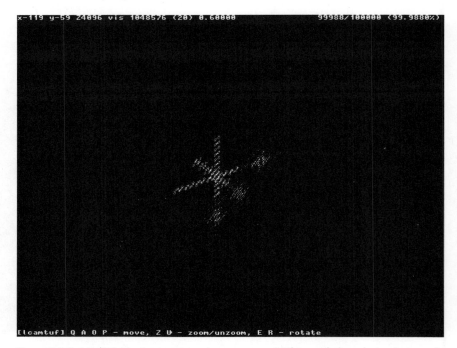

Figure 10-8: HP/UX 11. A strange x-wing structure, 18 bits wide but obviously irregular, likely a sign of high-correlation levels of a flawed PRNG

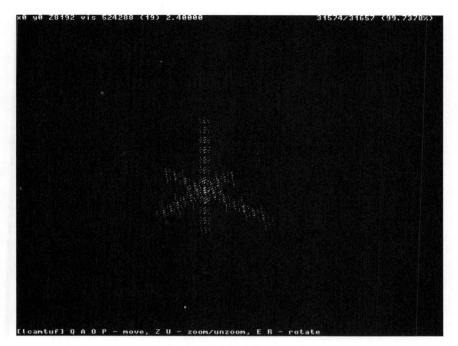

[lcamtuf] Q A O P — move, Z U — zoom/unzoom, E R — rotate

Figure 10-9: Mac OS 9. A similar but slightly different 17-bit structure

[lcamtuf] Q A O P — move, Z U — zoom/unzoom, E R — rotate

Figure 10-10: Windows NT 4.0 SP3. Again, a strong attraction pattern and a tiny 8-bit-wide attractor

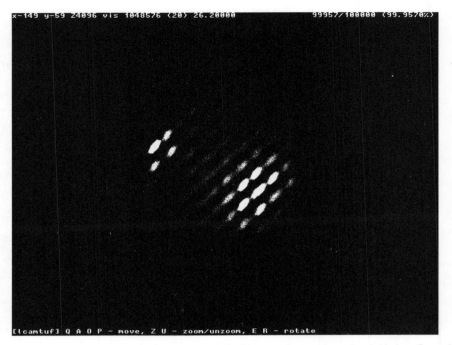

Figure 10-11: IRIX 6.5. A 16-to-18-bit-wide highly irregular random cloud; likely a flawed algorithm

Figure 10-12: NetWare 6. A seemingly random system, with a 32-bit-wide attractor cloud, but consisting of a large number of high-density spots and not uniform

Figure 10-13: UNICOS 10.0.0.8. A strange, 17-bit-wide cloud with irregular stretches of higher hit probabilities

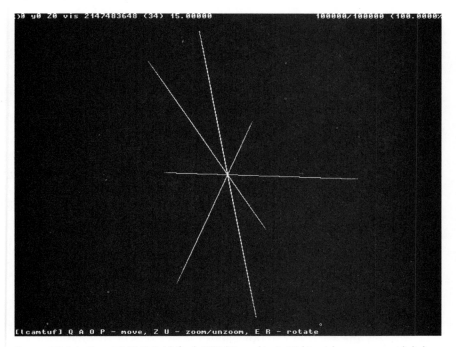

Figure 10-14: OpenVMS 7.2 (default TCP/IP stack). A 32-bit-wide structure with little randomness, showing strong but fairly unusual correlation patterns indicative of a broken PRNG design

Attacking with Attractors

Now, back to the question of sunflowers versus bricks. Yes, the relevance of the pretty pictures goes beyond visual delight for hard-core computer geeks. As it turns out, the attractor structure captured for each system creates a matrix of possible ISN behavior patterns, with densities that correspond to probabilities of a specific type of time dependency or statistical pattern appearing over time. Higher-density regions within the attractor correspond to historical correlations, which are also more likely to occur in the future; less populated areas are less likely to be visited. As such, once the approximate attractor for a specific system is mapped out, the attacker can guess at future results. But how, precisely, do those shapes map back to exact ISN values?

The key to a successful attack is recognizing that the x coordinate of every point in the attractor depends on the value of D_t—that is, on the sequence numbers observed at time t and $t-1$ (because $D_t = S_t - S_{t-1}$). The y coordinate, on the other hand, depends on D_{t-1} (ISNs at $t-1$ and $t-2$), and z depends on D_{t-2} (ISNs at $t-2$ and $t-3$).

Let's assume an attacker has sent three probes to a remote system, for whose operating system the attractor structure has been mapped. The probes correspond to times $t-3$, $t-2$, and $t-1$ and—naturally—are sufficient to reconstruct the y and z coordinates of the point that would mark the behavior of the system at this particular time on the attractor structure.

The attacker can use this information to deduce values of x for known y and z that are more likely to occur than others, based on the observation of the irregularities in the attractor structure noticed thus far. The y and z coordinates correspond to a single line in the attractor space, perpendicular to the x plane (as shown in Figure 10-15)—the collection of points with all possible x values, but known remaining coordinates. The collection of points at which the line intersects with or nears the high-density areas of the attractor forms a set of most likely values for the x coordinate. The areas of lowest density are, obviously, least likely to correspond to the correct value of x; after all, the attractor points did not show up there during previous measurements.

The ability to construct a set of candidates for the x value for known y and z is a major step toward a successful attack: knowing S_{t-1} (which, you will recall, was previously acquired by the attacker), the attacker can easily calculate S_t for every candidate x (D_t) value, as follows:

$$S_t = x + S_{t-1}$$

Having sampled three previous sequence numbers, S_{t-3}, S_{t-2}, and S_{t-1}, the attacker can thus determine a set of likely candidates for the next sequence number, S_t, which will likely be chosen for the next connection by the attacked system—the one the attacker did not initiate, but which he hopes to interfere with. The attacker can then execute an attack by sending

TCP/IP packets with the candidate sequence numbers; he does not have to get it right from the beginning because all wrong guesses will simply be disregarded by the remote implementation. However, as soon as the value of any of the spoofed packets agrees with the expected number, within the expected window size, the traffic will be accepted, thereby defeating the session integrity protection offered by TCP/IP.

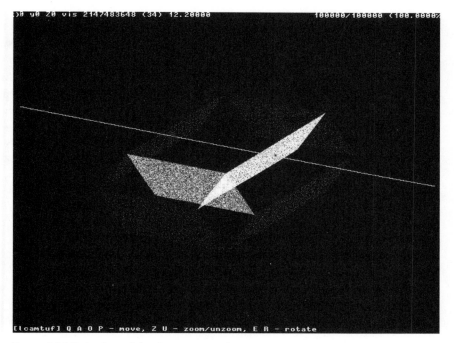

Figure 10-15: An "attack line" intersecting the attractor

The attack has some caveats, of course:

- Their observed dynamics might be local to the observation conditions or source itself—though judging from the achieved success ratio when this technique is deployed against common implementations, this is unlikely.

- If the candidate set is particularly large—as with algorithms that produce uniform attractor clouds with no clear irregularities—the technique becomes fairly impractical because it requires too many attempts to make a correct guess.

- Because it is often impractical to sample the entire sequence of values generated by an ISN implementation in a system (some systems have long or even unlimited cycles), it is impossible to construct a complete attractor. To counter this, you must use an approximate approach: the value is chosen as a candidate if a point is present within a given radius from a specific point on the (y,z) line, thus compensating for the fact that even fairly dense areas of the attractor can still contain gaps.

To keep the results meaningful and to establish a method for comparative assessment of the quality of a ISN generator, I decided to empirically estimate the success ratio with a limited number of tries. Specifically, I wanted to determine the likelihood of hitting the correct number given 5,000 attempts, based on the assumption that an attacker using a low- to mid-end network connection could send at most 5,000 packets in a short period of time.[*]

To test the validity of the approach, I chose to estimate the probability of success by dividing the input data acquired from remote systems into two parts: one part to construct the attractor and the other to perform actual tests. The test read four subsequent sequence numbers at once and then fed three of them to an implementation that, based on the attractor data, had to then generate a set of as many as 5,000 values. Finally, the output was compared with the fourth number acquired from the test data set. The test was repeated hundreds of times for subsequent ISN quadruplets for every attractor to determine an approximate successful guess percentage, which, in practice, denotes how likely the attacker is to succeed using this approach.

Following are some of the results for the systems in the attractor gallery:

Operating System	Attack Feasibility
IRIX 6.5.15	25% (25 out of 100 attempts)
OpenVMS 7.2	15.00%
Windows NT 4.0 SP3	97.00%
Windows 98	100.00%
FreeBSD 4.2	1%
HP/UX 11	100.00%
Mac OS 9	89.00%

This approach was obviously fairly effective[†] and prompted many vendors to redesign their algorithms or revisit their claims about algorithm security. (Follow-up research that I published one year later (2002) reviewed some of these changes, of which not all were satisfactory.)

But the real question is, What does this have to do with passive operating system fingerprinting?

---

[*] The smallest SYN packet has 40 bytes; hence, sending 5,000 SYN packets consumes at least 200 kilobytes of bandwidth. This amount of data can be successfully sent out over a modem line with V42.bis modem compression in a matter of 10–20 seconds. The choice of this threshold is quite arbitrary, but seems reasonable.

[†] These results apply to scenarios in which a precise data injection or spoofing is necessary. If less precision is required or if the only goal of an attacker is to cause a disruption, the remote party is not only going to accept packets with the exact sequence number, but also those that fit within the window size, as specified in TCP/IP parameters (see Chapter 9). In other words, DoS attacks will be even more successful.

Back to System Fingerprinting

Indeed, a couple of truly fascinating consequences result from our ability to map out the dynamics of a sequence number generator in a particular system and from the fact that most implementations exhibit certain more or less unique phase-space patterns. The most obvious trick is the application of ISN probing to old-school system fingerprinting.

By observing a couple of sequence numbers acquired from a remote system (for example, when a party attempts to establish several connections to a server) you can attempt to find an attractor to which this data fits best, by comparing the observed sample against a library of known attractors. (The numbers don't need to be predictable using the attack technique described; the attractor for a system need only be distinct.)

When compared with traditional, passive fingerprinting, this method usually provides us with less detailed insight into the system's configuration, but it is also nearly foolproof. To thwart the technique, you would have to modify the way sequence numbers are generated, but it is usually impossible to significantly tweak ISN-generation settings from the user space, and a modification of the kernel without degrading security usually requires a good dose of knowledge and skill (not to mention, access to the sources).

But, is that all? Of course not!

ISNProber—Theory in Action

Pictures and theory aside, it would be good to see how an ISN sampling works in the real world and how can it help to assess the configuration of a remote system or identify its instances. Fortunately for me, there is a program worth mentioning.

After reading my TCP/IP ISN analysis paper, Toni Vandepoel wrote a great tool called ISNProber. ISNProber uses sequence number analysis to differentiate among several instances of the same system, based on the observation that two distinct systems are likely to be at different locations in the attractor.

At its most trivial, ISNProber can tell that two systems are hiding behind a shared address, based on the appearance of observed ISNs. For the sake of simplicity, let's assume that system Y uses an increase-by-one ISN-generator design. We approach an IP address of a website www.example.com and want to determine how many systems there are. We first identify www.example.com as system Y, establish several subsequent connections, and then observe ISNs as follows: 10, 11, 534, 13, 540, 19.

It should be obvious that the lower numbers form a sequence originating from a computer that either handled less traffic or has a lower uptime (10, 11, 13, 19), whereas the higher numbers correspond to the other system. Hence, two computers are "co-serving" the same public IP, perhaps behind a load balancer. Furthermore, by varying sampling intervals, we can carefully examine the type of load balancer, its request distribution policy, and the traffic it receives.

This approach can not only differentiate systems hiding behind a common address, but also track users of system Y as they hop from one IP to another, for as long as they do not reboot their machine (and hence reset the ISN counter). For systems that offer ISN-generation schemes more sophisticated than the one in our example, the distinction can be more difficult, but it is certainly possible, as long as the ISNs are not purely random on all 32 bits. (If they are, collision-related concerns arise.)

The approach used here simply requires that a dose of predictability be present in the ISN-generation algorithm. As such, TCP/IP initial sequence analysis seems to be a promising alternative or addition to traditional passive fingerprinting—and can, quite regrettably, serve as a useful tool for privacy invasion and user tracking, too.

Preventing Passive Analysis

Defending against sequence-number prediction is fairly trivial, and good solutions, such as Steven M. Bellovin's RFC1948[2] specification, have been available for a long time. However, preventing passive analysis of the numbers is quite difficult, because the problem results not only from the weakness of the algorithms, but also from the diversity of the algorithms used, which causes few systems to share the same ISN footprint. Even among systems that implement RFC1948 or that use other cryptographically secure, external entropy-based generators, behavioral patterns may vary significantly, depending on the subtleties of the algorithm and the implementor's assumptions as to the values that would be sufficient to thwart an attack.

A degree of prevention can be achieved by deploying a stateful packet firewall that rewrites all sequence numbers in outgoing packets[*]; this makes all systems within a protected network appear roughly the same. Unfortunately, only some offer this functionality, and only some can benefit from it.

---

[*] Solar Designer points out that, technically, this can also be implemented as a clever hack in a stateless firewall. The firewall may combine (through XOR, for example) the original sequence number with a secure hash of a secret key, combined with a quadruplet of addresses and ports that uniquely identify a connection. Returning packets could then have the hash removed (by subsequent XORing), making the packet match the internal host's idea of the connection upon delivery, but existing only in an unpredictable, random 32-bit form while outside the firewall. This would work for all but the most broken (frequently repeating and collision-prone) ISN implementations.

Food for Thought

The technique of phase-space analysis is useful in fields that go far beyond sequence-number generation. Other parameters that are chosen pseudo-randomly or according to some internal scheme—such as IP packet ID fields, DNS request identifiers (as shown in Figure 10-16), application-generated "secret" cookies that identify user sessions, and so on—can be analyzed successfully, either to find flaws in a design or to identify an implementation and simplify further analysis or facilitate an attack.

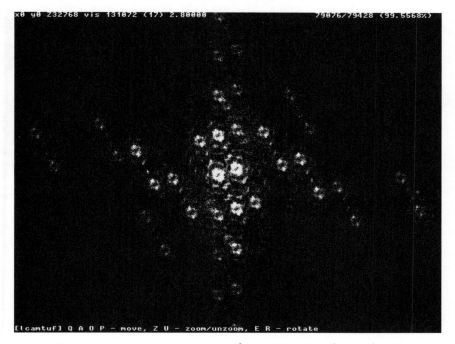

Figure 10-16: An interesting attractor pattern for Linux name-resolver implementation

Some work in this direction had been done or is under way; in a paper partly related to my original research, Joe Steward provides insight into some of the DNS system problems[3] that arise with the advancement of sequence number-prediction mechanisms. He notes that not only a UDP-based DNS protocol offers request verification methods that are simply not enough to withstand even "low-budget" spoofing attacks, but also the low quality of unique request identifiers generated by various implementations further weaken the scheme to make it trivially vulnerable to malicious data injection. Given that DNS is one of core services of the Internet, and that the perspective of spoofing a DNS response for a popular site to redirect all users of a specific network to a different web page is not exactly not tempting, DNS poisoning tops my list of downplayed threats on the Internet.

Dan Kaminsky provides some interesting, more advanced visualizations of supposedly random data at http://www.doxpara.com/pics/index.php?album=phentropy (Figure 10-17), definitely a worthy read.

Figure 10-17: Dan's rendition of BSD kernel randomness (courtesy of www.doxpara.com)

IN RECOGNITION OF
ANOMALIES

Or what can be learned from subtle imperfections of network traffic

In the previous chapters, I dissected and analyzed a number of ways to extract chunks of potentially and likely valuable information from seemingly irrelevant, "technical" parameters supplied along with every message transmitted by a suspect over the network. As I hope you have seen, we can obtain a considerable amount of data on the sender that the sender is surely unaware of providing (or, at the very least, not very happy about often being unable to opt out of providing that data). Using a wide array of packet and stream analysis tricks, in a perfect and happy world we can measure many characteristics of the remote party and can map their behavior to a specific system's signature and network configuration.

However, the reality is a bit different: some of the observed parameters deviate at least slightly from the expected set of values normally associated with a specific device or network configuration that the suspect is using. Although you may simply ignore these seemingly senseless and accidental discrepancies and still successfully identify the originating system or track its users, it is not necessarily wise to do so. We learn to pay no attention to seemingly meaningless annoyances like this, but nothing in the world of computing happens without a good reason (given a fairly lax definition of "good," at least), and exploring the mechanism behind these apparently random anomalies and minority patterns, rather than ignoring them, can provide valuable information about the previously unseen specifics of network configuration.

In this chapter I take a closer look at some of the processes that can affect the observed characteristics of a system. I explain the underlying reason for, the purpose of (or lack thereof), and the consequences of the technologies that prompt such behavior.

Needless to say, most of the reproducible modifications to IP packets discussed here originate from more advanced types of IP-aware intermediate systems. Therefore, I'll begin with a consideration of two long-neglected subjects: firewalls in general, and network address translation (NAT) in particular.

Firewalls are intended to remain stealthy bastions, and the less that is known about what the other guy uses, the better for him. Yet, despite rigorous firewall policies and settings, as these devices increase in complexity and become better suited to handle today's security challenges, they also become easier to examine using indirect or passive probe techniques.

Packet Firewall Basics

Popular firewalls[1] are, in essence, a class of intermediate router devices engineered to violate the fundamental design of an intermediate router device. As opposed to routers proper, systems that are expected to make nondiscriminatory routing decisions based on the information encoded on the third OSI layer, firewalls usually interpret, act upon, or even modify information on higher layers (such as TCP or even HTTP). Firewall technology, although fairly recent, provides a well-established and well-understood set of solutions and can be found in home networks and in large corporations. Firewalls are configured to reject, allow, or redirect specific types of traffic addressed to specific services and are (not surprisingly) used to limit access to certain functions and resources for all traffic traveling across such a device. Hence, they provide a powerful, albeit sometimes overhyped and overly relied upon, security and network management solution.

The key to the success of firewalls in all network environments is that they protect an array of complex systems using a single and comparatively more robust component and provide a fail-safe security measure if a configuration problem exposes a vulnerable service or function on a protected server. (In extreme cases, firewalls are used simply to cover for poor configuration and lack of maintenance of a protected system, usually with disastrous results.)

Stateless Filtering and Fragmentation

Basic firewalls are stateless packet filters. They simply inspect certain features of every packet, such as the destination port on Transmission Control Protocol SYN connection attempts. They then decide, based on these characteristics alone, whether to allow the packet to go through. The stateless design is extremely simple, reliable, and memory and resource efficient. For example, a stateless firewall can limit incoming connections to a mail server to only those addressed to port 25 (SMTP) by dropping all SYN packets but those addressed to this port. Because no connection can be established without this initial SYN packet, the attacker cannot interact with applications on other ports in a meaningful manner. To achieve this, the firewall does not have to be nearly as fast and complex as the mail server itself, because it does not need to keep a record of currently established connections and their exact state.

The problem with this type of completely transparent protection is that the firewall and the final recipient might understand some of the parameters differently. For example, say an attacker convinces the firewall that it is connecting to an allowed port, but crafts its traffic so that the final recipient reads it differently and establishes a connection to a port that the firewall is supposed to be protecting. An attacker can thus access a vulnerable service or an administrative interface, and we are in trouble.

Although causing such a misunderstanding might sound unlikely, it turned out to be fairly easy to achieve with the help of our old friend, packet fragmentation, using an approach commonly referred to as the "overlapping fragment attack"[2] (described in 1995 by RFC1858). In this situation, the attacker sends an initial packet, containing the beginning of the Transmission Control Protocol SYN request, to a port that is allowed by the victim's firewall (such as the aforementioned port 25). The packet is missing only a tiny bit at the end and has a "more fragments" flag set in its IP header, but why should the firewall bother about the trailing data in a packet?

The firewall examines the packet, and because it is a SYN packet, its destination port is also examined and found acceptable. The packet is passed through, but the recipient does not interpret it immediately (remember the reassembly process discussed in Chapter 9?). Instead, the packet is kept, pending the successful completion of defragmentation, which will not occur until the last trailing chunk of the packet arrives.

Next, the attacker sends a second packet fragment. This second packet is created to overlap with the original packet just enough so that it overwrites the destination port (one of the fields of the TCP header) at its location in the reassembly buffer. The fragment is crafted so that it starts at a nonzero offset and lacks most of the TCP header, except for the overwritten bit.

Because of this (and because it lacks the information needed to examine the flags of a TCP packet or other vital parameters the firewall could use to determine whether to allow or block this traffic), the second fragment is usually relayed as is by a stateless firewall. When combined with the first packet by the recipient, this second packet overwrites the original destination port to a more naughty value chosen by the attacker and actually opens a connection to a port that should be protected by the firewall.

Whoops.

NOTE *To protect against this attack, a well-designed stateless firewall performs initial defragmentation before analyzing packets. This, however, makes it somewhat less "stateless," and less transparent.*

Stateless Filtering and Out-of-Sync Traffic

Another problem with stateless packet filters is that they are not nearly as tight as we might hope. The filtering can only be carried out when a single packet contains all the information necessary for the filter to make an informed decision on how to handle it. Because, following the initial handshake, a TCP connection is largely symmetrical, with both parties having equal rights and using the same type of traffic (ACK packets) to exchange data, it is not easy to apply meaningful filters to anything other than the initial phase of a connection. There is no way to determine who (if anyone) initiated the connection through which ACK packets are being swapped without actually tracking and recording connections. Thus, it is a bit hard to define in a meaningful way the filtering policy that the firewall should attempt to apply to traffic such as ACK and other midway packets such as FIN or RST.

The inability to filter past SYN is not normally a problem. After all, if an attacker cannot deliver the initial SYN packets, they cannot establish a connection. But there's a catch: how systems handle non-SYN traffic to a specific port depends on whether a port is closed or the system is listening on that port. For example, some operating systems reply with RST to stray FIN packets and generate no reply on ports that are in open (listening) state.[*]

Techniques such as a FIN or ACK scan (the latter initially described by Uriel Maimon[3] in *Phrack Magazine*), as well as NUL and Xmas scans (scans with illegal packets with no flags set and all flags set, respectively) can thus be used against stateless packet filters to gather preattack evidence about which ports are open on a remote system or to map out what traffic is being dropped by the firewall. The ability to learn that a specific port is open without the ability to establish a proper connection to it is not an immediate threat by itself. However, a scan of this nature often discloses extremely valuable information about network internals (such as the operating system and services being run), which can be used to facilitate a better, more efficient, and more-difficult-to-detect attack once the first line of defense is compromised or bypassed. Thus, this is perceived as a potential weakness of a stateless firewall.

---

[*] Some aspects of this behavior (the tendency to reply with RST to stray and unexpected packets to closed ports and simply disregarding the same traffic addressed to ports on which a service listens for connections) is mandated by RFC793, and some is just a practice chosen by a specific group of implementors.

Perhaps a more grave threat is associated with the mechanism of SYN cookies when combined with stateless filtering. SYN cookies are used to protect operating systems against resource starvation attacks, in which the attacker sends a very large number of spoofed connection requests to the host (not itself a difficult operation to perform). This forces the recipient to send bogus SYN+ACK replies, and additionally to allocate memory and consume other resources when adding this connection-to-be to its TCP state tables. Most systems under such an attack would either consume excess resources and slow to a crawl or deny service to all clients at some point until those bogus connections time out.

To deal with this potential problem, SYN cookies use a cryptographical signature (a shortcut, actually, identifying the connection uniquely) in all SYN+ACK responses inside the ISN field, and then forget about the connection altogether. Only once the ACK response arrives from the host, and only if the acknowledgement number validates against the cryptographic procedure, will the connection be added to the state table.

The problem with SYN cookies, however, is that, in such a design, there is the possibility that SYN (and SYN+ACK response) was never sent in the first place. If the attacker can create an ISN cookie that validates against the host's SYN cookie algorithm (perhaps because the attacker has enough bandwidth, or because the algorithm is weak), he can send an ACK packet that would trigger the remote host to add a new connection to its state table despite, as mentioned, not ever sending SYN and receiving SYN+ACK. A stateless firewall would have no way of knowing that a connection has just been established, because it never received the opening request in the first place! Because there is no initial SYN packet, the destination IP and port could not be checked by the firewall and either approved or rejected, and yet, a connection is all of a sudden established.

That's really bad.

Stateful Packet Filters

To solve the problems of stateless filters, we need to store some of the information about previous traffic and the state of established streams on the firewall. This is the only way to transparently predict the outcome of defragmentation or to obtain the context for midconnection packets and decide whether they are illegitimate and should be discarded or are expected by the recipient and should be delivered.

With the increase of affordable high-performance computing, it has become possible to devise firewall systems that are much more complex and advanced than we could ever imagine. Thus, we have progressed to stateful connection tracking, a situation in which the firewall not only examines single packets, but remembers the context of a connection and validates every packet against this data. This allows the firewall to seal the network tightly and to disregard undesirable or unexpected traffic without relying on the recipient's ability to always tell good traffic from bad. Stateful packet filters try to track connections and allow only the traffic that belongs to one of the active sessions; as a result, they provide better protection and logging capabilities.

The task of stateful filtering is, of course, more challenging than stateless filtering and consumes considerably more resources, especially when a sizable network is protected by such a device. When protecting a large network, the firewall suddenly requires plenty of memory and a fast processor to store and look up the information about what is happening on the wire.

Stateful analysis is also more likely to cause problems or confusion. Issues ensue as soon as the understanding of the current state of a given TCP/IP session differs between the firewall and the endpoints; a situation that is not unlikely given the ambiguity of specifications and the variety of stacks used. For example, upon receiving an RST packet that is not within sequence number limits accepted by the recipient, a firewall that applies sequence number inspection less stringently than the final recipient does might conclude that a connection is closed, whereas the recipient might conclude the session is still open and be willing to accept further communications pertaining to this connection, and vice versa. In the end, stateful inspection comes at a price.

Packet Rewriting and NAT

The solution to improving packet interpretation, and to providing better protection against attacks such as those that use packet fragmentation to bypass firewall rules, was to give firewalls the ability to not only forward, but also rewrite portions of the traffic transmitted. For example, one approach attempts to resolve ambiguity by performing a mandatory packet defragmentation (reassembly) before comparing the packet against any access rules configured by the network administrator.

With the development of more sophisticated solutions, it became obvious that packet rewriting would not only benefit the network, but also provide a quantum leap for network security and functionality by deploying extremely useful technologies such as NAT. NAT is the practice of mapping certain IP addresses to a different set of IPs prior to forwarding them and demangling the responses sent back by a protected system. A stateful NAT mechanism can be used, among other applications, to implement fault-tolerant setups in which a single, publicly accessible IP address is served by more than one internal server. Or to save address space and improve security, NAT can be implemented to allow the internal network to use a pool of private, not publicly accessible, addresses, while enabling hosts on the network to communicate with the Internet by "masquerading" as a single public IP machine.

In the first scenario, NAT rewrites destination addresses on incoming packets to a number of private systems behind the firewall. This provides a fault-tolerant load-balancing setup, in which subsequent requests to a popular website (http://www.microsoft.com, perhaps) or other critical service can be distributed among an array of systems, and if any one fails, other systems can take over. The task is sometimes achieved with dedicated devices (not surprisingly called *load balancers*), but often also supported by NAT-enabled firewalls.

The latter scenario, commonly referred to as *masquerading*, relies on rewriting source addresses on outgoing packets so that a number of private, protected systems (that might be using private addresses not routed to this network from the Internet, such as 10.0.0.0) can connect to the external world by having their outgoing connections intercepted and rewritten by the firewall. The systems are hidden behind a firewall, and their actions appear to recipients outside the NAT-protected network as originating from the firewall. The connection is mapped to a specific public IP address and a specific port, and then the traffic is pushed out. All traffic returning from the destination to this IP and port is rewritten to point back to the private system that initiated the connection and forwarded to the internal network. This allows the entire private network of workstations that are not intended to offer any services to the Internet to remain not directly reachable from the external world, thus greatly increasing the network's security, concealing some of its structure, and preserving expensive public IP address space that would otherwise have to be purchased to accommodate every system. Using this system, a party that has only one public IP routed to them can still construct a network of hundreds or thousands of computers and provide them with Internet access.

Lost in Translation

Once again, address translation is more complex than it might sound: some higher-level protocols are not as straightforward as just connecting to a remote system and sending a bunch of commands. For example, the ancient but wildly popular File Transfer Protocol[4] (FTP), in its most basic and most widely supported mode, relies on establishing a return (reverse direction) connection from the server back to the client for the purpose of transferring the requested data; the initial connection initiated by the client is used only to issue commands. Many other protocols—most notably some chat protocols, peer-to-peer collaboration or data-sharing tools, media broadcast services, and so forth—also use weird or unusual designs that call for reverse connections and port hopping or allowing specific session-less traffic (such as User Datagram Protocol [UDP] packets) back to the workstation.

To address these challenges, every implementation of masquerading that does not aim to render these protocols useless must be equipped with a number of protocol helpers. These protocols inspect the application data exchanged within a connection, even sometimes rewriting some of it and opening temporary holes in the firewall to allow for a return connection.

And herein lies another problem, first spotted in FTP helper by Mikael Olsson several years ago[5] and later researched in other protocol helpers by, among others, the author of this book.[6] The problem is that these helpers decide to open holes in the firewall based on the information sent by a workstation over a specific protocol to a remote system. They assume that the traffic generated by the system is being transmitted on the user's behalf and with the user's knowledge. Needless to say, some programs, such as web browsers, can be tricked into sending certain types of network traffic, including traffic that "looks like" a protocol the program does not natively support, and can even be forced to do so automatically by crafting specific malicious content and sending it to the application. This spoofed traffic can fool a helper program into poking a hole in the firewall.

A classic example of such an attack is an abuse of a generic web browser: by adding a reference to a web page or a web element supposedly located on an attacker's system on a nonstandard HTTP port (which is, however, quite standard for FTP traffic), the client can be forced to connect to this resource and attempt to issue an HTTP request. Because the port to which the connection is established is normally used by FTP, the firewall's FTP helper starts listening to the conversation, hoping to give a hand when necessary.

The following example URL would cause the HTTP client to connect to the FTP port and issue what appears to be an FTP PORT command, which would be picked up by the firewall helper:

```
HTTP://SERVER:21/FOO<RETURN>PORT MY_IP,122,105<RETURN>
```

The request issued by the client would be just meaningless gibberish to a legitimate FTP service on the other end, and the service's response would be incomprehensible to the web client issuing this request—but that's not the point. What matters is that the attacker can control a part of the request—the file name the client will request from the server. This fictitious file name, chosen by the rogue, can contain any data the rogue wishes. By making the file name contain substrings normally identified with FTP requests, the attacker can trick an FTP protocol helper that is listening to this connection for a specific text command (PORT) into believing that the user is attempting to download a specific file. Hence, the remote server is temporarily allowed to connect to the victim (here, to a naughty sounding port 31337—122*256+105=31337). And so we let the attacker in without the victim knowing. Oops—again, more than we bargained for.

The Consequences of Masquerading

All of the aforementioned scenarios are related to masquerading abuse, but the mere presence of masquerading itself can provide us with interesting information about another party.

As noted earlier, masquerading is not nonintrusive. Its basic operating principle is to alter the outgoing traffic by rewriting portions of it. In so doing, it goes beyond merely tweaking the address and not only makes it possible to conclude that masquerading is taking place, but also enables a careful observer to identify the particular firewall system in use. Specifically, when using masquerading, we may encounter some of the following changes:

- There will be an observed discrepancy between the TTL on arriving packets and the expected or measured distance to the destination network. Traffic that originated behind a masquerade is at least one hop "older" than a packet originating from a system that gets its IP address for outgoing connections directly from a protected network.

- In most cases, various operating systems or slightly different system configurations (or uptimes) can be found in the originating network. These systems have slightly different TCP/IP characteristics, as discussed in Chapters 9 and 10. If we observe various TCP/IP fingerprints in connections seemingly originating from the same IP, we can get a strong hint as to whether NAT is present at a particular machine with an internal network behind it.

- Finally, a remote observer is likely to notice *source port shift*. This is an otherwise unusual occurrence that arises because connections coming from the network are using ephemeral source ports that are not in the particular operating system's normal range.

  Every operating system reserves a specific range of source ports for establishing a local endpoint identifier for all outgoing connections. However, a firewall often uses a different range of ports for mapping masqueraded connections that is specific to the NAT device's operating system. In this case, if the observed ranges differ from what is expected for the detected operating system (for example, if Linux, which normally operates in the range of 1024 to 4999, appears to be using very high port numbers instead), it is possible to deduce the presence of address translation and sometimes even determine the type of firewall in use.

These techniques are commonly used and form the basis for masquerade detection and masqueraded network reconnaissance. But several other means of detecting packet rewriting are also available.

Segment Size Roulette

One of the less obvious and hence less popular ways to detect packet rewriting devices and learn more about network configuration is analyzing the maximum segment size field in incoming traffic.

Because IP packet fragmentation adds noticeable overhead to the fragmented traffic, it is often perceived as a performance nightmare, and many implementers try to prevent it. On the other hand, as discussed earlier, fragmentation is difficult to eliminate, as it seems to be nearly impossible to accurately, quickly, and reliably determine the maximum transmission unit (MTU) over a path in advance of actual communications. Even the best method available, path MTU discovery, is far from perfect and still impacts performance when triggered. In order for it to detect the correct MTU setting by trial and error, some packets that do not fit might have to be discarded and be resent.

To prevent the performance and reliability impact of path MTU discovery and reduce the overhead of fragmentation, many NAT firewalls that rewrite certain parameters of outgoing traffic also change the declared Maximum Segment Size (MSS) parameter in TCP headers on connections originating from the private network to one more suitable for the external link from the network. This new setting is likely to be slightly narrower (have a lower MTU) than that of the LAN. This modification ensures that the receiving party does not attempt to send data that would not fit over the link if that link is across the particular part of the infrastructure with the lowest MTU, thus making fragmentation less likely to occur. (This assumes that any MTU incompatibility is most likely to occur near the sender or recipient system on the so-called last mile, where various types of low MTU links, such as DSL connections or wireless lines, are often found, and packets might need to be "downsized" to fit through those pipes.)

This reduction in the MSS alone is not particularly easy to detect. In fact, it is impossible to tell whether the MSS was set to a given value by the sender or modified somewhere down the road. That is, except for one minor thing. Recall from Chapter 9 that there is something special about the window size selection algorithm on many of today's systems:

> The window size setting determines the amount of data that can be sent without acknowledgment. The specific setting is often chosen according to the developer's personal voodoo rules and other religious beliefs. The two most popular approaches say the value should be either a multiple of the MTU minus protocol headers (a value referred to as Maximum Segment Size, or MSS) or simply something sufficiently high and "round." Older versions of Linux (2.0) used values that were powers of 2 (for example, 16,384). Linux 2.2 switched to a multiple of MSS (11 or 22 times MSS, for some reason), and newer versions of Linux commonly use 2 to 4 times MSS. The Sega Dreamcast, a network-enabled console, uses a value of 4,096, and Windows often uses 6,4512.

An ever-increasing number of today's systems (including newer versions of Linux and Solaris, certain versions of Windows, and SCO UnixWare) uses a window size setting that is a multiple of the MSS. Thus, it's easy to tell when the MSS setting in a packet has been tampered with because the window size on the resulting packet will no longer be a specific multiple of MSS. In fact, it's likely that it will no longer divide by MSS at all.

By comparing the MSS to window size, you can reliably detect the presence of a group of firewalls that support MSS *clamping* (readjusting to match the link) on a variety of systems. Although clamping is optional on

Linux and FreeBSD, it is often performed automatically on home firewalls and on smart DSL routers or other home networks. Hence, the presence of an anomalous MSS setting indicates not only a packet-rewriting device, but an association also with NAT capability, which can be taken as an indicator of the sender's network connection.

Stateful Tracking and Unexpected Responses

Another important consequence of stateful connection tracking and packet rewriting is that some RFC-mandated responses are generated by the firewall, not the sender. This enables an attacker to discover and probe such a device quite efficiently. When a connection is dropped from the NAT state table (whether due to a time-out or to a termination by one of the endpoints with an RST packet that did not reach the other end), further traffic in this session will not be forwarded to the recipient, as it would with stateless packet filters. It is handled directly by the firewall, instead.

The TCP/IP specification mandates that a recipient reply to all unexpected ACK packets with RST, to inform the sender that the session they are attempting to continue is no longer honored by the recipient or never was. Some firewalls might violate the RFC and refuse to reply to this traffic at all, simply dropping packets that do not seem to belong to an existing session. (This is not always wise, because it can cause unnecessary delays when a legitimate connection is dropped due to intermittent network problems.)

Numerous devices, however, reply with a legitimate and expected RST packet. This opens yet another avenue for the detection and careful fingerprinting of the firewall device. Because the packet is created from scratch by the firewall, its parameters relate to the firewall, not to what the firewall is protecting. This allows the traditional fingerprinting techniques discussed in Chapter 9 (such as examining DF flags, TTL, window size, option types, values and ordering, and so on) to be used to identify the firewall.

There is also another possibility, per RFC1122:[7]

> 4.2.2.12 RST Segment: RFC-793 Section 3.4
>
> A TCP SHOULD allow a received RST segment to include data.
>
> DISCUSSION: It has been suggested that an RST segment could contain ASCII text that encoded and explained the cause of the RST. No standard has yet been established for such data.

And indeed, even though no standard had been established, some systems choose to reply with verbose (albeit often cryptic) RST messages upon encountering a stray ACK, hoping that the other party will find comfort in knowing what went wrong. These replies often include internal keywords or, it would seem, attempts at some strange genre of geek humor that may be operating system specific, such as `no tcp, reset; tcp_close, during connect` (Mac OS); `tcp_fin_wait_2_timeout; No TCP` (HP/UX); `new data when detached; tcp_lift_anchor, can't wait` (SunOS).

Whenever we see such a verbose RST packet in response to network problems or unexpected traffic sent to the host, and we otherwise know that the remote system from which it originated does not use such verbose messages, we get a hint. We can deduce that there is a device between us and the recipient, likely a stateful firewall, and we can tell its operating system by matching the response against known messages produced by common and not-so-common operating systems.

These two fingerprinting techniques prove to be extremely effective in detecting the presence of stateful packet filters whenever network traffic can be observed during short-term network problems. These techniques can also be used for active fingerprinting without targeting the firewall device itself by sending a stray ACK packet to a target to differentiate stateless and stateful filters. Based on the target's response to the packet, the attacker can then devise the best method to approach the firewall (or use the knowledge gained in other ways).

Reliability or Performance: The DF Bit Controversy

Path MTU discovery (PMTUD) is a fingerprinting venue that is closely related to the IP fragmentation avoidance scheme described in Chapter 9.

Recent versions of the Linux kernel (2.2, 2.4, 2.6) and of Windows (2000 and XP) implement and enable PMTUD by default. Thus, unless this setting is changed, all traffic originating from them has a don't fragment (DF) bit set. Again, the path discovery algorithm tends to cause issues in some rare but not entirely unheard of situations.

Path MTU Discovery Failure Scenarios

The problem with PMTUD is that it depends on the ability for the sender of a packet to receive the ICMP error message "fragmentation required but DF set" and to determine the optimal settings for a connection. The packet that triggered the message is discarded before reaching the destination and has to be resized and sent again.

If the sender does not receive this message, they remain unaware that their packet did not get through. This prompts a delay at best or an indefinite lockup of the connection at worst, since retransmissions are also not likely to get through a link for which the maximum allowed size of a packet is smaller than what the sender is trying to push through.

The ICMP message generated when a packet is too large for a link is not guaranteed to reach the sender, however. In some networks, as a result of an ill-conceived attempt to improve security, all ICMP messages are simply dropped. Finally, even if a device sends one, it might not be delivered.

Why would ICMP messages be dropped? Because historically, many such messages were known to cause security problems: certain oversized or fragmented ICMP packets corrupted the kernel memory in many systems (also called the "ping of death"). ICMP messages sent to broadcast addresses were also used to trigger a storm of responses to a spoofed source address in an attack named "Smurf," as well as to carry out DoS attacks. Too, incorrectly configured systems often interpreted a specific type of ICMP broadcasts, a router advertisement message,[*] as a command to modify their network settings. Because they would accept it, regardless of whether those messages could be trusted, this opened yet another interesting attack route. And so, ICMP is feared and blocked by many.

NOTE   *A suggestion to reject all ICMP traffic can often be found in naive security guides, and some system administrators follow it. I have even seen it in a professional pen-test recommendation from an acclaimed auditor, whose name I regrettably cannot reveal here.*

Another issue that can make PMTUD unreliable is that some received error messages come from devices that use private address space. Sometimes, in order to preserve limited public IP address space (which is usually expensive), interfaces on the cable that connect the router and the firewall of a remote network are chosen from a pool of addresses reserved for private, local use, instead of from ones actually routed to the particular network from the outside world.

Unfortunately, the use of private address space can break PMTUD. Why? Because if a packet coming from the external world is too big to be forwarded by the recipient's firewall to the destination, the firewall sends an ICMP error message with a source address of the firewall itself, which belongs to the private pool. The firewall of the sender of the original packet can then reject such a response packet, because it appears to come from the external world, but with an IP address from a private pool (perhaps even from the same pool as the sender's private LAN). The firewall rejects this traffic because it is usually a sign of a spoofing attempt intended to impersonate a trusted, internal host. However, in this case, this decision breaks a relatively recent PMTU discovery mechanism and leaves the original sender unaware that their packet did not get through.

To make things worse, even if all conditions are right, and the packet reaches its destination, many of today's devices limit ICMP response rates and will not send more than a given number of messages during a particular time period. This, too, has been implemented as a security measure. Because ICMP messages were designed for informational purposes only and were not critical to communication before the introduction of PMTUD algorithms, rate limiting seemed like a sensible way to fend off certain types of DoS or bandwidth starvation attacks.

---

[*]Router advertisements were intended to allow the autoconfiguration of network hosts without the need to enter any settings by hand. The router periodically—or on request— broadcast a message saying, "Here I am. Use me." By default, some systems accepted unsolicited advertisements without much hesitation—a bad idea.

The Fight against PMTUD, and Its Fallout

In light of the foregoing, some regard PMTUD as a fairly bad design. It offers a slight performance improvement but at the price of infrequent but persistent and usually hard-to-diagnose problems that can prevent users from accessing specific servers or cause their connections to stall unexpectedly. Although many "black-hole detection" algorithms were devised to detect hosts or networks for which PMTUD should be disabled (and these work with varying success), this does not fully solve the problem and can introduce additional delays—usually when least desirable.

To solve these problems and avoid complaints, some commercial firewall vendors configure their solutions to perform a dirty trick: They clear the DF flag on all outgoing traffic. This is a subtle and often appreciated modification, but it is also a great way to identify the presence of a packet-filtering and rewriting device. If the characteristics of PMTUD-enabled systems are observed at a given address or a given network, but the incoming packets lack a DF flag as expected, the careful observer can deduce the presence and type of a firewall, thus obtaining another tiny bit of data without any interaction with the victim.

Food for Thought

This concludes my little story about how making firewalls better and more powerful to prevent infiltration and direct reconnaissance also made them easier to examine with indirect assessment. But allow me this brief digression.

Perhaps the most bizarre and interesting discovery is one I encountered somewhere back in 1999. Although not directly related to the design of firewalls, it still provides interesting food for thought for anyone interested in the problem of passively fingerprinting interim systems.

Jacek P. Szymanski, with whom I worked briefly and with whom I later had the pleasure of discussing certain unusual and suspicious network traffic patterns,[*] noted a sudden increase in badly broken TCP/IP packets coming to port 21536 (and, to a lesser extent, to ports such as 18477 or 19535). The broken packets always originated from ports such as 18245, 21331, or 17736 and came from a large number of systems in the dial-up address space operated by Poland's national telco, Telekomunikacja Polska.

Once a couple of those packets were captured, the traffic was badly and strangely mangled. The packets arrived with IP headers in place (with protocol type set to TCP), but the headers were immediately followed with TCP payload—the TCP headers were simply gone. The observed port combinations resulted from interpreting the first four bytes of the payload as a pair of numbers (which, had there been a TCP header there instead, would

---

[*] A cooperation that, at some point, resulted in the creation of a loosely knit group of Polish researchers who worked through 1999 and 2000 to correlate, track, and seek to explain many bizarre types of unexpected traffic patterns across the network.

correspond to the source and destination port combination). The pair 18245 and 21536 was merely a representation of the text string "GET "—four characters that open most HTTP requests transferred over the network. Similarly, 18477 and 21331 stood for SSH-, an opening phrase of every Secure Shell session. And 19535 and 17736 represented EHLO, a command that opens all ESMTP (Extended SMTP) sessions.

But the reason this type of traffic suddenly began to appear remained a mystery. Too, why did it come only from this particular network? And why did this type of packet mangling not result in connectivity problems or other inconvenience for the users, if some network equipment did indeed produce it?

The answer soon followed. As it turned out, all the observed traffic originated from Nortel CVX devices, a modem access system that this telco had begun to use. The problem occurred only sporadically, under heavy load. Consequently, only a small percentage of incomplete packets were sent, and only this small number reached the recipients (to their utmost surprise). The most likely reason was improper queue locking or buffer management, a problem that could be noticed only when numerous sessions were processed nearly simultaneously. In such cases, certain packets seemed to be sent out too early, while still "under construction," or were otherwise mangled by the implementation.

The company fixed their TCP/IP implementation shortly after the deployment in Poland, and all lived happily ever after. But, as you can imagine, they were not the first and not the last to accidentally leave a unique footprint of their systems in packets they trafficked.

The moral of this story is that it is once again naive to disregard what we typically ignore. In today's networking world subtle hints and unusual or unexpected and unexplained observations are extremely valuable. They are easy to find, but difficult to analyze.

Perhaps food for thought and a field worth further exploration are the various methods deployed to thwart system fingerprinting. Various firewall vendors have attempted to incorporate antifingerprinting measures that alter some packet characteristics by tweaking various TCP/IP parameters (such as Internet Protocol IDs, TCP sequence numbers, and so on). Needless to say, such a solution actually helps the attacker and produces an outcome precisely opposite to what they hoped for: unless all characteristics susceptible to fingerprinting are changed and homogenized (including sequence numbers, retransmission timings, time-stamp values, and so on), it is not only possible to detect the underlying operating system, but also the firewall being used to protect the network.

C'est la vie.

12

STACK DATA LEAKS

Yet another short story on where to find what we did not intend to send out at all

Sometimes, all it takes to find subtle but fascinating and helpful hints about your co-Netizens and their whereabouts is some luck. At least that was the case with a fairly interesting and extremely elusive information disclosure vector that I discovered in 2003, after several weeks of a daunting hunt.

Kristjan's Server

First things first. Several years ago, I asked a friend of mine, Kristjan, to let me use some disk space on one of his machines so that I could host a bunch of my projects on a reliable and fast system. He agreed, and soon after, I began to gradually move most of my programs and papers to their new home. Among the projects I transferred was a new version of p0f, my passive operating system fingerprinting tool (which you may remember from Chapter 9). This humble tool implemented some interesting passive analysis techniques, but to be truly powerful, it needed to ship with a strong and current database of operating system signatures. Maintaining it manually was difficult, and I soon ran out of obscure systems to fingerprint and add to it.

Fortunately, whereas gathering signatures for active fingerprinting software required often objectionable interaction with the target (stirring controversy and straining the network link and sometimes crashing particularly poorly implemented TCP/IP stacks), passive fingerprinting required no such action and could be performed effortlessly on all systems that connected to Kristjan's system to fetch my page. To encourage submissions, I set up a subpage where any user could immediately see their fingerprint and correct the way their system was being reported or add a new signature. This page proved to be a great way to collect signatures and improve the software, but this is not where the story ends.

In a bizarre turn of events, Kristjan decided to host a different, for-profit site on his system so that his system could pay its own bills. The site, as you might imagine, was not at all devoted to network security, gardening, or some other noble cause. Rather, it focused on some less prestigious, yet perhaps more appealing aspects of our lives: sex, nudity, and everything related. I rejoiced, as any self-respecting geek would, not because of the contents he served, but because millions of connection signatures started pouring down in a matter of hours, to be analyzed by the software I was developing. Hallelujah!

Surprising Findings

Better safe than sorry: While designing the new code for p0f, I decided to implement a number of sanity checks to detect even the most bizarre, unlikely, or unheard of patterns in incoming traffic, covering all possible illegal or meaningless combinations of TCP/IP settings. Although common sense suggested I should never encounter packets that have their parameters mangled in bizarre ways (at least not when communicating with popular and thus well-tested systems), there seemed to be no harm in implementing this functionality. Too, if a system indeed turned out to be sending packets that exhibited a particular type of anomaly, the ability to detect it would provide an excellent way to tell this particular OS from similar-looking implementations that do not share this flaw.

During the merry months of this blessed signature storm, I saw the strangest things. I eventually managed to explain some of these and document them for p0f, and some remained a mystery. Most of the anomaly checks I implemented previously hit the spot, and I immediately located systems that indeed were sharing more unusual TCP/IP implementation quirks. But one thing was particularly disturbing and hard to believe, so I decided to pay more attention to it.

Two of the tests—one a check for the ACK value set in TCP/IP headers when the ACK flag is not set (indeed a futile action), and the other a test for the URG value set when the URG flag is not set—seemed relatively meaningless at first, never yielding interesting results, until I noticed something quite unusual. I found that some Windows 2000 and XP systems that connected to Kristjan's server had, from time to time, nonzero URG or ACK values in packets that had neither flag set (most notably, SYN packets that open a new connection).

Having URG or ACK values set when a respective flag is not set is not strictly a problem. According to RFC793, when this is the case, the values simply lose all significance; for example:

> Urgent Pointer: 16 bits
>
> This field communicates the current value of the urgent pointer as a positive offset from the sequence number in this segment. The urgent pointer points to the sequence number of the octet following the urgent data. This field is only be interpreted in segments with the URG control bit set.

RFC793, in its very special way, tells us that this anomaly is not likely to cause any networking problems, and as such it might have gone unnoticed forever. But I took notice, simply because it was kind of odd.

I initially thought that a specific piece of network equipment was to blame, as was the case with most of the problems described in Chapter 11, but this was not so. The hits were coming from single systems, not entire networks, and they were not persistent; they just showed up in a couple of packets (with values either still or changing randomly) and then disappeared, never to show up again on subsequent connections. Also, the problem seemed to be exclusive to Windows; there were no minority operating systems represented at all in the group of systems exhibiting this issue.

I found myself spending week after week trying to trace the problem. As part of my hunt, I deployed some other installations in more controlled environments; and, to my amazement, the problem showed up, even in local networks and even from the most up-to-date systems, though only for short periods of time. Users could not recall doing anything unusual when this type of traffic occurred from their systems, and I could not track down any particular type of communications or set of actions that would trigger it; there seemed to be no pattern.

Puzzling.

Revelation: Phenomenon Reproduced

I was close to giving up. I posted my observations to several public mailing lists (most notably VULN-DEV, a popular vulnerability discussion list hosted by Security Focus), seeking further analysis and feedback from other researchers, but this failed to yield any results. And then, only by sheer luck, I caught one of my own test stations generating this exact behavioral pattern while working on a wholly different problem. I happened to have a sniffer running in the background (don't we all).

Soon, I had a diagnosis: the problem occurred when the workstation was performing a background file transfer or other network-extensive operations when attempting to establish a connection. In almost every OS, the packet to be sent out on a wire was first constructed in the system's main memory, using either a *static buffer* (a fixed location in memory used exclusively for this purpose) or a *dynamic buffer* (one allocated as needed using memory that could have been used previously for some other purpose). In this particular scenario, when two connections occur at roughly the same time, the buffer used to construct outgoing packets before sending them to the network card appeared to not be initialized properly prior to use; that is, it was not cleared of any leftover contents because the buffer was last used for a different purpose. The implementation code assumes that all contents of the buffer are zero and does not bother to touch those it does not need to initialize to any particular value (as is the case with ACK and URG values when respective flags are not set). As a result, some of the leftover contents are sent out on the wire.

Naturally, all other IP and TCP fields were properly initialized, as they ought to be; only URG and ACK were left out, as they had no relevance in this particular context. But this omission meant that a small portion of data that belonged to a different connection (or a different aspect of computer operations) was being sent out to another party. The problem manifested itself only during multiple sessions (common during web browsing, background downloads, and similar scenarios), but not when the system was idle.

The relevance of the information disclosed in this situation is twofold:

- It can be viewed as a traditional information disclosure scenario. Although the amount of information disclosed in every packet that does not have URG and ACK values initialized properly is fairly small and is not guaranteed to be meaningful (unless the buffer held something interesting to begin with), it may be of value in certain scenarios, particularly when a simultaneous session that can contain sensitive information, and effectively the bug itself, can be induced by an external entity.

- The vulnerability can be considered a convenient fingerprinting metric that reveals additional information about the operating system and the state it is in—a simple way to differentiate systems that extensively use the network from idle ones.

That's it. And although the significance of this discovery is perhaps easy to overestimate, I decided to include it here for its amusement value and to illustrate how easy it is to obtain even sophisticated data from a remote party without even asking.

Food for Thought

It is easy to lay blame for this on the developers. Although the developers are naturally at fault for not initializing memory properly, the entire notion of having a separate "enabler" for a field in the header is perhaps a design flaw in TCP itself and might contribute to this kind of problem. Similar subtleties plague protocol specifications, as demonstrated in Chapter 7, in which a similar type of a vulnerability was caused by following a specification too closely, without giving much thought to its potential side effects.

13

SMOKE AND MIRRORS

Or how to disappear with grace

Many of the information disclosure scenarios discussed so far require careful analysis of the information sent by a remote system in order to deduce certain facts about the sender or to intercept additional data they are not aware of sending in the first place. In several cases, however, only circumstantial evidence of the presence of some form of activity can be gathered. As discussed in Chapters 1 and 2, by precisely interpreting this evidence, you can determine the probable whereabouts of the user or an application that processes sensitive data, thus indirectly uncovering secrets of the victim's machine without having to access the data itself.

Some features of the IP make many of its implementations susceptible to circumstantial evidence information disclosure vulnerabilities, quite similar to what we witnessed earlier with certain types of system pseudo-random number generators or variable complexity data-processing algorithms. Carefully observing and then deciphering this information can be advantageous, providing us at the very least with much-needed intelligence regarding our adversary's general habits or a particular activity in which they are engaged.

Until now, this part of the book has focused on IP-layer attacks that require direct observation of the traffic coming from a sender, though typically without interacting with the victim. In this chapter, however, we take a peek at a spectacularly active but indirect IP-based attack in which an attacker profiles their victim by making an educated guess about what they cannot see. They do so by interacting with an innocent bystander who is not the real subject of the test and without this party's consent or knowledge, learning what they can about the actual victim.

Such an approach does not sound like the easy way to gather data. So, in the spirit of a geekdom, why not take the scenic, albeit a bit longer, route and look at it in more detail?

Abusing IP: Advanced Port Scanning

Rogue Internet users frequently use port scanning for pre-attack reconnaissance and system fingerprinting. When port scanning, a would-be attacker attempts a short connection to every port on a system and maps out all programs that listen for network traffic. In this way, they can determine where to attack by finding any vulnerable or otherwise potentially interesting network service on the system. Too, in many cases, they can determine which operating system their victim is using, because default services are often operating-system specific.

The first problem with traditional scanning is that it is quite noisy—the victim is likely to notice a storm or even a steady flow of connection attempts to unusual ports. Hiding is not easy, either; the attacker must be able to see the responses to their SYN packets to determine whether a port is open or closed. Open ports respond with SYN+ACK, closed ones with RST, and ports filtered by a firewall are likely to generate no response or an Internet Control Message Protocol (ICMP) message. Consequently, the attacker cannot simply spoof a source address on all outgoing packets; they must reveal their identity by providing source addresses that route back to the network they are listening on for incoming traffic.

Tree in the Forest: Hiding Yourself

Whether the party scans out of curiosity (for example, to see what operating system a competitor is running) or follows with an attack attempt, they usually want to leave as few traces as possible and avoid alerting the victim. Network administrators and certain authorities generally perceive host and network scans quite negatively. Although debate is ongoing about whether these scans should be considered malicious, the person doing the probing almost always loses when an annoyed systems administrator decides to file an abuse report or if your competitor identifies one of your employees as trying to probe their networks, regardless of the true intent and further plans of the curious tester.

One common way to camouflage port scans is to deploy a "decoy" scan, whereby the attacker sends SYN packets from a number of fake addresses, as well as from their actual IP, to each port. The victim handles these bogus packets just like real ones, except that the responses to bogus ones, of course, are sent out into the void. As a result, the victim has a much more difficult time determining who really is behind the scan, because to do so they have to eliminate all the decoy systems from the list of packet sources through either careful analysis or simple trial and error. Still, with some determination it is possible to locate the sender without help from the authorities, though the attacker hopes to discourage the victim by making it too time-consuming to fully resolve such a minor incident.

Idle Scanning

The ultimate defense against being discovered came—as it often does—from a guy who had too much time on his hands and wasted it reading through protocol specifications instead of doing something productive. And so a technique called "idle" scanning was born. Initially devised by Salvatore "antirez" Sanfilippo in 1998, it was soon widely implemented and became quite popular among hackers (both the simply curious and the malicious).[1]

Idle scanning is based on an important observation. To quote RFC793:

> As a general rule, reset (RST) must be sent whenever a segment arrives which apparently is not intended for the current connection. A reset must not be sent if it is not clear that this is the case.

Transmission Control Protocol RST packets are used to unconditionally terminate a connection and to tell the sender to cease any further attempts to communicate. The system, without much hesitation, sends an RST when encountering unexpected traffic, according to the rule in RFC793. (Naturally, RST packets themselves, even when unexpected, are not replied to; if they were, an endless stream of RSTs would bounce back and forth upon the slightest network hiccup.)

Idle scanning uses and cleverly abuses the fact that a bystander, a *witness host*, will handle all unexpected packets in this way. The attack enables rogue Netizens to scan a victim with whom they do not intend to directly communicate. When idle scanning, the attacker uses an unsuspecting and randomly chosen system on the Internet to scan a third system (the real victim), without ever revealing their own identity.

Idle scanning works like this: The attacker spoofs a SYN packet to a given port they want to check on the victim's system. This packet is addressed to the victim host, but with a spoofed return address of the witness system instead of the attacker's system. This alone does not sound like a good way to get anything done, but wait just a moment.

What happens next depends on whether the port is open:

- If the probed port on the victim system replies with RST to the witness host, the witness host receives it and simply ponders the RST in silence, without generating any traffic back to the victim.

- If the probed port is open, the victim replies with SYN+ACK. The witness, with utmost disbelief, concludes that it had never sent a SYN packet to begin with, so it sends RST to instruct the victim that they are grossly mistaken and that they had better stop now. The victim sheepishly accepts the response and drops all records for the connection it hoped to accept.

The relevance of this distinction is difficult to appreciate at first. But return to Chapter 9, and recall the following information about one of the fields in an IP header:

> The identification number (ID) is a 16-bit value that differentiates IP packets when fragmentation occurs. Without IP IDs, if two packets are fragmented at once, reassembly would severely mangle, interchange, or otherwise damage fragments of two packets that were fragmented simultaneously. IP IDs uniquely identify several reassembly buffers for different packets. The value used for this purpose is often chosen simply by incrementing a counter with every packet sent; the first packet sent by a system has an IP ID of 0, the second an Internet Protocol of ID 1, and so on.

Because the attacker has chosen a witness host that indeed uses this IP ID selection scheme (and there are many candidates to choose from), they can now easily determine whether the witness host has sent an IP packet within a given time frame. They do so simply by sending some meaningless traffic to the witness system before and after the actual probe and comparing IP ID values in the responses it sends. If two observed IP IDs differ only by 1, no packets were sent out by the witness system in between. However, if the difference is more than 1, some packets were indeed exchanged, though we cannot be sure with whom.

The attacker can also issue a probe just before sending a spoofed packet to the victim and shortly thereafter. Thus, they can determine whether a port is open or closed based on the witness host's replies. If the witness had an increased IP ID, it most likely replied with an RST to the victim, which means that the victim must have sent SYN+ACK in the first place in response to the spoofed packet. The attacker can then conclude that the port is open. If, on the other hand, the witness produces the next IP ID as expected, it did not receive any traffic from the victim, or it decided to ignore the received RST packet.

There are, of course, some practical considerations. Most important, the witness host should be relatively idle during the idle scan, and the test should be repeated several times to eliminate false positives; otherwise, we can incorrectly interpret some third-party communications on the witness's side as telling us that a specific port on the victim's machine is open.

NOTE *Neither issue has proven to be much of a deal, however, and many advanced tools (beginning with idlescan in 1999, and now the ingenious NMAP) implement idle scanning and do it well.*

The importance of idle scanning is that it can obfuscate the origin of a scan not by merely trying to discourage the victim, but by actually inhibiting any identifiable communications from the attacker. This makes it more difficult to track the attacker without the help of the owner of a witness host (which itself can be queried by the attacker for IP IDs as a part of legitimate traffic such as an HTTP session and hence can have a hard time figuring out whether it was used as a tool for an attack at all) or from external entities (law enforcement and ISPs). Because law enforcement response is usually initiated only once the system is compromised, not merely probed (curious competitors can sleep soundly) and requires the victim to admit to being compromised (which is not always convenient for certain large corporations), the attacker feels rather safe.

NOTE *Despite at first appearing no different from a regular SYN scan in the results it can offer, idle scanning offers a fairly unique scanning perspective. The use of witness scans makes it possible to see the destination system from the viewpoint of a witness. If the witness has higher access privileges to the victim's system (if, for example, it is a system within a protected network behind a firewall, or a system for which certain lax IP filtering rules are set for easier access to a corporate network, and so on), you can use idle scanning to discover the inner workings of a protected network.*

Defense against Idle Scanning

There is at present no immediate defense against an idle scan, and no easy way to tell it from a regular SYN scan. However, it is quite easy to defend against being a witness host by using random or constant IP IDs, as discussed in Chapter 9. Although doing so won't make attacks against you—or attacks in general—any more difficult (plenty of systems will always use sequential identifiers), it will prevent your network from being abused for this purpose.

To avoid the firewall bypassing ("perspective") attack, use common sense when designing access channels for external systems, and use proper ingress filtering on gateway systems, dropping all packets that arrive from the Internet with source addresses that seem to belong to a protected network. Although, as discussed previously, this type of filtering might break path maximum transmission unit (PMTU) discovery mechanisms, it usually fixes more problems than it breaks.

Food for Thought

Although less feasible, it is still possible to use IP IDs for the general profiling of IP activity. In fact, when the victim establishes an interactive session to a remote system, IP IDs can even be used to time keystrokes or similar actions, thus turning this technique into one of the previously discussed timing attack scenarios. Similarly, you can enhance user-racking capabilities by measuring the number of packets sent by a specific host between two subsequent visits to a monitored network.

You can also use TCP sequence numbers on certain systems to achieve the same functionality as IP ID analysis, depending on the ISN-generator design. I encourage you to explore this idea in more detail.

As for tracking down the source of an idle scan (or any other spoofed attack), see Chapter 17.

14

CLIENT IDENTIFICATION: PAPERS, PLEASE!

*Seeing through a thin disguise may come in handy
on many occasions*

The challenge of determining the true identity of
software and its legitimacy can be rather easily resolved
locally on the computer running the software. But it's
not so easy to do so over a network.

Both system administrators and application developers often attempt to
identify software being used at the other end of a network-based session, with
varying degrees of success. We attempt to identify software for several reasons.
For the WWW (World Wide Web), the most common goal is to optimize the
content served to a client based on the rendering engine being used—whether
that content is legitimate or malicious. The goal for client identification within
numerous other communication schemes—instant messengers, mail clients,
and so on—is to ensure policy compliance and to detect communications
originating from possibly dangerous or otherwise unacceptable applications.
And last but not least, programmers themselves attempt to identify software to
prevent unapproved (or unlicensed) software from using a particular network
service (possibly stripping them of some of their income) or to detect cases
such occurrences and take corrective actions.

The most trivial and common way to identify the other party relies on examining the information voluntarily advertised by the remote system. This information can include simply noticing a "welcome" banner provided by a server, taking a look at protocol headers sent by a client (such as *X-Mailer* in emails, *User-Agent* within WWW sessions, and so forth), and analyzing textual status and error or warning messages used by the service in response to certain types of traffic.* Unfortunately, the first method is extremely unreliable and easily sabotaged by users who have something to hide; the last method is intrusive and quite difficult to use against clients without causing problems. (Most client software is designed to bail out and complain upon encountering the first error condition; users who, as a result of an attempt to identify their software, encounter an error message and cannot legitimately access a service, will not be impressed.)

Camouflage

Examining textual announcements produced by the client is unreliable not simply because users *can* camouflage their Internet software (web browsers, mail clients, and so forth) in order to mimic the responses of the most popular clients, but because they often also have a good incentive to try: either to blend in with the crowd or simply to fool servers that tend to know better what version of a program the visitor needs to be running. It's simple to do so, either by using a client's built-in functionality or by modifying a program's sources or binaries with one of a multitude of freely available tools.

Too, because many corporate environments have begun to implement more rigorous content filtering in order to block unwanted traffic, some coders who work on more questionable applications have, in response, begun to impersonate harmless software. Not long ago, peer-to-peer music-sharing applications, malicious Trojan horses, and spyware began to pretend to be the most prevalent web browser, Microsoft Internet Explorer, in their outgoing communications. The same was true for many address-gathering web crawlers used by shoddy marketing businesses around the globe.

Other protocols are also plagued by impersonators. Not surprisingly, a majority of much despised bulk-mailing software used by spammers and con artists pretends to be programs such as Microsoft Outlook, PINE, Mutt, Eudora, The Bat!, or Netscape Mail. The basic premise is to hide behind camouflage to sneak past network administrators who, were they to become aware of the software's presence, would find it easy to block them. No sane spammer will announce that their emails are coming from "Uncle Bernie's Notorious Mass-Mailer, Extreme Edition," simply because it would be too easy for a user or spam filter to filter them out.

---

* A popular tool that uses fingerprinting to analyze responses is AMAP by THC; you can find out more at http://www.thc.org/releases.php. Fyodor's NMAP can identify services by analyzing banners.

Approaching the Problem

Because it is trivial to modify the basic text responses and banners returned by a program, we need to find a better way to detect trickery than trivial textual response matching in order to identify client software with reasonable accuracy. Solutions that simply check less obvious parameters or responses are bound to fail at one point or another: although in almost all cases, it is possible to devise a single check to identify a specific type of undesirable software, three heads will grow back in place of the one just cut off.

It soon becomes impractical to try to address every single incarnation of malicious software. In some cases, a general malicious client detection can be achieved by simply checking for patterns that are clearly indicative of the type of abuse we hope to prevent: The difference between a legitimate mail client and a spammer's software is that the former is unlikely to attempt to send out 10,000,000 mails in one shot. Yet, this approach is very limited: while for some protocols and some clearly defined attacks, this may work like a charm; for WWW traffic, it is another story, and it is difficult to hit the right spot without ending up with an excessive number of false positives or missed programs.

Because it is perceived as the core of all Internet services available to end users, the WWW is one of few protocols that simply must be open for almost all, and, thus web traffic is most commonly chosen by naughty applications to masquerade their behavior in a system and the data they are transferring to a remote host. It is not uncommon for web browsers to trigger bursts of connections to various sites or to perform thousands of requests per hour. At the same time, it is not impossible to send out sensitive information to a remote host in a single, brief connection. Here, traffic profiling falls just short of providing an answer.

Towards a Solution

Given all this, it would appear that differentiating spyware or a Trojan horse from a legitimate application can be extremely tricky. However, as it turns out, some good tools are available for precisely identifying this kind of software, thus enabling interested parties to more accurately and precisely identify client applications. The most promising and universal approach, generally referred to as *behavioral analysis* (a fancy term for old and busted "timing patterns") aims to analyze the subtle internal dependencies between subsequent portions of traffic, as opposed to looking at the actual data exchange in a single request or in the sheer volume of connections over time. Because these dependencies are closely associated with internal algorithms and a program's performance, they are much more difficult to spoof than most of the other metrics we could examine. I'll discuss this approach in this chapter and propose a basic analysis toolset to achieve this level of accuracy and detail, using World Wide Web traffic as a convenient example.

But before we dive into the details, we need a bit of background. Let's take a quick look at the history of the WWW, the design of web clients, and the protocols they use to talk to servers. It all began earlier than you might think. . . .

A (Very) Brief History of the Web

The concept of the World Wide Web is not particularly difficult to grasp: the idea behind the Web is to give users instant access to a number of cross-referenced, linked documents that combine different types of information. Simple enough.

The Web as we know it today consists primarily of text with metadata (such as references to other files, formatting elements, annotations, dynamic or interactive elements), often enhanced with all kinds of multimedia (video, music, and various applications). It represents the spirit of our times and signifies a brand new method of communicating and finding information. But the idea of the Web is not new. It was born many years before technology made it possible to achieve this set of features for electronic documents—perhaps long before electronic documents were even considered a serious possibility.

According to a timeline[1] published by the World Wide Web Consortium (W3C), the concept of hyperlinking was first discussed in the *Atlantic Monthly*[2] back in 1945 by Vannevar Bush, a director of the Office of Scientific Research and Development during and after World War II.

Bush proposed a device called Memex, a personal, electromechanical unit that could, in fact, be seen as an early predecessor of today's PDAs. Memex provided storage for a user's documents and personal files and aimed to provide intuitive mechanisms for accessing the data. One of Memex's features was its ability to create and follow links between documents stored on microfilm. For some reason, the idea of an insanely complex mechanical device running on microfilm did not really catch on back then.

The concept of hyperlinking popped up several times in later years, resulting in the first computer-based implementations in the 1960s. These attempts were not particularly successful though, largely because the computing power needed to make the technology appeal to users was still years in the future.

The right time came in the late 1980s. After the microcomputer boom, and shortly before the frontal assault of the PC platform, a number of humble proposals made the rounds at Conseil Europeén pour la Recherche Nucléaire[*] (CERN) concerning the possibilities of hyperlinking. Tim Berners-Lee, one of the CERN researchers, is by all accounts the one to officially blame for spawning HyperText Markup Language (HTML), a set of controls for embedding metadata, links, and media resources in text documents. (Truth be told, HTML, the core of the Web as we know it, is

---

[*] European Laboratory for Particle Physics, Geneva, Switzerland.

hardly an entirely new design and borrows some ideas from SGML, an ISO 8879 Standard Generalized Markup Language of 1986.) The first web browser was born shortly thereafter on what is now a barely known, but was then an innovative and advanced computer platform, NeXT. The browser was given the ubiquitous name World Wide Web.

Now that we came up with a catchy name, the revolution was unstoppable. In 1992, Berners-Lee filed an initial specification draft[3] for HyperText Transfer Protocol (HTTP), a tool for encapsulating HTML data and other resources in server-to-client communications. In 1993, several web browser engines became available, and a handful of web servers were already serving their contents to curious visitors. Of course, HTTP accounted for only a smashing 0.01% of all backbone traffic, but it was rising!

The first popular web browser, Mosaic, was developed at the National Center for Supercomputer Applications, at the University of Illinois. It borrowed from Berners-Lee's code, but added support for contents other than text, and introduced fillable forms and many other features that we now take for granted. Mosaic's code eventually evolved into Mozilla, which, in turn, served as the core code for Netscape Navigator (later to fork into the open-source project Mozilla, whose codebase would be then used as a foundation for subsequent generations of Netscape Navigator—simple, isn't it?). At the same time, just to further confuse users, a company called Spyglass transformed Mosaic into the core of what was to become Netscape's main competitor, Microsoft Internet Explorer.

In 1994 the W3C, a body devised to oversee the development of the Web, was formed. The first official, much-improved, and extended version of the protocol was filed by Berners-Lee, Roy T. Fielding, and Henrik Frystyk in 1996, soon followed by the HTML 3.2 specifications. In subsequent years we saw newer, enhanced versions of HTTP and HTML, now governed by the W3C. And you all know the story's ending; or is it only the beginning?

A HyperText Transfer Protocol Primer

HTTP[4] is a surprisingly straightforward, text-based protocol built on top of TCP/IP. A client for this protocol connects to an HTTP-capable service on a remote server and makes a request, asking for a specific resource on the server. An HTTP request includes the following parameters in the first line of a query:

- A method for accessing the resource. Most often, the client simply asks to retrieve a file, by issuing a GET request (though other methods exist for tasks such as submitting form data, performing diagnostics, storing data on a server, or executing certain extensions).

- A universal resource identifier (URI). This is a path to a static file or to a dynamic executable that is the subject of the request. If the file is a dynamic executable, it is also possible to pass additional, appropriately encoded parameters to this program as a part of the URI.

- The version of the protocol the client supports and wants to use. The server can choose to reply with a lower protocol version if the one used by the client is unsupported. (If this information is missing, the client is assumed to be using HTTP/0.9, an early and obsolete version of the protocol, which we won't address here.)

For example, an HTTP request might look like this:

```
GET /show_plush_toys.cgi?param1=value&param2=this+is+a+test HTTP/1.1
Host: www.plush-penguins.com
User-Agent: Joe's Own Web Client (UnixWare)
Accept: text/html, text/plain, audio/wav
Accept-Language: pl, en
Connection: close
```

This request asks for a resource called /show_plush_toys.cgi at www.plush-penguins.com. Judging by the file's cgi extension, this is a dynamically executed program that is invoked with two parameters (param1 and param2), as listed following the question mark.

The client request can be (and in this example indeed is) followed by a number of text headers, one on each line, that specify additional parameters. These can be anything from client identification (User-Agent field, as mentioned earlier), to the preferred language for the contents (here Polish and English), to the specification of a virtual server the client is referring to. (If several domain names point to a single IP address, this specification makes it possible for the server to determine whether the user is looking for www.squeaky-ducks.com and www.plush-penguins.com, both of which might be hosted on the same system.)

The protocol mandates some of these headers. The set of required headers depends on its version, but most servers are fairly lax and make no fuss if some are omitted. This aside, some headers specify features that go beyond the protocol's specification itself.

Each request must end with an empty line, denoting the end of the client headers, at which point, for most types of requests, the server is expected to process the query and produce a reply. The server usually responds with a message in a structure similar to the query, starting with an HTTP return code and some descriptive text, like this one:

```
HTTP/1.0 404 Not Found
Content-Type: text/plain
Server: Uncle Mary's Cookie Recipe Server (Linux and proud of it!)
Date: Mon, 09 Feb 2004 19:45:56 GMT

The document you are looking for is nowhere to be found.
```

The return code or message might report various conditions, such as the successful completion of the request, an instruction for the browser to look somewhere else, or an error message such as "File Not Found" or "Permission

Denied." This information is followed by a set of headers, similar to the format accepted for the request. These describe various parameters such as the server software version, the location the browser should proceed to next, a content type specification for the returned file, a setting used to differentiate images from plain-text or HTML documents from binary files, and so on. The actual contents follow, if available.

As you can see, basic HTTP is fairly simple. Although it does offer some advanced features, most are either slightly bizarre, or just rarely used. (I'm guessing that you do not see the "402 Payment Required" error message every day.) Still, it would be naive to trust that the basic protocol is sufficient to meet the needs and expectations of today's users.

Making HTTP Better

The days when a typical website consisted of several kilobytes of static text and perhaps some minor graphic elements are long gone. As computers have become more powerful, and 300 bps modems have become easier to find in a museum than in every household, form has begun to dominate substance on the Web. Hundreds of kilobytes of images and subpages, subframes, and client-side scripts are commonly used to make sites more attractive and professional, with varying degrees of success. For many sites, multimedia contents have actually become the primary type of information served, with HTML providing only a placeholder for images, video, embedded Java programs, or games. The Web in general is no longer merely a way to tell others about your private projects or interests; the driving force behind it is the ability to market and sell products and services cheaper and faster than ever. And marketing demands the eye-catching presentation of products and services.

Web browsers, web servers, and HTTP itself have had to adapt to this changing reality to make it easy to deploy new technologies and follow new trends. Conveniently enough, many of the technologies introduced in this process have interesting security implications for mere mortals and can also help us identify the client on the other end of the wire in a transparent way. As such, we must consider the optional features and extensions introduced since the day the Web was born.

Latency Reduction: A Nasty Kludge

The problem with the Web and some other current protocols is that the content presented to a user by a single multimedia site must be obtained from various sources (including wholly different domains) and then combined. Web pages have their text and formatting information separate from actual images and other sizable goodies (a practice truly to be praised by those who have a limited bandwidth and just want to get to the point).

This situation makes it necessary for clients to make several requests in order to render a web page. The most naive way to achieve this is by requesting each piece, one by one, in sequence, but this is not the best practice in the real world because it leads to bottlenecks: Why wait for a page to load simply because the banner server is running slowly? Hence, to improve the speed of content retrieval, the browser issues numerous requests at once.

And herein lies the first shortcoming of HTTP: it offers no native ability to serve simultaneous requests. Instead, requests must be issued sequentially.

The *sequential* (also called *serial*) *fetch* model results in a considerable performance penalty if one of the web page elements needs to be downloaded from a slow server or over a spotty link or if it takes a while for the server to prepare and deliver a particular element. If sequential fetching were the only option, any such slow request would prevent subsequent requests from being issued and served until it (the slow request) is filled.

Because newer versions of HTTP have not improved this situation, most client software implements a kludge: the web browser simply opens a number of simultaneous, separate TCP/IP sessions to a server or a set of servers and attempts to issue many requests at once. This solution is actually quite sane when the page is requesting resources from several separate machines. However, it's not a good fix when the requested resources are on a single system, where all requests could be made in a single session and reasonably managed by the server. Here's why:

- The server has no chance to determine the best order in which to serve requests. (If it could, it would serve time-consuming, sizable, or simply the least relevant objects last.) It is simply forced to do all nearly at once, which can still cause the most important stuff to be needlessly delayed by increased CPU load.

- If several larger resources are served at once, and the operating system scheduler switches between the sessions, the result can be considerable negative performance impact due to the need for the disk drive to seek between two possibly distant files repeatedly and in rapid succession.

- Considerable overhead is usually associated with completing a new TCP/IP handshake (though this is somewhat lessened by keep-alive capabilities in newer versions of HTTP). It's more efficient to issue all requests within a single connection.

- Opening a new session and spawning a new process to serve the request involves overhead on the operating system level and strains devices such as stateful firewalls. Although modern web servers attempt to minimize this problem by keeping spare, persistent processes to accept requests as they arrive, the problem is seldom eliminated fully. A single session avoids unnecessary overhead and lets the server allocate only the resources absolutely needed to asynchronously serve chosen requests.

- Last but not least, if the network, not the server, is the bottleneck, performance can actually deteriorate as packets are dropped as the link saturates with data from several sources arriving at once.

Alas, good or bad, this architecture is with us for now, and it is still better than serial fetch. We should acknowledge its presence and learn to take advantage of it.

How can this very property help us to identify the software that the client is using? Quite simply. The significance of parallel file fetching for the purpose of browser fingerprinting should be fairly obvious: no two concurrent fetch algorithms are exactly the same, and there are good ways to measure this.

But before we turn our attention to parallel fetching, we need to take a look at two other important pieces of the security and privacy equation for the Web: caches and identity management. Although seemingly unrelated, they make a logical whole in the end. Thus, a brief intermission.

Content Caching

Keeping local caches of documents received from the server is one of the more important features of the Web during its rapid expansion in recent years.[*] Without it, the cost of running this business would have been considerably higher.

The problem with the increasing weight and complexity of a typical website is that it requires more and more bandwidth (which for businesses remains generally quite expensive), as well as better servers to serve the data at a reasonable speed.

If performance is not impacted by bandwidth bottlenecks, solutions such as concurrent sessions (as described earlier) put additional strain on service providers instead. The reason might be fairly surprising: if a person on a fairly slow link (such as a modem) opens four subsequent sessions to fetch even a fairly simple page, four connections and four processes or threads need to be kept alive on the server, taking away those resources from those with faster connections.

Finally, to make things worse, heavier and more complex websites don't always mesh with user expectations. Relatively long web page load times that were once considered fairly decent now seem annoying and drive users away. In fact, research suggests that the average web user won't wait more than 10 seconds for a page to download before they move on.[5] The result is that corporations and service providers need more resources and better links to handle the incoming traffic. In fact, had things been left the way they were initially designed, the demand for serverside resources would have likely exceeded our capacity to fulfill the demand some time ago.

Of some help is that the contents served to web surfers is static or changes seldom, at least when compared with the rate at which a resource is retrieved by users. (This is especially true for large files, such as graphics, video, documents, executables, and so on.) By caching data closer to the end user—be it on the ISP level or even on the endpoint browser itself—we can

---

[*] Its importance is slowly decreasing, however: as more and more web pages are generated dynamically, and our Internet backbone becomes more mature and capable, caching is bound to lose its significance.

dramatically decrease the bandwidth used for subsequent visits from users who share a common caching engine and make it easier on the servers handling the traffic. The ISP benefits from a lowered bandwidth consumption, as well, being able to serve more customers without having to invest in new equipment and connections. What HTTP needs, however, is a mechanism to keep the cache accurate and up-to-date. The author of a page (either human or machine) needs to be able to tell the cache engine when to fetch a newer version of a document.

To implement document caching, HTTP provides two built-in features:

- A method for telling, with minimum effort, whether a portion of data has been modified since the most recent version held by the cache engine (the document recorded at the time of the last visit).

- A method for determining which portions of data should *not* be cached, whether for security reasons or because the data is generated dynamically every time the resource is requested.

This functionality is in practice achieved fairly simply: The server returns all cacheable documents with the regular HTTP session, but with an additional protocol-level header, Last-Modified. To no surprise, this header represents the server's idea of the time this document was last modified. Documents that cannot be cached are, on the other hand, marked by the server with the header Pragma: no-cache (Cache-Control: no-cache in HTTP/1.1).

The client browser (or an intermediate cache engine run by the ISP) is supposed to cache a copy of every cacheable page based on the presence of an appropriate header, along with the last modification information. It should keep the cached page for as long as possible, either until the user-configured cache limit is exceeded or the user manually purges the cache, unless specifically instructed to discard it after a specific date with an Expires header.

Later, when the site is visited again, the client concludes that they have a previous instance of the page cached on the disk and follows a slightly different procedure when accessing it. As long as a document lives in the cache, the client attempts to fetch the file every time the user revisits a site, but specifies the If-Modified-Since header with every request, using the value previously seen in the Last-Modified header for <Since>. The server is expected to compare the Modified-Since value with its knowledge of the last modification time for a given resource. If the resource has not been changed since that time, the HTTP error message "304 Not Modified" is returned instead of the requested data. As a result, the actual file transfer is suppressed, thus preserving bandwidth (with only a couple of hundred bytes exchanged during this communication). The client (or intermediate cache engine) is expected to use a previously cached copy of the resource instead of downloading it again.

NOTE   A *more up-to-date approach, ETag and If-None-Match headers, a part of entity tagging functionality of HTTP/1.1, works in a similar manner but aims to resolve the ambiguity surrounding the interpretation of file modification times: the problems that stem* *from a file being modified several times in a short period of time (below the resolution of the clock used for Last-Modified data). of files being restored from a backup (with a modification time older than the last cached copy), and so on.*

Managing Sessions: Cookies

Another important and seemingly unrelated requirement for HTTP was that it be able to differentiate between sessions and track them across connections, store session settings and identity information. For example, some websites greatly benefit from the ability to adapt to one's personal preferences and to restore the look and feel chosen by the user each time they visit the site. Naturally, a user's identity can be established by prompting for a login and password every time a page is viewed, at which point the user's personal settings can be loaded, but this bit of extra effort dramatically reduces the number of people who would be willing to do this to access the page.

A transparent and persistent way to store and retrieve certain information from the client's machine was needed to ensure seamless and personalized access to web forums, bulletin boards, chats, and many other features that define the browsing experience for so many people. On the other hand, the ability for web server administrators to recognize and identify returning visitors by assigning them a unique tag and retrieving it later meant the surrender of anonymity in exchange for a little convenience. Such a mechanism would give companies with second-grade ethics a great tool to track and profile users, record their shopping and browsing preferences, determine their interests, and so forth. Search engines could easily correlate requests from the same user, and content providers that serve resources such as ad banners could use this information to track people even without their permission or the knowledge of site operators.[*] Regardless of the concerns, however, there seemed to be no better, sufficiently universal alternative for this mechanism. And so web cookies were born.

Cookies, as specified in RFC2109,[6] are small portions of text that are issued by a server when the client connects to it. The server specifies a Set-Cookie header in the response to the visitor. This portion of text is, by its additional parameters, limited in scope to a specific domain, server, or resource and has a limited lifespan. Cookies are stored by cookie-enabled client software in a special container file or folder (often referred to as a *cookie jar*) and are automatically sent back to the server using a Cookie header whenever a connection to a specific resource is established again.

Servers can choose to store (or push out) user settings in Set-Cookie headers and just read them back on subsequent visits; and here is where cookie functionality would end in a perfect world. Unfortunately, computers

---

[*] If an advertisement banner or any other element of a website is placed on a shared server, such as http://banners.evilcompany.com, the operator of evilcompany.com can issue and retrieve cookies whenever a person visits any legitimate website that uses banners supplied by them. Needless to say, most banner providers do issue cookies and track users, albeit primarily for market research purposes.

have no way of telling what is stored in a cookie. A server can choose to assign a unique identifier to a client using the Set-Cookie header and then read it back to link current user activity to previous actions in the system.

The mechanism is wildly regarded as having serious privacy implications. Some activists downright hate cookies, but the opposition to this technology is getting less and less vocal nowadays. Browsing the Web with cookies disabled gets increasingly more difficult—with some sites even refusing traffic from clients that do not pass a cookie check. Thankfully, many browsers offer extensive cookie acceptance, restriction, or rejection settings and can even prompt for every single cookie before accepting it (although the latter is not particularly practical). This makes it possible to mount a reasonable defense of your privacy, if only by defining who the "good guys" are and who to trust.

But is our privacy in our hands then?

When Cookies and Caches Mix

The privacy of web browsing has long been considered a hot issue, and not without reason. Many people do not want others to snoop on their preferences and interests, even if their whereabouts are not particularly questionable. Why? Sometimes, you simply do not want a shoddy advertising company to know that you are reading about a specific medical condition and then be able to link this information to an account you have on a professional bulletin board, particularly because there is no way of knowing where this information will end up.

Cookie control makes our browsing experience reasonably comfortable, while keeping bad guys at bay. But even turning cookies off does not prevent information from being stored on one's system to be later sent back to a server. The functionality needed to store and retrieve data on a victim's machine has long been present in all browsers, regardless of cookie policy settings. The two necessary technologies work in a similar manner and differ only in terms of their intended use: cookies and file caching.

Somewhere back in 2000, Martin Pool posted a fairly short but insightful message[7] to the Bugtraq mailing list, sharing an interesting observation and supporting it with some actual code. He concluded that there is no significant difference between the Set-Cookie and Cookie functionality versus Last-Modified and If-Modified-Since, at least for systems that do not use centralized proxy caches and that store copies of already fetched documents locally on disk (as is the case with most of us mere mortals). A malicious website administrator can store just about any message in the Last-Modified header returned for a page their victim visits (or, if this header is sanity-checked, it might simply use a unique, arbitrary date to uniquely identify this visitor). The client would then send If-Modified-Since with an exact copy of the unique identifier stored by a rogue operator on their computer whenever a page is revisited. A "304 Not Modified" response ensures that this "cookie" is not discarded.

Preventing the Cache Cookie Attack

Using your browser to slightly tweak Last-Modified data in response might seem like a neat way to prevent this type of exposure (while introducing some cache inaccuracy), but this is not the case. Another variant of this attack is to rely on storing data in cached documents, as opposed to using tags directly: a malicious operator can prepare a special page for the victim when a website is visited for the first time. The page contains a reference to a unique file name listed as an embedded resource (for example, an image). When a client revisits this page, the server notices the If-Modified-Since header and replies with the 304 error message, prompting the old copy of the page to be used. The old page contains a unique file reference that is then requested from the server, making it possible to map the client's IP to a previous session in which that file name had been returned. Oops.

Naturally, the lifetime of cache-based "cookies" is limited by cache size and expiration settings for cached documents configured by the user. However, these values are generally quite generous, and information stored within metadata for a resource that is revisited once every couple of weeks can last for years, until the cache is manually purged. For companies that serve common components included on hundreds or thousands of sites (again, banners are a good example), this is a nonissue.

The main difference with these cache cookies, compared with cookies proper, is not a matter of the functionality they offer, but rather the ease of controlling the aforementioned exposure. (Cache data must also serve other purposes and cannot be easily restricted without a major performance impact associated with disabling caching partly or completely.)

In this bizarre twist, you can see how two aspects of the Web collide, effectively nullifying security safeguards built around one of them. Practice shows that intentions are not always enough, because rogues are not always willing to play by the rules and use the technology the way we want them to. Perhaps turning your cookies off does not make that much of a difference after all?

But then it is about time to go back to the main subject of our discussion.

Uncovering Treasons

The subject of detecting trickery and accurately fingerprinting client software, that is. I have thus far mentioned that the task of detecting deceptive clients is complex, but not impossible and that behavioral analysis, a careful monitoring of the sequence of events produced by the browsers in question is a route worth exploring.

HTTP is a particularly generous subject of study, because, as we have seen, much of the activity occurs in parallel or nearly in parallel, and the exact queuing and data-processing algorithms are fairly subtle and unique for each client. By measuring the number of files downloaded at once, the relative time delays between requests, the ordering of requests, and other fine details of a session, it is possible to measure the unique characteristics of a system on a level that is much more difficult for the user to tamper with. Hence, you can distinguish impersonators from law-abiding citizens with no effort.

To provide a real-world example of this approach in the simplest possible way, and to stay as close to real applications as possible, I decided to see how much could be told from existing, fairly limited samples of data that many of you probably have on hand, so I reached for the standard logs of slightly more than 1 million requests to a relatively popular website. The data used for this analysis was a typical Apache web server access log, containing request completion times, requested URIs, advertised browser data from the User-Agent header, and other basic information of this nature. The page for which the log was kept consists of a set of relatively small pictures of comparable size and a single HTML document that calls for them all.

A Trivial Case of Behavioral Analysis

Apache's practice of logging requests when they are completed, as opposed to logging them when issued, could be perceived as a problem, but is actually quite helpful, assuming the requested set of files is relatively homogeneous. Request initiation order is usually more influenced by the sequence in which resources are referenced within the main page, whereas completion timing is a more complex beast.

Completion order probabilities depend on the number of requests, inter-request delays, and other parameters that subtly but noticeably vary from browser to browser. In particular, browsers that always keep only one connection open always issue requests in a known order, A-B-C-D; browsers that open three connections at once and issue requests rapidly are just as likely to produce B-A-C-D, C-B-A-D, C-A-B-D . . . and in those later cases, requesting queuing and session management matters most.

Naturally, we cannot forget that the observed sequence is also heavily affected by network latency and reliability and other random issues. Still, it is reasonable to expect that, for such a large set of samples, these non–browser-specific effects would either average out or affect data for all clients in a similar way. And when this happens, we will hopefully see subtle differences between browsers that lie underneath a friendly user interface.

Figure 14-1 shows a statistical distribution of attempts to load the ten-element web page mentioned earlier for the four most popular web clients in the dataset. Each graph is divided into ten major segments. The first corresponds to the main HTML file, which is directly requested and naturally makes the first element of the site. The remaining nine major segments correspond to nine images referenced from this HTML, in the order in which they are called for in HTML.

Each of the segments is further divided into ten discrete locations on the X axis (not explicitly shown here to avoid cluttering the chart). The height of the graph at the nth discrete location within a given segment represents the likelihood of this particular file being loaded as the nth item in sequence.

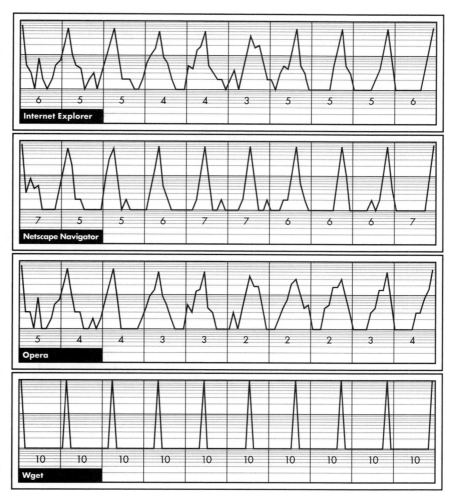

Figure 14-1: Behavioral pattern differences for popular web clients

To make the graph more readable, distribution probabilities are given as percentages between 1 and 100 (corresponding to percentages, with all values less than 1 percent rounded up), and discrete points are connected with lines. The graphs are then plotted on a logarithmic scale (log10, with major guides at 1, 10, and 100) to make subtle features more pronounced and easier to visually compare.

In a perfect world, with fully sequential and predictable browsers, the first segment would contain only a peak at the first (leftmost) discrete location; the second segment would contain a peak only at the second location, and so forth. In practice, however, some browsers issue many requests at once, and thus the order is more easily shuffled: the third referenced file can end up being loaded before the second or after the fourth. The less pronounced a single spike is in each segment, the more aggressive the browser fetch algorithm appears to be—for the more even the probability of this file being loaded out of order is.

The differences should be clearly visible, even between browsers historically based on the same engine: Mozilla and Internet Explorer. All clients appear to observe the order in which files were referenced in the main document, and so subsequent spikes move slowly from left to right across the segments. Yet, as you can see, Mozilla is generally considerably less impatient than Internet Explorer and more often finishes downloading files in the order in which they were requested. Opera, on the other hand, touted as the fastest browser on earth, is considerably less sequential (with many files having two or three nearly identically pronounced spikes, suggesting that a set of requests is issued so rapidly that the completion sequence is almost arbitrary, and most heavily influenced by network jitter). Wget, a popular open-source web spider, is for comparison perfectly sequential (a pattern common for automated crawlers), uses a single connection, and loads all files in the same order.

Giving Pretty Pictures Meaning

Pictures and graphs are nice, but have little or no value for automated policy enforcement or abuse detection. To quantify observed patterns somehow, and to make fingerprinting a bit more realistic, I decided to introduce a simple metric that gives a segment a better score (in the range of 0 to 10) when only a single peak is present and gives a lower score when the distribution is more arbitrary. This could allow for creating a simple, ten-value fingerprint for a specific piece of software and then match observed activity against a set of signatures to determine the best fit.

To construct a metric that expresses a relative quality (linearity) Q of observed behavior at major segment s, I used the following formula (f_n denotes the probability of file appearing at position n in fetch sequence, expressed in percentage values for convenience and to upset purists):

$$Q_s = 1.42 \left(\frac{\sqrt{\sum_{n=1}^{10} f_n^2}}{10} - 3 \right)$$

This equation, although scary at first sight, is actually straightforward. I wanted the formula to give preference to the situation when this particular file is most often loaded at a fixed position in a sequence (that is, one f value is near 100 percent, and remaining probabilities are close to 0 percent) over those when all positions are equally likely to occur (all f values at 10 percent).

Because the sum of all elements of f is fixed (100 percent), the easiest way to achieve this is to use a sum of squares: for any sequence of nonzero numbers; a sum of squares of those numbers is always less than a square of the sum. The highest and lowest results are as follows:

$$10^2 + 10^2 + 10^2 + 10^2 + 10^2 + 10^2 + 10^2 + 10^2 + 10^2 + 10^2 = 1,000$$
$$100^2 + 0^2 + 0^2 + 0^2 + 0^2 + 0^2 + 0^2 + 0^2 + 0^2 + 0^2 = 10,000$$

The remaining math, besides the main sum, is used merely to map results to a reasonable scale of 0 to 10 (when rounded).

The results of calculating this metric for each segment of observed traffic for each browser are superimposed on Figure 14-1, as a numeric value describing every segment of the graph. As expected, Wget scores perfectly for each segment. Scores for the other browsers confirm previous visual observations and make them more tangible. Although Internet Explorer and the Mozilla/Netscape engines appear to have roughly similar graphs, strong differences can be observed around load charts for items 4 through 6 and to a lesser degree across the entire fetch sequence. Opera clearly distances itself from the bunch, with consistently lower scores for each segment.

As a result, by applying a fairly trivial analytic tool, we ended up with a framework for devising a practical method to identify browsers and detect trickery in a statistically significant sample of user's HTTP traffic. You can enhance the model by analyzing other auto-load elements such as scripts, HTML style sheets, image maps, frames, and other files that exhibit even greater browser-to-browser variance. The Santa might find it easier this year to prepare the naughty user list.

Beyond the Engine . . .

I merely hope to show how easy it is to detect hidden characteristics of an unknown application by observing its behavior, without making any specific assumptions or dissecting the internals of such a program. The above exact numbers are likely not directly applicable to any website other than the one I used, and so you are encouraged to do your homework should you find a potential use for this technique. Once you profile a site or a set of sites, you can use the data to efficiently recognize systems based on their activity patterns over time.

Needless to say, the method I've used here is a (perhaps overly) simplistic approach to behavioral analysis and is based on perhaps the most trivial of all possible scenarios; I provide it as encouragement and to tempt you to search for more. In advanced cases, you can readily use the process of rendering contents in frames, tables, and other visual containers or fetching and rendering special types of files to determine which browser is being used even without performing statistical matching—in various highly specific aspects of browser activity, differences become far more striking. A clever application of differential timing is also promising.

And consider this: You can take more thought out forms of behavioral analysis a step further and deploy them not to tell one rendering engine from another, but to tell machines from humans or even identify single users. As discussed in Chapter 8, keyboard use patterns are often so unique for an individual that it is possible to use them for biometrics. Similarly, research suggests we can use the ways users click links, make choices, read information, and so on to indicate who or what is behind a set of requests.[8] Although now closer to scientific speculation than fact, this is a wonderful field to explore and play with.

... And Beyond Identification

Browser activity and behavioral analysis applications go beyond the detection of browser software—in fact, some enter the domain of user privacy and anonymity.

An interesting piece of research published in 2000 by Edward Felten and Michael Schneider[9] makes a fascinating contribution to the possible applications for the technique, an ability that is closely allied with caching mechanisms deployed in today's engines, bringing us to the point where all the elements discussed so far finally meet.

The basic premise of their research is that, by inserting a reference to a file on a particular site and then measuring the delay the browser encounters while downloading it, it is possible to tell whether the user had visited a particular site in recent days. Simple enough.

I'll spare you a lengthy excursion into the world of theory, predictions, and speculations (just this once) and instead propose a nearly real-world example. Assume that I am running www.rogue-severs.com. I've decided that my main page will, for some reason, refer to a picture (such as a front-page logo) taken from www.kinky-kittens.com; I make the visual element difficult to find or scale it down so that it is not visible, but it will be still loaded by a browser.

An unsuspecting user visits my site. If they have never been to www.kinky-kittens.com, it takes them a while to download the image I have referenced. If they are a frequent visitor, however, the image is already present in their cache and is fetched almost instantly.

Because the reference to the www.kinky-kittens.com resource is preceded and followed by requests for other visual elements I happen to host on my site, by deploying clever timing heuristics, it is possible to reliably measure whether the entire logo had been fetched or whether it was already in the cache. All this suffices to determine whether a newcomer to my page is indeed a frequent visitor to a specific website (or a particular section of a website) and effectively brutally invades their privacy. Although the scenario is not likely to be used for widely deployed routine espionage (primarily because clear evidence is left behind and might be noticed by the operator of the server on whose users we desire to snoop), targeted attacks might be quite effective.

In the end, all pieces of the puzzle fit together, perhaps loosely, but still fit together. Users, programs, and habits can all be easily exposed through a careful abuse of modern features of a popular Internet protocol. Something not necessarily always comforting to the valued visitors of www.kinky-kittens.com.

Prevention

Fully anonymizing one's web-browsing experience appears to be a battle already lost. Although some practices for improving the privacy and anonymity of online web users are commonly accepted, these features can be easily circumvented by a malicious website.

The problem is, unfortunately, too serious to dismiss. It is one thing to have an entity we have decided to trust (such as an ISP) be aware of our activity, but an entirely different issue when parties we'd rather not deal with routinely gather sensitive profiling information and probably just as routinely resell it to others as a part of their business model. This is enough to concern even those who do not wear a tinfoil hat and aluminum underwear on a daily basis.

On the other hand, the relative difficulty of remaining fully anonymous or appearing completely harmless is important in environments where HTTP traffic must be allowed and yet where users should be protected and supervised without violating their privacy beyond bare necessity. In corporate networks, the ability to track offending systems without the need to manually inspect data is truly invaluable and appreciated both by users and system administrators alike.

Food for Thought

No single component of HTTP is ill conceived, broken, or unwarranted. Yet, when we put it all together, many security and privacy features seem to cancel out, and the user is left quite exposed to eavesdroppers running rampant. Sadly, we can do little without starting over from scratch, and there is no guarantee that the results would work as well or provide even as much privacy as HTTP, HTML, and WWW clients do now.

15

THE BENEFITS OF BEING A VICTIM

*In which we conclude that approaching life with due optimism
may help us track down the attacker*

I have discussed a variety of problems that can have a significant cumulative impact on all daily communications, risks that we are not always comfortable with. You have seen how others can exploit the network to steal information or to get more than you expect or would allow them to, as well as how to use these techniques to gather more information about your enterprise or home network, and attackers that target it.

I hope I have offered both useful insight into how problems like these are born and how to avoid them whenever possible. I've tried to show that security and privacy implications are simply a part of every activity and that they cannot be fully eliminated simply by making the correct design decisions, installing the right software, or establishing and enforcing the proper policies. Information disclosure simply cannot be fully suppressed, and our only hope is to have enough information and knowledge about potential leak or attack scenarios to mitigate the most significant ones as much as possible in a particular application.

This, the third part of the book, has focused on wide area networking and the threats that lurk there. Although this is the longest part and is only now about to conclude, it is the furthest from offering a complete view of all the issues that can arise in an open network. In fact, it would be quite difficult and largely pointless to discuss all variants of problems; thus I've chosen to cover only the most complex, challenging, or fascinating aspects of host-to-host communications. I've focused on discovering attack scenarios on different protocol layers and different abstraction levels, instead of enumerating concepts and attack vectors that rehash old ideas and add nothing new to the subject. I hope that the information provided thus far will help and encourage you to find other incarnations of these issues in other areas of networking and computing—and perhaps even beyond.

We make a significant paradigm shift in the next part of the book as we explore how careful observation of the network as a whole, rather than as single systems, can be used to defend ourselves or to attack others. But before we do, let's look at some other possibilities in one of the more unusual areas of network surveillance: passive counterintelligence—that is, learning more about the attacker or their aims by analyzing their actions. The data gathered this way can provide a powerful set of investigative leads that make it easy to identify an attacker's intentions, toolset, or even the attacker themself. The task of building an attacker profile, attempting to read their mind, and perhaps even playing a game of deception with them is often a thrilling experience in and of itself.

Defining Attacker Metrics

As expected, you can acquire a good deal of information about a remote rogue party by merely applying some of the common TCP/IP traffic metrics discussed previously—such as passive operating system fingerprinting—to the observed traffic. You can, for example, identify the specific tool used to perform a port scan.

Similarly, we can also apply behavioral analysis to characteristics of the attacker's behavior such as inter-request delays and request ordering (for example, the order in which ports are scanned and how fast). We can use behavioral analysis with some success to track programs or, during a manually performed break-in or unauthorized assessment attempts, even to determine the individual characteristics of an attacker (such as their computer proficiency).

One particularly interesting method we can deploy to identify the tool the attacker used to scan our network relies on applying one of the methods discussed in Chapter 9—port sequence fingerprinting—to a wholly new task; this is based on the observation that a majority of scanners in use today either scan networks and systems from lowest to highest ports or addresses (sequentially) or randomize the order in which resources are accessed. The latter approach is more often used and is regarded as the better because it can balance loads and make scanning detection slightly more difficult. But, in a surprising twist, the use of randomness can fire back at the attacker in a couple of bizarre ways.

The problem arises because their authors do not consider network scanning tools mission-critical applications with high-security requirements. The most common (and easiest) way to implement a pseudorandom number generator in programs that do not require cryptographically secure output is to invoke standard system or built-in language facilities. The ISO standard[1] for the most prevalent programming language in the world, C, suggests that a simple linear congruent algorithm be used to implement a standard C library pseudorandom number generator (discussed in Chapter 1). The recipe for building and using the generator devised by the standard is as follows:

1. The generator should be seeded with an initial 32-bit value (S_0) by invoking a standard library function srand(). If the generator is not seeded, it will begin with a fixed default seed and will produce identical result sequences in all cases.

2. In each call to rand(), the main function that is repeatedly invoked to obtain subsequent pseudorandom numbers for use in user applications, the seed S is recomputed as follows: $S_{t+1} = S_t * 1103515245 + 12345$. The result is truncated to 32 bits (modulo 4294967296).

3. The return value for each rand() call is the more significant word of S_{t+1}, modulo 32768. In a 32-bit variant, one of the algorithms more commonly used on today's computers, the procedure in this and the previous step is repeated several times to calculate subsequent bit portions of the result value.

All linear congruent generators, including the one described here, are susceptible to the general cryptanalysis methodology proposed by H. Krawczyk in the '90s, as mentioned in Chapter 1. Based on the observation of a couple of subsequent (or otherwise ordered) outputs, it is possible to reconstruct the internal state of the generator and thus predict all its previous and future outputs.

Naturally, the immediate implication of this possibility—the victim's ability to determine, based on a knowledge of prior attempts, in what order the attacker will try to target other resources on the machine or network—is not particularly exciting or valuable itself. Still, this possibility has two important consequences in the context of network probe attempts:

- We might be able to determine S_0. If we know or can estimate when the generator began its work (or, alternatively, which general properties the initial seed should exhibit), it is possible to reconstruct the value used to initialize the generator. Because S_0 is the only input to the algorithm, it must produce identical behavior for identical seed values—and so, we can trace the seed by observing PRNG output.

- We might be able to determine t increments. Once we reconstruct the generator state, it is possible to determine how many random values were requested by the scanner by calling rand() in between two calls that the scanner used to obtain values (port numbers or host addresses) for packets the observer captured.

The importance of the first consequence of this design, our ability to reconstruct the value used to initialize the generator, might be not immediately apparent. But we have another bit of the puzzle to consider. One common way to initialize a random number generator is to use a handy 32-bit value that changes often enough not to risk identical PRNG behavior too frequently. The system time counter is often used for this purpose, and it is sometimes combined with another small number, such as the current process ID (PID), to decrease the likelihood that two programs run in a short time interval will produce similar results.

By applying this knowledge to the calculated S_0, the probe victim can discover the attacker's system time (GMT or local, depending on the operating system settings and scanner type). Knowledge of the system's local time can give the observer a hint about the attacker's origin and identity in a most trivial way. If they are trying to confuse us by spoofing packets from various sources, we can get lucky ruling out those perceived sources for which S_0 would indicate a time zone not matching the geographical region to which the source address belongs. For example, if by comparing the attacker's estimated system time with GMT we determine that attacker's time is five hours behind Greenwich Mean, we might conclude that they are likely on the east coast of the United States and not in China. Thus, by comparing our best guess of the time zone with records for various IP address blocks, we can tell that, of all observed "decoy" scan sources, the attacker's true identity is more likely to be behind packets originating from a Boston ISP than ones from an ISP located in Beijing.

Additionally, once we know the attacker's local time, we can track them by measuring the distance of their system clock from the real time (and, in the long run, how fast it drifts). Because computer clocks are usually not particularly accurate and tend to drift quite a bit when they are not regularly synchronized with an external source (as much as several minutes a day in some cases), this might be a good way to correlate attacks carried out by the same person. Different machines are likely to be systematically off by a different amount of time that would be changing at a distinctive ratio.

Finally, when the PID is used as a part of the initialization seed along with system time, and the attacker's system time is known to be within a certain range, the PID can be used to determine the approximate system uptime or the number of tasks executed between two scans. Because every new process on a machine is assigned a higher PID number, this dependency is rather straightforward.[*]

---

[*] Although some systems offer optional PID randomization for the purpose of making certain unrelated types of local attacks more difficult.

By reconstructing the PRNG state, we can also see how many random numbers were generated between the generation of two packets received by the recipient. When only one system is being scanned, there should be no gaps whatsoever or only marginal discrepancies due to network problems. However, when more than one system is being scanned, these gaps (caused by packets that are being sent to different targets) can be easily detected. By detecting them we can determine how many systems are being targeted simultaneously.

Furthermore, when the scanner software generates fake decoy packets that appear to come from random hosts, it is possible to eliminate spoofed addresses—ones that were made up using PRNG (and thus match its possible output) and determine which one does not match and hence must be real—pointing conclusively to the real perpetrator of an attack. For example, if our reconstructed PRNG data shows traffic coming from addresses such as:

198.187.190.55 (decimal representation: 3334192695)

195.117.3.59 (decimal representation: 3279225659)

207.46.245.214 (decimal representation: 3475961302)

we can determine that both 3334192695 and 3475961302 were one of the first outputs we would see of a generator seeded with S_0; whereas 3279225659 does not seem to be any of the first outputs of a reconstructed PRNG and hence is likely a real address.

We can use all this information to determine an attacker's intentions and the software they are using. We can even use it to track the system they are working on, correlate it with other data to determine their true identity and geographical location, and sometimes even determine how they are using their computer as the scan progresses.

NOTE *NMAP, in response to the uptime and scan history disclosure problems discussed above, attempts to use secure system RNG facilities (such as /dev/random, as discussed in Chapter 1) to generate random numbers instead of relying on standard C library tools. However, this method is not available on many operating systems (such as Windows), and other scanners have not taken similar steps to defend an attacker.*

Protecting Yourself: Observing Observations

The Internet has become a giant battlefield in the last ten years. Newly connected machines are being instantly flooded with automated attack probes, worms, and other types of information that stress their security. The traditional, and now fairly trendy, intrusion detection and prevention movement aims to find out about and stop attacks, by warning the administrator when pre-attack probes are being carried out using specially crafted traffic analysis tools. In heterogeneous or simply sufficiently complex environments, these often produce more noise and false positives than one can handle.

In some cases, however, the ability to observe attacks and the responses they trigger is a great way for the administrator to learn about network problems and attacks as they occur (even though those incidents themselves are hardly noteworthy, usually). For one thing, in some networks, active discovery and asset scanning to ensure policy compliance and system configuration is difficult to initiate or too troublesome to perform, whether due to policy regulations, slow turnaround times, rarely open network maintenance windows, and so forth. In such an environment, the ability to peek and determine what rogues are seeing may be an invaluable substitute for locally initiated active reconnaissance.

Too, periodic active discovery might not be fast enough to respond to certain threats; thus, the ability to learn that something has suddenly gone wrong by merely observing the results others get could be quite valuable. And, of course, this is a two-edged sword—a hacker who has compromised or plans to compromise a network, but wants to keep a low profile and plan their steps in advance, can watch traffic generated by other discovery attempts in order to build their knowledge about a particular system.

The task of stealing knowledge acquired by an attacker appears to be simple only in theory; the challenge of correlating and processing results, particularly when analyzing large environments or when based only on partial information from separate attack attempts from different locations, is not trivial. Some tools to facilitate network and system mapping using "passive scanning" are nevertheless slowly showing up on the horizon—with Preston Wood's DISCO[2] being a prime example.

Food for Thought

I find it strange that the techniques described in this chapter are often not supported by comprehensive research, published white papers, or readily available tools. With the attack tracking craze initiated by Lance Spitzner's honeypot research, and only fueled by products such as intrusion detection systems, one would expect to see fewer efforts to identify attacks (which are usually not particularly exciting themselves and which typically use well-documented vectors and flaws) and more attempts to determine the intent and origin of an attack and to correlate events that are meaningless alone, but that can signal a problem when combined.

I can only shed some light on the tip of an iceberg, but needless to say, this may be one of the more exciting areas to research and contribute to.

And now, for something completely different. . . .

PART IV

THE BIG PICTURE

Our legal department advised us not to say
"the network is the computer" here

16

PARASITIC COMPUTING, OR HOW PENNIES ADD UP

*Where the old truth that having an army of minions is better
than doing the job yourself is once again confirmed*

I hope you've enjoyed the ride so far. I've discussed a number of fancy problems that affect the security and privacy of information from its input at the keyboard to its ultimate destination hundreds or thousands of miles away. But it is too early for either of us to throw a party; something is missing from the picture—something far bigger than what we have discussed so far. The dark matter.

The problem with our story so far is simple: communications do not occur in a void. Although the process of exchanging data is usually limited to two systems and a dozen or so intermediate ones, the grand context of all events simply cannot be ignored; the properties of the surrounding environment can shape the reality of a chitchat between endpoints in profound ways. We cannot ignore the relevance of systems that are not directly involved in communications or the importance of all the tiny, seemingly isolated bits of individually trivial events that data meets along its path. It can be fatal to focus only on what appears relevant to a specific application or a particular case, as I hope this book has shown you thus far.

Rather than fall into this shortsighted trap, I've chosen to embrace the grand scheme of things in all its glory. Thus, the fourth and last part of this book focuses exclusively on the security of networking as a whole and discusses the Internet as an ecosystem, instead of a collection of systems accomplishing specific tasks. We pay tribute to the seemingly inert matter that binds the world together.

This part of the book begins with an analysis of a concept that appears to be the most appropriate way to make the transition. For many computer geeks, this concept, called parasitic computing, has revolutionized the way we think of the Internet.

Nibbling at the CPU

A humble research paper published in letters to *Nature* by Albert-Laszlo Barabasz, Vincent W. Freeh, Hawoong Jeong, and Jay B. Brochman in 2001[1] could easily have gone unnoticed. At first glance, this letter did not seem worthy of much attention; in fact, it posed a seemingly laughable proposition. The authors suggest that traffic could be created within well-established network protocols such as TCP/IP that would pose (as a message) a trivial arithmetic challenge—a problem to be solved—to a remote computer; the remote system would unwittingly solve the problem while parsing the message and preparing a response. But why would anyone waste time casting riddles at emotionless machines? What could one gain from this? Wouldn't it be as much fun to solve them yourself? Of course, the answer is quite interesting.

First, there is a business to solving puzzles with a computer: much of today's cryptography is based on the relative difficulty of solving a set of so-called non-polynomial* (NP) problems. NP-complete problems seem to take pleasure in crashing every codebreaker's party at the least opportune times. The ability to solve them efficiently—whether with enormous computing power, clever algorithms, or both—would likely take a lucky inventor one step closer to world domination. There's the incentive, then, but how would one do it?

The method proposed in the research is quite novel. The paper first states that many NP problems in mathematics can be easily expressed in terms of Boolean satisfiability (SAT) equations. SAT equations represent

---

* In complexity theory, polynomial problems can be solved by a Turing machine in time that is polynomially proportional to input length (number or size of variables for which the answer must be found). This means that the time needed to solve a polynomial problem corresponds directly to the input length raised to a constant exponent, which can be zero (causing the time not to depend on input length at all, as with testing for parity). Non-polynomial (NP) problems have no known solutions of this nature and may require dramatically more time to solve as the input length increases, exhibiting, for example, exponential dependency. A subset of NP problems, known as NP complete, are proven to have no polynomial time solutions. NP problems are generally regarded as "hard" for nontrivial inputs, whereas P problems are less expensive to solve.

these problems as Boolean logic operations, effectively constructing a sequence of parameters and variables (a Boolean formula). A classic example of an SAT formula might be

$$P = (x_1 \text{ XOR } x_2) \text{ AND } (\sim x_2 \text{ AND } x_3)$$

Here, P is the formula (problem) itself, and x_1 to x_3 are binary inputs, or parameters.

Although there are 2^3 possible combinations of values for x_1, x_2, and x_3, only one of them makes P true: $x_1 = 1$, $x_2 = 0$, $x_3 = 1$. Hence, we say that only this triplet is a solution to P. Finding solutions to SAT problems boils down to determining a set of values for all variables in the equation, for which the whole formula that incorporates those variables has a logic value of truth. Although trivial SAT problems like the one shown earlier are easy to solve, even without invoking any solving mechanism other than trial and error, more complex multivariable cases are indeed NP complete, and, consequently, other NP problems can be reduced to SAT problems in polynomial (meaning sane) time.

And here lies the problem. We can formulate a hard NP problem in terms of SAT, but this does not buy us much. As of this writing, when it comes to a non-trivial equation, even the best SAT-solving algorithms known aren't much more effective than a brute-force search whereby all possibilities are tried, and the value of the formula is evaluated for each possibility. This means that if we have a SAT problem and enough computing power to even consider approaching it, attempting a solution using brute force is not such an insane approach, and we would not get much further by with a more sophisticated one. Anyway, there's not much to lose by trying.

And here's the revelation that binds SAT problems and TCP/IP networking. The basic observation made by the researchers is fairly obvious (or should be, if you subscribe to *Nature*): the checksumming algorithm of TCP (or IP), as discussed in Chapter 9, although in principle designed for a wholly different purpose than solving equations, is nothing more than a set of Boolean operations subsequently performed on bits of the input message. After all, at the low level, the algorithm boils down to pure Boolean logic carried out on words of the transmitted packet. They conclude that, by providing specific contents of the packet ("input"), the remote system can thus be forced to carry out a set of arithmetic operations and then evaluate its correctness—its agreement with the checksum declared in the TCP or IP header.

Although the operation performed by the remote system during the checksumming process is in every single iteration exactly the same, it has a functionality sufficient to serve as a universal logic gate, a mechanism we remember from Chapter 2. By interleaving the actual tested input with carefully chosen "control" words that invert or otherwise alter the partial checksum computed thus far, it is possible to carry out any Boolean operation.

This, in turn, means that SAT logic can be easily re-created using a specific sequence control and "input" bits in a packet once the data is exposed to a checksumming algorithm; equation variables (chosen this or the other way) are interleaved with fixed words that are used to transmogrify the current checksum value so that the outcome of the next operation mimics a specific Boolean operator. The final result—the value to which a packet sums—denotes the final outcome: the logic value of a formula to be evaluated.

Thus, the satisfiability test is quite accidentally carried out by the remote recipient when, upon arrival, it attempts to validate the checksum. If the checksum comes out as 1 (or as some other value that in our SAT computation system corresponds to an SAT statement evaluating true), it passes the satisfiability test for the variable values chosen for this particular packet (and the traffic is passed to higher layers and acted upon). If the checksum fails, the formula has not been satisfied, and the packet is dropped silently. In other words, if our input bits denoted a specific hypothesis, the recipient had either verified it or proved it wrong, taking different actions depending on the outcome.

Further, a party wanting to solve an SAT problem quickly can prepare a set of all possible combinations of variable values (inputs) for a given formula, interleave it with information that causes the inputs to combine with others in the most desirable way, stuff this information into TCP packets, and send them out (nearly in parallel) to a large number of hosts around the globe. The checksum for a packet would be set manually to a value we know the "hypothesis" would produce if proven true, instead of actually calculating it. Only hosts that receive packets with variable values for which the formula evaluates to the desired value would respond to the traffic; other systems would simply disregard such traffic as corrupted due to the checksum mismatch. The sender can thus determine the correct solution without performing massive computations and can simply look up the set of values used in packets sent to those hosts that replied to a request.

The research goes further and reports on a successful attempt to solve an NP problem using real-world hosts across the globe, thus providing not only theoretical background, but also actual confirmation of the approach.

The impact of this technique is quite subtle, but also important: it proves that it is possible to effectively "outsource" computations to unaware and unwilling remote parties on the network, including sets of operations needed to solve real-world computing problems, without actually attacking these systems, taking them over, installing malicious software, or otherwise interfering with legitimate tasks. One person can thus, effectively, divide a specific computational task among a large number of systems. In the process, they can consume only a tiny and negligible fraction of a system's computing power that could nevertheless add up to the equivalent of a decent supercomputer, when millions of systems work on a problem together.

World domination at hand? Not so fast.

Practical Considerations

. . . or, perhaps, not just yet. The approach suggested in the aforementioned research is revolutionary and interesting, but not necessarily a particularly practical way to build a supercomputer by stealing from the rich. The amount of bandwidth needed to sustain a reasonable computing rate, and the amount of computations needed to prepare trivia for other systems to solve, is quite high. As a result, this scheme is not efficient enough to outsource the solving of complex mathematical problems to a global supercluster of unwilling victims.

In the scheme outlined earlier, the requirement of exponential computing power is exchanged for the requirement of exponential bandwidth. This is not necessarily a decent trade-off, particularly because only relatively simple tests can be pushed out, considering the packet size limitations of most networks. (All of them could likely be solved in the time it takes to transmit this data over Ethernet.) This technique proves that the attack is possible and provides a truly universal venue to facilitate it, but using more specific attack scenarios might yield much more useful results.

Other ways of stealing negligible amounts of individual computing power are perhaps more interesting as ways to achieve impressive computing power at a low cost. For example, certain types of client software (such as web browsers) can be easily used to execute even fairly complex algorithms in a relatively trivial way. One such example, a "Chinese lottery" computing scheme detailed in RFC 3607,[2] is used by a tiny Java applet that Jean-Luc Cooke's md5crk.com website encourages webmasters to add to their web pages. Once this applet is added to a site, every visitor to it can execute the applet on their system, borrowing a negligible amount of CPU cycles in order to contribute them to a project aimed at finding MD5 shortcut function collisions. (Collisions are two different messages that produce the same shortcut. They are elusive and anecdotal, although most definitely possible,[*] beings that can allow us to better understand the weaknesses of shortcut functions and could empirically prove and demonstrate that MD5 is too weak to be a match for today's computers.)

Java applets are small pieces of machine-independent programs that are by default executed by web browsers in special, restricted "sandbox" environments. They have no access to local disk storage and (only in theory) no ability to do any harm, though they can use limited network connectivity to perform computations and to add certain visual elements to a web page. They are most commonly used to enhance websites with additional features, such as interactive games, visual effects, and so on. But Jean-Luc used these

---

[*] While this book was being prepared for printing, a team of Chinese researchers from Shandong University—Xiaoyun Wang, Dengguo Feng, Xuejia Lai, and Hongbo Yu—advised of a technique for finding and provided samples of MD4, MD5, HAVAL-128, and RIPEMD-128 collisions. This is one of the more important bits of news in modern cryptography, and confirmation that those functions are inadequate for some security-related applications. While the md5crk.com project has closed down, its contributions to exploring the field of parasitic computing remain valid.

applets to do something else: to find likely candidates for collisions using the joint computing power of hundreds or thousands of systems around the world, simultaneously.

The principle behind the applet's operation was trivial: The applet was executed on client systems worldwide whenever a cooperating website was visited; then, once launched, the applet tried to calculate MD5 shortcuts for different randomly chosen messages. This continued until a shortcut that matched a certain arbitrarily chosen and fixed masking pattern was found. Such a pattern could be "any shortcut with zero for the last four bytes" or something similar. The pattern was chosen so that it does not take too long to find a suitable shortcut by trial and error (so that the person does not have to leave the web page and stop the code before it is found), but so that only a small fraction of all possible shortcuts would match the rule.

Once a suitable message was found, the program "phoned home" with the candidate. The author could then examine the submissions. The applet had already examined and rejected a number of collision candidates, and only submitted those that matched a predefined condition (ones that were partly identical). Because much less variation is possible in the data collected this way, the likelihood of a collision in a chunk of n entries is considerably higher than for purely random data. By analogy, the likelihood of running into two visually indistinguishable apples in an amount of fruit we are capable of going through within one day is higher if we order for delivery only those apples that have nearly the same weight and color, as opposed to purchasing a wagon of arbitrary fruit.

Although somewhere in the gray area of cyber-ethics, this ingenious approach first openly deployed by md5crk.com really worked and provided a good demonstration of how parasitic computing can be both quite effective and stealthy. It appears that the ability to steal processor cycles originally intended to be used for "rightful" purposes is well within reach, and perhaps used more often that we want it to be. And this possibility is here to stay.

But, a cranky skeptic continues, can parasitic computing do more than just nibble tiny bits of CPU power to facilitate cracking encryption schemes, a task few of us are truly interested in?

Parasitic Storage: The Early Days

When you shout, acoustic waves move through the air, gradually losing energy and dispersing in all directions. However, if they encounter a solid obstacle along the way they will likely bounce, and, if the angle is just right, they will bounce back to you. The audible result is that a split second after shouting you will hear an echo of your own voice.

But what happens when an information theory geek reads their code aloud standing on the top of a mountain, directing their words toward a rocky valley? I thought you'd never ask. In such case, they cannot help but make a clever observation: if they read it fast and then immediately forget about what they just recited (because they become preoccupied with other matters), they can still eventually recover the information he when it bounces back off the bottom of the valley and is echoed back. Voilà—a convenient data storage mechanism.

Sounds ridiculous? Maybe we are just too young. Early types of computer memory modules used a similar acoustic technique that allowed the processor to store some information "offline" and recover it later. Instead of using air (through which waves spread a bit too fast to provide reasonable storage capacities without building extremely large memory units), a mercury-filled drum was used (an environment in which acoustic waves propagate much more slowly). The principle remained the same, however, and even gave an interesting meaning to the term *memory leak*. Such a device, *mercury delay line memory*, was used, for example, in the famous UNIVAC I.[*]

Naturally, this slow, bulky, dangerous, and inconvenient sort of memory was dropped in favor of other solutions as soon as the technology matured. However, the invention itself had some charm to it, and wouldn't fade into oblivion that easily. A short presentation by Saqib A. Khan at the DefCON conference in Las Vegas in 2002 revived it and gave us the first hints about how to use the properties of a large-scale network to construct similar types of momentary storage using the Internet as a medium. But this time, the description of acoustic memory did not sound ridiculously primitive, but rather unbelievably cool to all hackers and geeks watching this short slide show. Acoustic memory had made its comeback in style.

Because the round-trip times for packets (the time needed for a message to arrive at a remote system, and for a response to come back) are nonzero, a certain amount of data can always be kept "on the wire" by repeatedly sending out and receiving portions of it and waiting for it to echo back. Saqib used ICMP (Internet Control Message Protocol) "echo request" (ping) packets to achieve this effect; most systems on the Internet respond to such packets with "echo reply," quoting the original payload they received.

This seemed like a cool trick. However, it was also far from practical for any reasonable application, because it required frequent retransmissions of portions of data. Because ICMP "echo reply" is sent back nearly immediately after the "echo request" is received, only a small amount of data could be pushed out before being sent back and needing to be recovered off the wire. As a result, the amount of data that could be stored this way could be no larger than the amount that the user could push out in, at best, a couple of seconds (and more commonly, under a tenth of a second).

Ah, but parasitic storage could be improved.

---

[*] Perhaps it is worth noting that a low-capacity, analog delay line memory was also used in early implementations of SECAM (Séquentiel Couleur avec Mémoire, or Sequential Color with Memory) TV receivers. Unlike NTSC or PAL, the SECAM signal uses a reduced color resolution; red and blue chrominance components are transmitted alternatively, never both at once. The other component must be taken from the preceeding line to determine how a specific pixel should look. To make this possible, a memory device needed to be implemented.

Making Parasitic Storage Feasible

In 2003, Wojciech Purczynski and I coauthored a paper called "Juggling with Packets: Parasitic Data Storage." We took the concept of parasitic storage a bit further and considered a number of methods that could be used to dramatically extend the Internet's storage capacity, while conserving the bandwidth needed to sustain the information. Our research focused on several other ways to store data on remote systems and classified them based on the properties of the storage medium (its visibility, volatility, and reliability). We also included a detailed discussion of the hypothetical storage capacities for each of the techniques.

The paper was quite short and—I hope—refreshing and humorous, and it's included here.

```
==================================================
Juggling with packets: floating data storage
==================================================


"Your dungeon is built on an incline. Angry monsters can't play marbles!"

Wojciech Purczynski <cliph@isec.pl>
Michal Zalewski <lcamtuf@coredump.cx>


1) Juggle with oranges!
------------------------


Most of us, including the authors of this paper, have attempted to juggle
with three or more apples, oranges, or other fragile ballistic objects. The
effect is usually rather pathetic, but most adept juggler padawans sooner or
later learn to do it without inflicting excessive collateral damage.

A particularly bright juggler trainee may notice that, as long as he
continues to follow a simple procedure, at least one of the objects is in the
air at all times and that he has to hold at most two objects in his hands at
once. Yet, each and every apple goes through his hands every once in a while,
and he can recover it at will.

After some fun with juggling, he may decide that the entire process is
extremely boring and go back to his computer. While checking his e-mail, an
educated juggler might notice that a typical network service has but one duty:
to accept and process data coming from a remote system and take whatever steps
it deems appropriate based on its interpretation of the data. Many of those
services do their best to behave robustly, to be fault tolerant, and to supply
useful feedback about the transaction.

In some cases, the mere fact that a service is attempting to process the
data and reply according to protocol can be used in ways that the authors
never dreamed of. One of the more spectacular examples of this, which our
fellow juggler might be familiar with, is research done at the University of
Notre Dame, titled "Parasitic Computing" and published in letters to "Nature."
```

Nevertheless, our hero concludes that such attempts are quite impractical in the real world. The cost of preparing and delivering trivia to be solved far exceeds any eventual gain since the sender has to perform operations of comparable computational complexity simply to deliver the request. "The computing power of such a device is puny!" he says.

A real juggler would focus on a different kind of outsourced data processing, one that is much closer to his domain of expertise. Why not implement a distributed fruit-based data storage? What if I write a single letter on every orange and then start juggling? I can then store more orange bytes than my physical capacity (the number of oranges I can hold in my hands)! How brilliant. . . . But, but, would it work without oranges?

2) The same, without oranges

This paper is based on the observation that for all network communications, there is a nonzero (and often considerable) delay between sending information and receiving a reply--a result of the physical constrains of the medium and the time it takes to process data on all computer equipment.

Like an orange with a message written on it, a packet used to store a piece of data travels for a period of time before returning to the source, and for this period of time we can safely forget its message without losing data. As such, the Internet has a nonzero momentary data storage capacity, and it is possible to push out a piece of information and effectively have it stored until echoed back. By establishing a mechanism for the cyclic transmission and reception of chunks of data to and from a number of remote hosts, it is possible to maintain an arbitrary amount of data constantly 'on the wire,' thus establishing a high-capacity, volatile medium.

This medium can be used for memory-expensive operations, either as regular storage or for certain types of sensitive data for which one does not want to have leave a physical trail on a hard disk or other nonvolatile media.

Since it is not considered bad programming practice to return as much relevant information to the sender as the sender sends to the service, and because many services or stacks maintain a high level of verbosity, our juggling experience tells us that it is not only possible, but also feasible, to establish this kind of storage, even over a low-end network hookup. Unlike traditional methods of parasitic data storage (such as P2P abuse, open FTP servers, binary Usenet postings, and so on), this particular method may or may not leave a trail of data (depending on how we implement it), and it does not put any single system under a noticeable load. Therefore, unlike the traditional methods, this technique is less likely to be detected and considered an abuse. Hence, the possibility of the data being intercepted and purposefully discarded is much less a problem.

3) Class A data storage: memory buffers

Class A data storage uses the capacity inherent in communication delays during the transmission and processing of live data as it travels across networks between two endpoints. The information stored herein remains cached in the memory of a remote machine and is not likely to be swapped out to a disk device.

Examples of class A memory are a variety of schemes that rely on sending a message that is known to result in partial or full echo of the original request, including the following:

- SYN+ACK, RST+ACK responses to SYN packets, and other bounces

- ICMP echo replies

- DNS lookup responses and cache data. It is possible to store some information in a lookup request and have it bounce back with an NXDomain reply or to store data in an NS cache.

- Cross-server chat network message relaying. Relaying text messages across IRC servers and so on can exhibit considerable latency.

- HTTP, FTP, web proxy, or SMTP error or status replies.

The most important properties of class A storage are:

- Low latency (milliseconds to minutes), which makes it more useful for near random access memory applications.

- Lower per-system capacity (usually kilobytes), which makes it less suitable for massive storage.

- Only one chance to receive or few retransmits which make it less reliable in case of a network failure.

- Lower likelihood of permanent recording. The data is not likely to be stored on a nonvolatile medium or swapped out, increasing privacy and deniability.

In particular, when using higher-level protocols, additional features appear that might solve some of the low-capacity and short- recovery window problems shared by various types of class A storage. For example, it is possible to establish a connection to a service such as SMTP, FTP, HTTP, or any other text-based service and send a command that is known to result in an acknowledgment or error message being echoed along with part of the original data. We do not, however, send a fully formatted message; we leave some necessary characters unsent. In most cases, end-of-line characters are required in order to complete the command. In this state, our data is already stored on remote service waiting for a complete command or until connection time-out occurs. To prevent time-outs, either on TCP or at the application level, no-op packets need to be sent periodically. A \0 character interpreted as an empty string has no effect on many services but is sufficient to reset TCP and service time-out timers. A prominent example of an application vulnerable to this attack is Microsoft Exchange.

The attacker can sustain the connection for an arbitrary amount of time, with a piece of data already stored at the other end. To recover the information, the command must be completed with the missing \r\n, and then the response is sent to the client.

A good example is the SMTP VRFY command:

```
220 inet-imc-01.redmond.corp.microsoft.com Microsoft.com ESMTP Server
Thu, 2 Oct 2003 15:13:22 -0700
VRFY AAAA...
252 2.1.5 Cannot VRFY user, but will take message for
<AAAA...@microsoft.com>
```

It is possible to store just over 300 bytes, including nonprintable characters, this way--and have it available almost instantly. More data can be stored if the HTTP TRACE method is used with data passed in arbitrary HTTP headers, depending on the server software. Sustained connections can give us arbitrarily high latency, thus creating large storage capacity.

This type of storage is naturally more suited for privacy-critical applications or low-latency lower to medium capacity storage (immediate RAM-extending storage for information that should leave no visible traces). The storage is not suitable for critical data that should be preserved at all costs, due to the risk of data being lost on network failure.

4) Class B data storage: disk queues

Class B data storage uses "idle" data queues that store information for an extended period of time (often on the disk). For example, MTA systems can queue e-mail messages for as many as 7 days (or more, depending on the configuration). This feature can give us a long delay between sending data to store on the remote host and receiving it. Because a typical SMTP server prevents the relay of e-mail from the client to itself, e-mail bounces can be used to have data returned after a long period of time.

For example, consider this potential attack scenario:

1. The user builds a list of SMTP servers (perhaps servers that provide a reasonable expectation of being beyond the reach of their foes).

2. The user blocks (with block/drop, not reject) all incoming connections to their port 25.

3. For each server, the attacker has to confirm its delivery time-outs and the IP from which the server connects back while trying to return a bounce. This is done by sending an appropriate probe to an address local to the server (or requesting a DSN notification for a valid address) and checking to see how long the server tries to connect back before giving up. The server does not have to be an open relay.

4. After confirming targets, the attacker starts sending data at a pace chosen so that the process is spread evenly over the period of one week. The data should be divided so that there is one chunk per each server. Every chunk is sent to a separate server to immediately generate a bounce back to the sender.

5. The process of maintaining the data boils down to accepting an incoming connection and receiving the return at most a week from the initial submission, just before the entry is about to be removed from the queue. This is done by allowing this particular server to go through the firewall. Immediately after the chunk is received it is relayed back.

6. To access any portion of data, the attacker looks up which MTA is holding this specific block and then allows this IP to connect and deliver the bounce. Three scenarios are possible:

   - If the remote MTA supports the ETRN command, the delivery can be induced immediately.

   - If the remote MTA was in the middle of a three-minute run in an attempt to connect to a local system (keeps retrying thanks to the fact its SYN packets are dropped, not rejected with RST+ACK), the connection can be established in a matter of seconds.

   - Otherwise, it is necessary to wait from five minutes to one hour, depending on the queue settings.

This scheme can be enhanced using DNS names instead of IPs for users on dynamic IP or to provide additional protection (or when it is necessary to cut the chain immediately).

The important properties of class B storage are:

   - High per-system capacity (megabytes), making it a perfect solution for storing large files and so on

   - Higher access latency (minutes to hours), likening it to a tape device, not RAM (with the exception of SMTP hosts that accept the ETRN command to immediately reattempt delivery)

   - Very long lifetime, increasing per-user capacity and reliability

   - Plenty of delivery attempts, making it easy to recover the data even after temporary network or hardware problems

   - Likely to leave a trace on the storage devices, making it a less-useful solution for fully deniable storage (although it would still require examining a number of foreign systems, which does not have to be feasible)

Class B storage is suitable for storing regular file archives, large append-only buffers, encrypted resources (with a proper selection of hosts, it remains practically deniable), etc.

5) Discreet class A storage

In certain situations, it might be necessary to devise a solution for discreet data storage that does not reside on the machine itself and that makes it possible to deny the presence of this information anywhere.

The basic requirement is that the data is:

- Not returned until a special key sequence is sent

- Permanently discarded without leaving any record on any nonvolatile storage media in the absence of keep-alive requests

It is possible to use class A storage to implement this functionality using the sustained command method discussed earlier. The proper TCP sequence number is necessary to release the data, and until this sequence is delivered, the data is not returned or disclosed to any party. If the client node goes offline, the data is discarded and likely overwritten.

The sequence number is thus the key to the stored information, and, if the lifetime of the data is fairly short when keep-alive \0s stop coming, it is often adequate protection.

6) User-accessible capacity

In this section, we attempt to estimate the storage capacity available to a single user.

In order to maintain a constant amount of data "outsourced" to the network, we must be able to receive and send it back on a regular basis.

The amount of time that data can be stored remotely is constrained by the maximum lifetime Tmax of a single packet (including packet queuing and processing delays). The maximum amount of data that can be sent is limited by maximum available network bandwidth (L). Thus, the maximum capacity can be defined as:

Cmax [bytes] = L [bytes/second] * Tmax [seconds] / Psize * Dsize

where:

Dsize - The size of a packet required to store an initial portion of data on a remote host

Psize - The size of a packet required to sustain the information stored on a remote host

Psize and Dsize are equal and thus can be omitted whenever the entire chunk of data is bounced back and forth; they differ only for "sustained command" scenarios. The smallest TCP/IP packet to accomplish this has 41 bytes. The maximum amount of data that can be sustained using HTTP headers is about 4096 bytes.

That all, in turn, gives us the following chart:

```
Bandwidth  | Class A | Class B
-----------+---------+---------
28.8 kbps  | 105 MB  |    2 GB
256 kbps   | 936 MB  |   18 GB
2 Mbps     | 7.3 GB  |  147 GB
100 Mbps   | 365 GB  |    7 TB
```

7) Internet as a whole

In this section, we attempt to estimate the theoretical momentary capacity of the Internet as a whole.

Class A

To estimate the theoretical class A storage capacity of the Internet, we assume the following:

- ICMP messages offer the best balance between storage capacity and preserving a remote system's resources.

- An average operating system has a packet input queue capable of holding at least 64 packets.

- The default PMTU is approximately 1500 (the most common MTU).

As an estimate of the number of hosts on the Internet we use an ISC survey for 2003, which lists 171,638,297 systems with reverse DNS entries (although not all IPs with reverse DNS have to be operational). To take this into account, we used the ICMP echo response ratio calculated from the last survey that performed such a test (in 1999). The data then suggested that approximately 20 percent of visible systems were alive, which, in turn, sets the number of systems ready to respond to ICMP requests at roughly 34,000,000.

By multiplying the number of systems that reply to ICMP echo requests by the average packet cache size and maximum packet size (minus headers), we estimate the total theoretical momentary capability for class A ICMP storage to be approximately 3 TB.

Class B:

> To estimate theoretical class B storage capacity, we use the example of
> MTA software. There is no upper cap for the amount of data we feed to a
> single host. Although it is safe to assume that only messages under
> approximately 1 MB will not cause noticeable system load and other
> undesirable effects, we assume that the average maximum queue size is
> 500 MB.
>
> Our own research suggests that roughly 15 percent of systems that respond
> to ping requests have port 25 open. We thus estimate the population of
> SMTP servers to be 3 percent (15 percent of 20 percent) of the total host
> count, or just over 5,000,000 hosts.
>
> This gives a total storage space capacity of 2500 TB.

Applications, Social Considerations, and Defense

But what now? What is the benefit of having practical parasitic computing
and storage schemes, if the benefits are still not nearly good enough to make
it a tempting alternative to just getting more hardware?

Despite advances in the practical exploitation of parasitic computing,
applications that aim to extend the sheer computing power or storage space
of a traditional system may appear pointless when we consider the abun-
dance of cheap memory and gigahertz processors.

The unseen potential of this technology may, however, lie in a wholly
different set of applications: *volatile computing*. The ability to build usable
distributed computers that can disperse at will, leaving no physical traces and
storing no meaningful data at any one location, might be a powerful privacy
tool and also pose some challenges for forensics and law enforcement. The
ability to build volatile store-and-keep memory that collapses shortly after
taking a single node offline, but that does not involve frequent retransmissions of data, might provide a good level of deniability for an offender (or
an oppressed entity, for that matter) and require many common evidence
collection procedures to change quite dramatically.

Furthermore, imagine volatile systems that could, once bootstrapped
and initialized, sustain themselves for extended periods of time, living in the
Internet and taking no localized physical presence. Two designs are possible
for volatile, distributed computer systems, and neither is that absurd:

- Systems can be designed so that they complete a complex task by finding
  a solution in parallel (already largely accomplished by the SAT computing scheme discussed previously). The disadvantage of such systems is
  that the computation result must be retrieved and the next iteration of
  processing must be initiated manually by occasionally "reseeding" the
  entire system from some location. Solutions that rely on low-level properties of protocols such as TCP would likely fall into this category.

- Systems can be designed so that they execute subsequent iterations of distributed computing themselves. All types of abuse of higher-level features (such as embedded document-rendering algorithms) and of some network services might be used to facilitate this type of activity.

In each case, the consequences can be quite profound. For example, how do you take down a redundant self-repairing machine that uses no single system, but rather borrows tiny bits of memory and processing power from others for fractions of a second—and uses no vulnerabilities to do so or clearly distinguishable traffic that can be filtered out? And isn't it also a bit disconcerting to realize that we would not be able to immediately discern the goals of such a distributed computer? Bowing respectfully to the masters of bad science fiction, I believe the domination of computers is imminent and want to welcome our new machine overlords.

Food for Thought

Defense against parasitic computing is generally extremely difficult. The ability to store data or to cause the other party to perform certain trivial computations is often bound to the fundamental functionality of network protocols. This is a characteristic that we cannot conceive of removing without wiping out the Internet as we know it and introducing a host of new problems more serious than the one remedied.

Protecting a single system against becoming a node for parasitic computing is also fairly difficult, because the number of resources stolen from a system is often a negligible fraction of the idle CPU time and memory and, hence, might easily go unnoticed.

Chances are good that parasitic computing has yet to show its full potential and that the threat—irrelevant or nonexistent for single systems but significant for the net as a whole—is here to stay.

TOPOLOGY OF THE NETWORK

*On how the knowledge of the world around us may help
track down friends and foes*

What is the shape of the Internet? No committee
oversees it or decides where, how, and why it should
expand or how new and existing systems should be
organized or managed. The Internet grows in all
directions in ways that are equally driven by demand,
economics, politics, technology, and blind luck.

Yet the Internet is not a shapeless blob: there are planned, locally
governed hierarchies of autonomous systems, with core routers surrounded
by lesser nodes, with links configured by automatic mechanisms or carefully
designed by humans. The Internet is a spectacular mesh, a complex and
fragile cobweb covering the entire industrialized and developing world. The
task of capturing this ever-changing topology appears challenging, but also
tempting, especially when we realize how we can benefit from the
information collected.

In this chapter, I'll first discuss two notable attempts to map the Internet's topology, and then I'll moralize once more on the potential uses for the
information gathered this way to do things that our ancestors could not even
dream of.

Capturing the Moment

The most comprehensive attempt to map the Internet was undertaken by the Cooperative Association for Internet Data Analysis (CAIDA), an organization funded, among others, by federal research agencies (NSF, DHS, DARPA) and the industry (Cisco, Sun). The organization was formed to come up with traffic and infrastructure analysis and tools for the common benefit of the Internet community, in hopes of making it better, more reliable, more resilient, and more robust.

Since 2000, one of CAIDA's flagship public projects has been the creation and maintenance of the autonomous system core network map (aka "Skitter"). As of this publication, their most recent capture represents data for 12,517 major autonomous systems, corresponding to 1,134,634 IP addresses and 2,434,073 links (logical paths) between them.

Despite sounding astonishingly arcane, the CAIDA Internet map was created with only publicly accessible router BGP configuration data, empirical network testing results (traceroute), and WHOIS records for network blocks. This map is organized using polar coordinates. Points representing each system are located at an angle corresponding to the physical location of a network's declared headquarters location and the radius corresponding to the "peering relevance" of this particular autonomous system. The latter parameter is derived by calculating the number of other autonomous systems observed to accept traffic from this particular node. Thus, massive core systems are located toward the center of the map, whereas systems that have direct contact with only a couple of nodes are located near the outer perimeter. Lines in the graph simply correspond to peering relations between routers.

NOTE *Quite regrettably, we were not allowed to use a graphical representation of CAIDA Skitter graphics in the book free of charge. I encourage you, however, to see this stunning picture online at http://www.caida.org/analysis/topology/as_core_network/pics/ascoreApr2003.gif where it is available to the general public at no cost.*

Another noteworthy attempt to map the network used an approach that relied on analyzing distances to various networks, as seen from a particular location (in this case, from Bell Laboratories), to build a treelike structure quite unlike the complex mesh created by CAIDA. Conducted by Bill Cheswick in 2000,[1] this analysis resulted in the map shown in Figure 17-1. This structure does not parametrize the graph depending on the physical or administrative location of a system; the relative distance from the center corresponds to the number of hops between that node and Bell Labs, however.

Although the two attempts appear to involve massive data collection and analysis, it is not prohibitively difficult for an amateur to attempt to map the network on even a fairly low-end link. Probing all publicly routable subnets with a single packet might require generating only a couple of gigabytes of traffic—the equivalent of a couple of hours to one day on a typical DSL connection. The only risk is that of upsetting some system administrators, but with the proliferation of computer worms and automated attacks, very few have a sensitivity threshold that low. Mapping the observed structure of the Internet is possible, and it can be rewarding, especially because it can tell us a lot about how the worldwide network is organized.

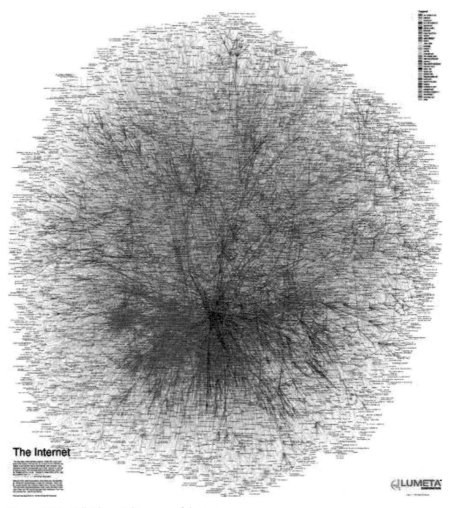

Figure 17-1: Bill Cheswick's map of the Internet

But, as it turns out, the data, such as the information acquired by CAIDA, Bill Cheswick, or just about any proficient user of the Net, can also be successfully used to better understand the nature and better examine the origin of a mysterious traffic we might one day stumble upon.

Using Topology Data for Origin Identification

Spoofed traffic is one of the Internet's major problems—or, at the very least, one of its more annoying woes. Blindly spoofed packets with bogus or specially chosen but deceptive source addresses can be used to abuse trust relationships between computers, inject malicious contents (such as unsolicited bulk mailings) without leaving conclusive traces and legitimate origin information, and so forth. Blind spoofing can also be used to hide the identity of an attacker conducting system probes ("decoy scanning" discussed earlier in Chapter 13). The worst plague of all is, however, spoofing used to carry out Denial of Service (DoS) attacks.

In a typical DoS attack, the administrator is given a chance to see the origin of malicious traffic directed against one of their services (and presumably intended to bring it down and cause inconvenience or loss to the operator). It is possible to randomly spoof offending packets, however, and in such cases the administrator is left helpless, unable to filter out the traffic coming from the attacker without cutting off other users. Their only hope is to work with the upstream provider to investigate the actual origin of the traffic on the link layer and pass the information to the offender's ISP; this, however, takes time, and lots of it. It also requires convincing all parties, without a court order, that the case is worthy of investigation (and their time and money). This situation makes it particularly important for the system administrator to be equipped with tools and methods to differentiate between spoofed and legitimate traffic.

When I used to live and work in the United States (I live in Poland these days), my colleague Mark Loveless decided to implement an idea originally proposed by Donald McLachlan: He would measure time to live (TTL) on network traffic between him and the presumed sender of a packet to automatically determine whether an incoming packet had been spoofed. The challenge of identifying the origin of a network packet in a world where the information cannot be trusted is important, and the ability to do so, even if only in a specific subset of cases, would greatly benefit many analytic and administrative tasks, for the reasons mentioned earlier.

To understand Donald and Mark's idea, consider that the remote system, from which we are seeing traffic, is at a specific logical distance from us, separated by a given number of network devices. Thus, all packets legitimately sent by this system exhibit a certain TTL on arrival, corresponding to the default initial TTL configured on that system, minus the number of intermediate systems the packet has gone through (as discussed in Chapter 9). However, for spoofed traffic that presumably originates on a wholly different network, the initial TTL and the distance is most likely different than the aforementioned observation would suggest. Mark's tool, despoof,[2] compares the TTLs observed on specially induced and previously received traffic in order to distinguish between legitimate and falsified traffic.

However, although this method might work well in individual cases when used against unsuspecting attackers, at least two problems are associated with it:

- A paranoid attacker can measure distances before the attack and choose a TTL that matches the expected value. Although possible, this trick is a bit difficult to implement. For one thing, the attacker might be physically unable to set TTL high enough to achieve a specific value that would match the expected value of a real packet once the packet reaches its destination. This attacker's plan could be thwarted if the system that he is trying to impersonate uses a default TTL at or near 255 (the maximum possible) and he is farther from the target than the system he is trying to impersonate (hence it is very much impossible for him to send a packet that would, upon arrival at the destination, have the desired TTL). Of course, few systems use the highest possible TTL, and it is rare for an attacker to want to impersonate a specific system to begin with.

The attacker's second challenge is that he might not be able to determine the exact distance between his victim and the impersonated system if he is nowhere near them and does not know the routing specifics between these hosts. But if the victim uses despoof to dynamically implement filtering rules to cut off malicious packets, the attacker might just try various TTLs from various sources until he sees that the victim is no longer capable of making the distinction. (This would be obvious: the system targeted would begin to exhibit the effects of a successful attack, such as a performance impact.)

- Each time a suspicious packet is received, the recipient must start an investigation and then wait for the results to arrive. This makes it impractical to use despoof as a basis for an automatic defense, especially in response to DoS attacks. However, this method is still quite useful for determining the actual origin of a "decoy scan."

Without the knowledge of a specific network's topology, it is difficult to do any better than with despoof; the TTL analysis technique implemented by this tool is good enough to recognize and stop many common probes and individual attacks, but what next?

Combine Mark's tool with real-time data on the network structure, and apply passive fingerprinting to determine the initial TTL of a system that sends specific requests, and this technique becomes much more powerful. This additional data allows us to perform an initial passive assessment of incoming traffic by comparing observed and initial TTLs with the expected distance indicated by the network map.[*] Because the distance we should be seeing can be determined without initiating any active probe of the network topology data, we can instantly distinguish between legitimate and malicious traffic without much effort. This, in turn, makes it possible to react to massive incidents quite reliably and to detect individual low-profile probes without alerting the attacker that a spoofing detection system is in place.

Obviously, there is plenty to be gained from taking the structure of a network into account when considering peer-to-peer relations. But spoofing detection is only the beginning.

---

[*] In such an approach, the comparison of TTLs must be performed with a certain error margin, because there can be several additional hops within internal networks. Too, some routes are asymmetric, and their lengths can differ slightly depending on the direction in which the traffic is being exchanged.

Network Triangulation with Mesh-Type Topology Data

Network triangulation is a considerably more interesting application of network topology mesh-type data for the purpose of traffic analysis. We can use network triangulation to determine the approximate location of an attacker who sends spoofed packets without the help of those operating the underlying routing backbone, as soon as they choose to attack more than one target at once or in succession—truly, happiness in misery.

Well, to be correct: although triangulation works best when the attacker chooses several targets, in some scenarios, it may work quite well even if they choose to attack only one service. In particular, we might be able to observe the same attack from different viewpoints when the object attacked has several IP addresses and the service is being served from several physical locations in order to distribute the load and make the entire structure fault tolerant (as is common with web services). In all other scenarios, we can get a range of data on an attack when system administrators notice that more than one system is being targeted by an attacker and share their data about the incident.

Regardless of the case, once data believed to come from a single source is seen at more than one destination, we can triangulate. For each destination at which the traffic is seen, only a specific set of networks are at a distance that can be determined by observing the distance through which the offending packet has traveled (again, possible to find out by examining TTL[*]). An intersection of all those sets for every observation point would yield a smaller set—or, often, only a single network—from which the attack could originate, as shown in Figure 17-2.

The ability to perform the trace on our own frees us from unconditional dependence on ISPs and helps to precisely pinpoint who is attacking or probing our network—and perhaps find out why.

Although this approach is much more difficult to thwart than traditional despoofing, a clever attacker might still be able to fool an observer by randomizing a different TTL (or range of TTLs) to be used for every target. True, we know of no tools to do this at present, but this might change.

The battle is lost? Nope—there is a way to keep perpetrators from fooling us that way.

Network Stress Analysis

The solution, dubbed "network stress analysis," comes in the form of a fine piece of research presented by Hal Brunch and Bill Cheswick at the LISA conference in 2000.[3] Brunch and Cheswick proposed an interesting use for

---

[*] Even if the tool uses random TTLs, it is possible to judge the distance by using the maximum TTL observed if a number of packets can be observed at each destination (which is almost always the case). For example, if the scan tool randomizes initial TTLs in the range of 32 to 255, but for several thousand packets received at the destination, none had a TTL higher than 247, the host is quite likely to be 255 – 247 = 8 systems away.

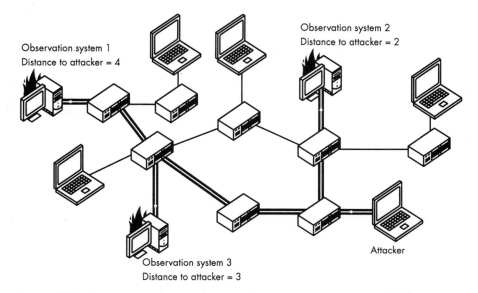

Observation system 1
Distance to attacker = 4

Observation system 2
Distance to attacker = 2

Observation system 3
Distance to attacker = 3

Attacker

Figure 17-2: A naive network triangulation: only one origin is consistent with all observations. The attacker may be spoofing source addresses, but can't fool the victims.

tree-type network topology data (similar to the graph shown earlier in Figure 17-1) obtained for a specific location. They came up with a way to use the data to detect the origin of a particular type of spoofed traffic: Denial of Service. The approach itself is fairly trivial and is based on the assumption that such an attack would stress not only the system against which it is being carried out, but also interim routers, and that this stress could be externally measured by the victim and used to—almost literally—go back and find a yarn by pulling the wire.

The job of stress-testing network links is achieved by first building or obtaining a tree of links from your location to all networks on the Internet and then going through subsequent branches of this tree structure when an attack occurs. For each branch (which, in reality, denotes a connection to a higher-order router), we can iteratively measure network load on this node by sending test traffic to or through the router associated with it. (In this particular paper, a UDP [User Datagram Protocol] chargen is used, but ICMP requests or any other type of messages could be also used.) We choose a more loaded node as a potential candidate for the incoming traffic and then list and test all branches that spawn from this node until we trace the traffic back to the origin.

Figure 17-3 illustrates a simple trace-back scenario. In the first phase, the attacked system attempts to measure the performance of the three nearest Internet routers when an attack occurs; it concludes that the first (topmost) router is the most saturated.

Based on this information, the victim chooses to test only those routers directly connected (peering) with this device. In this particular figure, only three devices are to be tested (the remaining six are not to be tested because they do not peer with this device), and, again, the first one is the most loaded. The process continues until a router that is directly connected to a specific network, for which a physical location and owner information can be discovered through public databases, is determined to be the final endpoint.

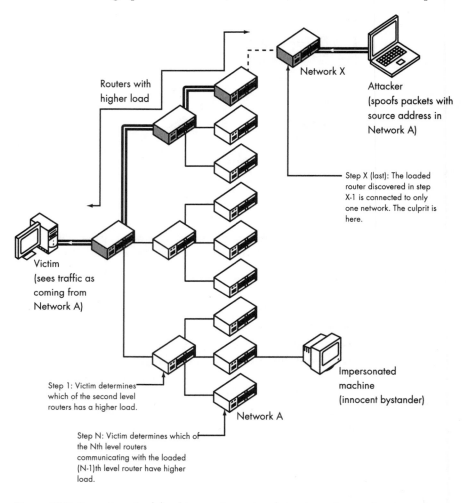

Figure 17-3: Recursive attack backtrace using network topology data and stress testing

A potential problem arises: some devices might be heavily loaded for reasons other than handling DoS traffic; other devices might have plenty of spare CPU cycles and would not be considerably affected by relaying malicious traffic.

To solve this issue, the research proposes putting an artificial short-term load on the router (by generating additional traffic) and then observing how this test affects the bandwidth and latency of the DoS requests; if this particular device is indeed involved in relaying malicious packets, the attack rate should drop when we put load on the device (again, likely by generating additional bogus TCP, UDP, or ICMP requests, designed more to consume a device's CPU power than to congest its interfaces). Hence, there should be a correlation only on those branches that are involved in servicing the malicious traffic.

This brilliant and simple scheme had been successfully used in test environments. However, because it involves interacting with routers and placing an additional load on them, certain ethical considerations come into play when we consider using it in the real world.

Food for Thought

The main difficulty in using the techniques discussed in this chapter for tracking down attackers is that we need to construct and update network maps for each location. It is not immediately clear how often such maps should be refreshed, and what methods would prove most reliable and least intrusive.

Another possible issue is that much of the core Internet infrastructure is redundant. Some alternative routes may be chosen only when the primary route fails or is saturated, though in some cases the switch may occur as a part of load balancing. Thus, some empirical maps may become obsolete in a matter of minutes or hours—although such cases are not very common.

In the end, although private, individual uses of various despoofing tactics may prove very successful, there are many open questions that need to be answered before we can deploy such techniques on a large scale—and some of the questions are not as much about technical issues.

18

WATCHING THE VOID

*When looking down the abyss, what does not kill us
makes us stronger*

We have looked at many ways to discover information
and intercept data by observing the communications
between two systems or by watching the side effects of
such communications. The story does not end here,
however. Sometimes, by averting our eyes from the
target we hope to probe, we can see even more.

An entire set of methods commonly referred to as "black-hole monitoring"
is dedicated to observing and analyzing unwanted or unsolicited traffic that
arrives accidentally, erroneously, or in mangled form at a specific destination.
These methods most often include simply running a packet dump utility and
then painstakingly analyzing and theorizing about every single observance.

Although in a perfect world, we should gain nothing by looking for data
where we are not supposed to find it, in reality we can use these methods to
gather abundant bits of information and invaluable hints as to the condition
of a network as a whole. Even though the information is mostly random and
we cannot choose who we listen to, we can still benefit from the effort.

Direct Observation Tactics

One application of black-hole monitoring lies in detecting and analyzing global attack trends. Many black hat hackers in possession of new attack techniques often simply scan large blocks of network addresses to find vulnerable targets that can be compromised and ultimately used for illicit activities (presumably to collect skip hosts[*] or to build attack drone networks for automated attacks). We can use black-hole monitoring to alert us to new vulnerabilities being exploited in the wild by simply observing increased standard network scan activity from various sources.

Many network administrators deploy black-hole monitoring. They sometimes combine it with honeypots (in which a fake "lure" system is put out on the network to catch attackers and intercept their tools and identify their techniques[1]) to produce an advance warning system that will allow them to be the first to know about impeding breakouts of worms and other malware. (You can also use black-hole traffic to calibrate "noise levels" and detect targeted attacks against your servers more efficiently, without picking up automated, indiscriminate malicious activity.)

Researchers such as Dug Song and Jose Nazario (Jose most recently in his book *Defense and Detection Strategies against Internet Worms*[2]) have attempted to analyze black-hole activity during massive outbreaks of network worms. Their goal is to better understand and model the distribution (initial propagation and reinfection) dynamics of the network and to test the efficiency and persistence of the worms' infection algorithms. Their research will help us to devise future defenses against massive, distributed threats, while providing valuable insight into the state of the network today. Some examples of their findings are shown in Figures 18-1 through 18-4.

Figure 18-1 shows how a worm propagates during an outbreak. The data is based on the number of observed attack attempts on TCP port 137, a part of the Windows NetBIOS implementation, which is installed by default on all Windows computers and targeted by many types of self-propagating malware. Notice in this figure how, after a week of initial propagation—when both the number of infected sites (sources) and systems attacked on the observed black-hole network were steadily and rapidly increasing—a stabilization period suddenly stretches for over a month with dramatic peaks and valleys. Such a propagation footprint is highly unique to a worm and the network conditions in which it operates; it also reflects the subtleties of the target selection and infection algorithms used by the author.

Figure 18-2 shows a different aspect of the worm propagation algorithm and depicts the properties of the target selection algorithm. In this case, a popular worm that targeted Microsoft SQL servers appears to have fairly continuous coverage of the address space (although addresses with octets between about 200 and 225 are chosen considerably more often, and the worm appears to skip values over 225 altogether).

---

[*] Skip host is a system used as an intermediate hop for carrying out further attacks or other illicit activity (such as sending spam). This technique makes it more difficult to track the ultimate offender, because their origin is not directly known, and a number of administrators or jurisdictions must cooperate to find them.

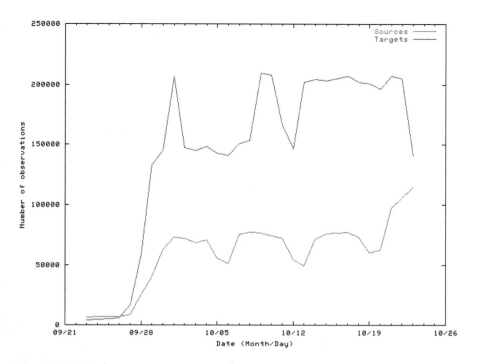

Figure 18-1: Windows worm propagation characteristics

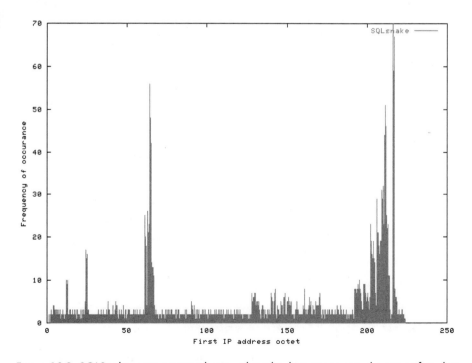

Figure 18-2: SQLSnake worm target selection algorithm histogram; note the nonuniform but generally continuous coverage of the address space

Figure 18-3 shows the same graph for a different network worm, Slapper. This worm targeted Linux systems, exploiting a flaw in a popular OpenSSL encryption library. The algorithm appears to offer considerably more uniform, but much less continuous coverage, with gaping holes across certain values.

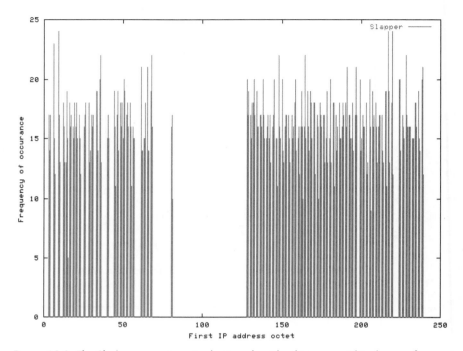

Figure 18-3: The Slapper worm target selection algorithm histogram. This shows a far more uniform distribution, but noncontinuous coverage with gaps suggesting that the least significant bits of each of the "random" addresses are constant—perhaps due to a programming glitch.

Figure 18-4 shows worm persistence patterns over time. For example, some worms appear to die off steadily as systems are patched and disinfected, while others use algorithms that cause sudden and recurring rise and fall patterns (familiar to anyone who has experimented with population or epidemiology models based on natural phenomena).

As Jose and his colleagues strive to demonstrate, black-hole monitoring may not be only a routine and perhaps completely needless activity, but also a great way to discover the secret life of all things malicious. Alas, the story does not end there. By observing only the traffic we consider aimed at us, we miss the most interesting bits of data.

Attack Fallout Traffic Analysis

The other application of black-hole monitoring relies on observing traffic that was never aimed at us in the first place, but which is merely a side effect of other activity.

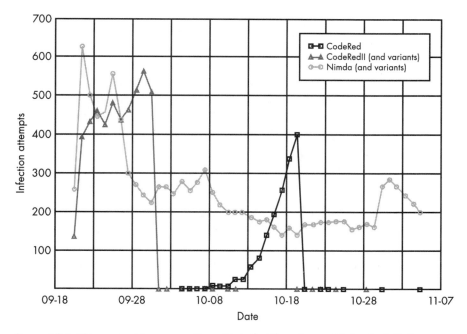

Figure 18-4: Worm persistence over time. Note that there is no trivial spike-falloff pattern for CodeRed and that the model behaves like a biological population model.

Here we can see how a number of common reconnaissance and attack schemes use address spoofing to conceal an attacker's identity. The assumption is that an administrator will have difficulty differentiating decoy traffic from bogus addresses from the attacker's actual probes. Although as I've shown in previous chapters, this approach does not guarantee the attacker complete anonymity; in order to successfully "despoof" the traffic, an administrator must implement extensive logging and additional measures at the time of the attack. Because these procedures are not always implemented, attackers can often spoof their attacks quite effectively and remain out of the spotlight.

Whether packets are spoofed or not, the attacked system will in good faith respond to all requests including those allegedly coming from made-up addresses. However, only the responses to packets with a proper source address arrive back at the sender; all other probes generate responses that are scattered all around the Internet, and we can often catch them.

Although it may seem unlikely that we will receive such a misdirected packet, remember that a considerable number of SYN+ACK, RST+ACK, and RST packets are generated in response to decoy scans or SYN flood attacks. The Internet address space appears vast, with millions of packets typically involved in such attacks, but it is quite likely that over time, some will reach every single network block. Although the likelihood of a single, randomly generated spoofed packet bouncing back to a specific address is only 1 in 4,294,967,296 (1 to 2^{32}), assuming that a typical small subnet assigned to a small company or organization usually consists of 256 addresses (class C network or equivalent), this probability is increased to 1 in 16,777,216 (1 to 2^{24}). This can be further improved by ruling out address ranges that are known to be reserved for special purposes or which are otherwise not noteworthy and thus excluded in certain types of attacks.

Because the face of a single SYN packet is about 40 bytes (and compresses well in bulk) and a typical network link available to a casual attacker has a throughput of approximately 10 to 150 kilobytes per IP layer per second (low-end DSL and T1 line, respectively), he can push out 250 to nearly 3,000 packets in this time frame—or 900,000 to circa 10,000,000 packets per hour.[*]

For a typical DoS attack to produce any noticeable results and cause major inconvenience to the victim, it usually has to be carried out for several hours or days. (The attacker wants to inconvenience their victim for as long as possible.) As a result, dozens to hundreds of millions of packets are sent, generating a similar number of SYN+ACK or RST+ACK replies.

Due to this huge amount of traffic, it's quite reasonable to expect that even a relatively small entity could notice the fallout of a small SYN flood attack as it happens, even if the recipient host drops many attack packets. Furthermore, administrators able to monitor class B equivalent networks (65,356 addresses, usually owned by larger companies, ISPs, research institutions, and so forth) would be able to pick up much smaller events quickly.

Because all the fallout replies in a spoofed DoS attack include certain details of the messages fabricated by the attacker to trigger those responses in the first place (such as port and sequence numbers, timing information, and so forth), we can use these replies to extract important information about the type and scale of attack. We can use these replies to determine whether a specific service has been targeted, how many systems have been targeted, the bandwidth available to the attacker, and the tool used to perform the attack (by examining source port selection, chosen sequence numbers, and "random" IP patterns[†]).

Finally, by analyzing the sources of these ricochet responses, we might notice that a particular network segment is under attack or be able to identify global "hostility trends," perhaps to better prepare if a specific industry or business is being targeted. We can also use this information to learn about attacks that are being covered up by the victim or to identify false claims of attacks. (Claims that certain targets are being attacked by cyber-terrorists are sometimes made as a PR stunt to justify financial losses or to push a specific political agenda. Of recent, some experts accused SCO of taking their servers off-line and pretending to be a victim of a coordinated DoS attack to discredit the Linux users community.)

---

[*] Note that determined, seasoned attackers proficient in Denial of Service attacks often have dozens or hundreds of "zombie" nodes at their command, thus increasing this estimate dramatically.

[†] For example, some tools only "spoof" packets from even or odd IP addresses due to coding flaws. Analyses similar to those conducted by Jose Nazario and others typically prove to be as good at pinpointing attack tools as they do at identifying worms.

Detecting Malformed or Misdirected Data

This application for monitoring black holes relies on monitoring traffic that does not seem to make any sense, but that still appears to reach a specific destination. To better illustrate the problem, allow me this digression.

In 1999, a group of friends, colleagues in Poland, and I began a humble after-hours project. Our goals were to track down a hard-to-explain set of RST+ACK packets that we had noticed arriving at networks we maintained and to monitor unusual and unsolicited traffic patterns arriving at unused network segments in general. It was great fun, and, as you might imagine, it resulted in a good deal of speculation when we tried to reasonably explain some of the most unusual cases. Our research also enabled us to learn more about the world around us as we encountered some exceedingly bizarre and seemingly inexplicable traffic that, once properly analyzed, provided more insight into the vast conspiraces of our wired world.

Although formally abandoned, this project ended up in my private "Museum of Broken Packets,"[3] a semihumorous web page dedicated to tracking down, documenting, and explaining packets that should never have reached their destination or that should never have looked the way they did. The stated purpose of the museum was as follows:

> The purpose of this museum is to provide a shelter for strange, unwanted, malformed packets—abandoned and doomed freaks of nature—as we, mere mortals, meet them on the twisted paths of our grand journey called life. Our exhibits—or, if you wish, inhabitants—are often just a shadow of what they used to be before they met a hostile, faulty router. Some of them were born deformed in the depth of a broken IP stack implementation. Others were normal packets, just like their friends (you or me), but got lost looking for the ultimate meaning of their existence and arrived where we should never have seen them. In every case, we try to discover the unique history of each packet's life, and to help you understand how difficult it is to be a sole messenger in the hostile universe of bits and bytes.

And this is what the last type of black-hole monitoring boils down to. Although the task can appear pointless at first, it is foolish to assume so. The museum made it possible to passively uncover dark secrets about various proprietary devices and well-protected networks, and running such an experiment elsewhere would undoubtedly result in the same or greater accomplishments.

Some of the exhibits in my museum include marvels such as the following:

- Packets originating from networks with a specific type of web accelerator, router, or firewall; the device appends, strips, or otherwise mangles some of the data. A good example is a flaw in certain Nortel CVX devices that is responsible for the occasional stripping of TCP headers from packets (as discussed in Chapter 11). The uniqueness of this flaw enables us to learn a good deal about a number of remote networks without having to actually go out and probe them.

- Several line noise exhibits, showing packets containing either utter garbage or data that certainly did not belong to a specific connection. One of the most surprising exhibits is unsolicited traffic containing data that appears to be a dump of .de DNS zone contents (a listing of all domains in Germany). The traffic could not have originated just anywhere, because mere mortals have no rights to obtain such a list. Instead, it must have originated at an authorized party able to obtain and transfer this data and must have been mangled either by the sender or by a device somewhere along the way. Although all cases shed little light on the nature of mishaps on the network, cases such as this one often enrich the observer with unexpected—and often valuable—findings.

Other noteworthy exhibits included cases of apparent espionage camouflaged to appear as regular traffic and many other coding or networking hiccups. But enough bragging—if you feel compelled to find out more, visit http://lcamtuf.coredump.cx/mobp/.

Food for Thought

Many regard black-hole monitoring as just another way to detect attacks against their systems (and perhaps an expensive way, given the scarcity of public IP space resources). But the real value of this technique is that it makes it possible to not only identify known attacks (something that can be done just as well in many other locations, without wasting IP space), but also detect and analyze subtle patterns that would otherwise be lost below the "noise level" in an extensively used network.

Naturally, performing this type of black-hole monitoring is not easy and remains expensive. It takes time to learn how to find that needle in the haystack of the usual worm and black hat activity that, in a sufficiently extensive network, usually bears no significance beyond statistical reporting.

Yet, for the joy of finally finding the needle, it is often worth a try.

CLOSING WORDS

Where the book is about to conclude

This is where the book ends, but where I hope your journey begins. I have taken pride in guiding you through the world of complex and uncommon security problems that I most enjoy, and I hope you have shared my passion. Whether you are a seasoned security professional—perhaps more experienced and knowledgeable than I—or just an enthusiast discovering this field, I hope that I have given you a new perspective on security, as a challenge and art all its own, not a set of obstacles that must be eliminated or worked around.

By understanding the subtle relationships between seemingly unrelated components and processes, you can effectively tackle the most dangerous and pervasive security problems and assess and mitigate everyday risks more efficiently. Security problems should be seen as a function of a solution to virtually every challenge in the world of IT, no matter how trivial or limited in scope; not as the adverse circumstances of doing business. Only by seeing the magic and charm of the complementary universes and the subtle ways they interact can we avoid routine and begin to really enjoy our work, or understand our hobby.

But then it is not the right time or place to hit high notes.

Thank you for playing.

BIBLIOGRAPHIC NOTES

Chapter 1

1. Alan Turing, "On Computable Numbers, with an Application to the Entscheidungsproblem," Proceedings of the London Mathematical Society, Series 2, 42 (1936).

2. R.L. Rivest, A. Shamir, L. Adleman, "A Method for Obtaining Digital Signatures and Public-Key Cryptosystems," Massachusetts Institute of Technology (1978).

3. Ueli M. Maurer, "Fast Generation of Prime Numbers and Secure Public-Key Cryptographic Parameters," Institute for Theoretical Computer Science, ETH Zurich, Switzerland (1994).

4. Donald E. Knuth, *The Art of Computer Programming, Volume 2: Seminumerical Algorithms*, 3rd ed. Addison-Wesley (1997).

5. H. Krawczyk, "How to Predict Congruential Generators," *Journal of Algorithms* 13, no. 4 (1992).

6. S. Bakhtiari, R. Safavi-Naini, J. Pieprzyk, "Cryptographic Hash Functions: A Survey," Centre for Computer Security Research, Department of Computer Science, University of Wollongong, Australia (1995).

7. Dawn Xiaodong Song, David Wagner, Xuqing Tian, "Timing Analysis of Keystrokes and Timing Attacks on SSH," University of California, Berkeley (2001).

8. Claude E. Shannon, "Prediction and Entropy of Printed English," *Bell Systems Technical Journal 3* (1950).

9. Benjamin Jun, Paul Kocher, "The Intel Random Number Generator," Cryptography Research Inc. (1999).

10. "Evaluation of VIA C3 Nehemiah Random Number Generator," Cryptography Research Inc. (2003).

11. Michael A. Hogye, Christopher T. Hughes, Joshua M. Sarfaty, Joseph D. Wolf, "Analysis of Feasibility of Keystroke Timing Attacks Over SSH Connections," CS588 Research Project, School of Engineering and Applied Science, University of Virginia (2001).

Chapter 2

1. Yurii Rogozhin, "A Universal Turing Machine with 22 States and 2 Symbols," *Romanian Journal of Information Science and Technology* 1 no. 3 (1998).

2. Milena Milenkovic, Aleksandar Milenkovic, Jeffrey Kulick, "Demystifying Intel Branch Predictors," Electrical and Computer Engineering Department, University of Alabama in Huntsville (2002).

3. Paul C. Kocher, "Timing Attacks on Implementations of Diffie-Hellman, RSA, DSS, and Other Systems," Cryptography Research Inc. (1999).

4. *Intel 80386 Programmer's Reference Manual*, section 7.2.IMUL, Intel Corp. (1986).

5. E. Biham, A. Shamir, "Differential Fault Analysis: Identifying the Structure of Unknown Ciphers Sealed in Tamper-Proof Devices" (1996).

Chapter 3

1. Wim van Eck, "Electromagnetic Radiation from Video Display Units: An Eavesdropping Risk?" PTT Laboratories, Netherlands (1985).

2. Ian A. Murphy, "Who's Listening?" IAM/Secure Data Systems (1988, 1997).

3. Winn Schwartau, *Information Warfare*. 2nd ed. Thunder's Mouth Press, New York (1996).

Chapter 5

1. John A.C. Bingham, *The Theory and Practice of Modem Design*. Wiley-Interscience (1988).

2. Electronic Industries Association, Engineering Department, "Interface Between Data Terminal Equipment and Data Circuit-Terminating Equipment Employing Serial Binary Data Interchange" (1991).

3. Charles E. Spurgeon, *Ethernet: The Definitive Guide*. O'Reilly and Associates (2000).

4. Joe Lughry, David A. Umphress, "Information Leakage from Optical Emanations," *ACM Trans. Info. Sys. Security* 5, no. 3 (2002).

5. Adi Shamir, Eran Tromer, "Acoustic Cryptanalysis: On Nosy People and Noisy Machines." Preliminary presentation available as of this writing at http://www.wisdom.weizmann.ac.il/~tromer/acoustic/ (2004).

6. Paul Kocher, Joshua Jaffe, Benjamin Jun, "Differential Power Analysis." Cryptography Research, Inc. (2000).

Chapter 6

1. J. Postel, J. Reynolds, "RFC-1042: A Standard for the Transit of Internet Protocol Datagrams Over IEEE 802 Networks," Network Working Group, http://www.ietf.org/rfc/rfc1042.txt (1988).

2. Ofir Arkin and Josh Anderson, "EtherLeak—Ethernet Frame Padding Information Leaks," @Stake, http://www.atstake.com/research/advisories/2003/atstake_etherleak_report.pdf (2003).

Chapter 7

1. David C. Plummer, RFC 826, "An Ethernet Address Resolution Protocol," Network Working Group (1982).

2. Louis Senecal, "Layer 2 Attacks and Their Mitigation," Cisco (2002).

Chapter 8

1. J. Case, M. Fedor, M. Schoffstall, J. Davin, RFC 1157, "A Simple Network Management Protocol," Network Working Group (1990).

2. Institut für Bankinnovation GmbH, "PSYLock: a typing behaviour based psychometrical authentication method," http://pc50461.uni-regensburg.de/ibi/de/leistungen/research/projekte/einzelprojekte/psylock_english.htm (2003).

3. Solar Designer, Dug Song, "Passive Analysis of SSH (Secure Shell) Traffic," Openwall Project, http://www.openwall.com/advisories/OW-003-ssh-traffic-analysis (2001).

4. Nikita Borisov, Ian Goldberg, David Wagner, "Intercepting Mobile Communications: The Insecurity of 802.11" (2001).

Chapter 9

1. J. Postel, University of Southern California, "RFC 791: Internet Protocol," Network Working Group (1981).

2. J. Postel, University of Southern California, "RFC 796: Address Mappings," Network Working Group (1981).

3. J. Mogul, S. Dearing, "RFC 1191: Path MTU Discovery," Network Working Group (1990).

4. J. Postel, University of Southern California, "RFC 768: User Datagram Protocol," Network Working Group (1980).

5. J. Postel, University of Southern California, "RFC 793: Transmission Control Protocol," Network Working Group (1981).

6. S. Bellovin, "RFC1948: Defending Against Sequence Number Attacks," Network Working Group (1996).

7. V. Jacobson, B. Braden, "RFC1232: TCP Extensions for High Performance," Network Working Group (1992).

8. M. Mathis, J. Mahdavi, S. Floyd, and A. Romanow, "RFC2018: TCP Selective Acknowledgment Options," Network Working Group (1996).

9. B. Braden, "RFC1644: T/TCP – TCP Extensions for Transactions – Functional Specification," Network Working Group (1994).

10. J. Postel, University of Southern California, "RFC 792: Internet Control Message Protocol," Network Working Group (1981).

11. Lance Spitzner, *Honeypots: Tracking Hackers.* Addison-Wesley Publishing Company (2002).

12. R. Morris, "A Weakness in the 4.2BSD UNIX TCP/IP Software," AT&T Bell Laboratories (1985).

Chapter 10

1. Michal Zalewski, "Strange Attractors and TCP/IP Sequence Number Analysis," BindView Corporation, http://www.bindview.com/Support/RAZOR/Papers/2001/ (2001).

2. S. Bellovin, "Defending Against Sequence Number Attacks," Network-Working Group, http://www.ietf.org/rfc/rfc1948.txt (1996).

3. Joe Steward, "DNS Cache Poisoning: the Next Generation," http://www.lurhq.com/dnscache.pdf (2002).

Chapter 11

1. Elizabeth D. Zwicky, Simon Cooper, D. Brent Chapman, *Building Internet Firewalls.* O'Reilly & Associates (2000).

2. G. Ziemba, D. Reed, P. Traina, "RFC1858: Security Considerations for IP Fragment Filtering," Network Working Group (1995).

3. Uriel Maimon, "TCP Port Stealth Scanning," *Phrack Magazine* no. 49 (1996).

4. J. Postel, J. Reynolds, "RFC959: File Transfer Protocol," Network Working Group (1985).

5. Mikael Olson, "Extending the FTP ALG Vulnerability to any FTP client," VULN-DEV mailing list, http://www.securityfocus.com/archive/82/50226 (2000).

6. Michal Zalewski, "Linux Kernel IP Masquerading Vulnerability," Bindview Corporation, http://razor.bindview.com/publish/advisories/adv_LkIPmasq.html (2001).

7. R. Braden (editor), "RFC1122: Requirements for Internet Hosts—Communication Layers," Network Working Group (1989).

Chapter 13

1. Salvatore Sanfilippo, "New TCP Scan Method," Bugtraq, http://seclists.org/bugtraq/1998/Dec/0082.html (1998).

Chapter 14

1. World Wide Web Consortium, http://www.w3c.org/History.html.

2. Vannevar Bush, "As We May Think," *Atlantic Monthly* 176, no. 1 (1945): 101-08.

3. Tim Berners-Lee, "Basic HTTP," http://www.w3c.org/Protocols/HTTP/HTTP2.html.

4. R. Fielding, J. Gettys, J. Mogul, H. Frystyk, L. Masinter, P. Leach, T. Berners-Lee, "RFC2616: HyperText Transfer Protocol—HTTP/1.1." Network Working Group (1999).

5. Various sources, references quoted after http://usability.gov/guidelines/softhard.html: Anna Bouch, Allan Kuchinsky, Nina Bhatti, "Quality Is in the Eye of the Beholder: Meeting Users' Requirements for Internet Quality of Service," CHI (2000);
Martin, Corl, "System Response Time Effects on User Productivity," Behaviour and Information Technology, vol 5, no. 1, 3-13 (1986);
Jakob Nielsen, "Top Ten Mistakes in Web Design," http://www.useit.com/alertbox/9605.html (1996);
Nielsen, "The Need for Speed," http://www.useit.com/alertbox/9703a.html (1997); Nielsen, "Changes in Web Usability Since 1994," http://www.useit.com/alertbox/9712a.html (1997);
Nielsen, "The Top Ten New Mistakes of Web Design," http://www.useit.com/alertbox/990530.html (1999).

6. Kristol, Montulli, "RFC2109: HTTP State Management Mechanism," Network Working Group (1997).

7. Martin Pool, "Privacy Problems with HTTP Cache-Control," Bugtraq, http://cert.uni-stuttgart.de/archive/bugtraq/2000/03/msg00365.html (2000).

8. Bamshad Mobasher, Robert Cooley, Jaideep Srivastava, "Automatic Personalization Based on Web Usage Mining," ACM Communications vol. 43 no 8, 142-151 (1999).

9. Edward Felten, Michael Schneider, "Timing Attacks on Web Privacy," ACM Conference on Computing and Communications Security (2000).

Chapter 15

1. ISO/IEC Standard 9899, "Programming Language – C," http://plg.uwaterloo.ca/~cforall/N843.ps (1999).

2. DISCO, http://www.altmode.com/disco.

Chapter 16

1. Albert-Laszlo Barabasz, Vincent W. Freeh, Hawoong Jeong, Jay B. Brochman, "Parasitic Computing," letter to Nature 412 (2001).

2. M. Leech, "RFC 3607: Chinese Lottery Cryptoanalysis Revisited," Network Working Group (2003).

Chapter 17

1. Bill Cheswick, Hal Burch, Steve Branigan, "Mapping and Visualizing the Internet", http://www.cheswick.com/ches/papers/mapping.ps.gz (2000).

2. Despoof, http://razor.bindview.com/tools/desc/despoof_readme.html.

3. Hal Brunch, Bill Cheswick, "Tracing Anonymous Packets to Their Approximate Source," http://www.usenix.org/publications/library/proceedings/lisa2000/burch/burch_html (2000).

Chapter 18

1. Lance Spitzner, *Honeypots: Tracking Hackers*: Addison-Wesley (2002).

2. Jose Nazario, Defense and Detection Strategies against Internet Worms: Artech House (2003).

3. Michal Zalewski, "Museum of Broken Packets," http://lcamtuf.coredump.cx/mobp (2001).

INDEX

biphase code, 67
bipolar encoding, 74–75
black-hole monitoring, 253
    attack fallout traffic analysis,
        256–58
    direct observation, 254–56
    malformed and misdirected data
        detection, 259–60
blind spoofing
    in connection hijacking, 147
    origin identification of, 245–47
blinkenlights, 78–79
    implications of, 80
    protecting, 85–87
    snooping devices for, 81–84
Boole, George, 21–22
Boolean logic, 21–22
    applications of, 25–26
    for calculations, 28–30
    in computer design, 27–28
    for flip-flops, 31–32
    in nonelectric computers, 26–27
    satisfiability equations, 228–32
    universal operators for, 22–25
bots in zero-effort exploits, 59–61
bottlenecks in HTTP, 207–9
branch prediction, 41
Brochman, Jay B., 228
browsers
    behavioral analysis for, 212–17
    development of, 203
Brunch, Hal, 248–49
buffers
    for Ethernet frames, 93–94
    leaking, 56
    for parasitic storage, 234–37
    URG and ACK values in, 190–92
Bush, Vannevar, 202

C

cable modems, 73
caching
    in behavioral analysis, 216–17
    for HTTP, 207–11
    for memory, 39

CAIDA Internet map, 244
calculations, Boolean logic for,
    28–30
CAM (content addressable
    memory), 97, 100
camouflaging software identity,
    200–202
Carrier Sense Multiple Access with
    Collision Detection
    (CSMA/CD), 75
carry bits in addition circuits, 29–30
CCDs (Charge Coupled Devices),
    19
CERN (Conseil Europeen pour la
    Recherche Nucleaire), 202
Charge Coupled Devices (CCDs),
    19
checksums
    in Ethernet, 75–76
    in ICMP headers, 134
    in IP fragmentation, 149–50
    in IP headers, 124
    in satisfiability equations, 230
    in TCP headers, 131
Cheswick, Bill, 244–45, 248–49
Chinese lottery computing
    schemes, 231
Chinese Remainder Theorem, 6
Church-Turing thesis, 32, 34
clamping, MSS, 182
clocks
    in data transmission, 66
    in port scanning attacks, 222
Code Red worm, 257
collisions
    in data transmissions, 75–76
    sequence number, 154
complexity in instruction sets, 41
computational effort analysis, 44–48
connection hijacking, 147
Conseil Europeen pour la
    Recherche Nucleaire
    (CERN), 202
content addressable memory
    (CAM), 97, 100

Internet Control Message Protocol
(ICMP)
headers in, 134–35
for parasitic storage, 233
in PMTUD failure, 184–85
Internet Explorer browser
behavioral analysis for, 213–14
development of, 203
Internet Protocol. *See* IP
interrupts
I/O, 8–10
in inter-keystroke timing, 17
IP (Internet Protocol), 96, 114–15
address space, 116–18
fragmentation in, 147–50
header structure in, 118–24
in passive fingerprinting, 135–41
port scanning in, 194–97
reliability of, 124–25
spoofing. *See* spoofing
IP identification numbers
in idle scanning, 196
profiling from, 198
IP Personality, 146
IRIX 6.5, sequence number
attractor patterns, 164
ISNProber tool, 169–70
ISNs. *See* sequence numbers

J

jam code mechanisms, 76
Java applets, 231–32
Jeong, Hawoong, 228
Jun, Benjamin, 19

K

Kaminsky, Dan, 171–72
keyboard and keystrokes, 3–4
entropy in, 11–14, 18
input timing in, 14–19
interrupts for, 8–10
one-way shortcut functions for,
11
randomness in, 4–8

remote timing attacks, 19–20
reproducible unpredictability in,
20
typing-pattern based biometrics
for, 105–6
keys in encryption, 6
Khan, Saqib A., 233
Kocher, Paul, 19, 42
Krawczyk, H., 221

L

Last-Modified headers, 208–11
latency reduction for HTTP, 205–7
leaks
Ethernet frame, 92–94
memory, 55–56, 233
lights and LEDs, 78–79
disk-activity, 88
implications of, 80
protecting, 85–87
snooping devices for, 81–84
link-level protocols, 91
linked documents, 202
load balances, 179
logging
on Apache servers, 212
passive fingerprinting for, 144
logic. *See* Boolean logic
logical indicators, 105–6
Loveless, Mark, 246–47
LPT interface for LED snooping,
82–84
Lughry, Joe, 80

M

MAC (Media Access Control)
addresses
in Ethernet protocol, 90, 96–97
spoofing, 100
Mac OS 9, sequence number
attractor patterns, 163
malformed data detection, 259–60
Manchester encoding, 67–69
mapping, Internet, 244–45

Electronic Frontier Foundation
Defending Freedom in the Digital World

Free Speech. Privacy. Innovation. Fair Use. Reverse Engineering. If you care about these rights in the digital world, then you should join the Electronic Frontier Foundation (EFF). EFF was founded in 1990 to protect the rights of users and developers of technology. EFF is the first to identify threats to basic rights online and to advocate on behalf of free expression in the digital age.

The Electronic Frontier Foundation Defends Your Rights!
Become a Member Today!
http://www.eff.org/support/

Current EFF projects include:

Protecting your fundamental right to vote. Widely publicized security flaws in computerized voting machines show that, though filled with potential, this technology is far from perfect. EFF is defending the open discussion of e-voting problems and is coordinating a national litigation strategy addressing issues arising from use of poorly developed and tested computerized voting machines.

Ensuring that you are not traceable through your things. Libraries, schools, the government and private sector businesses are adopting radio frequency identification tags, or RFIDs – a technology capable of pinpointing the physical location of whatever item the tags are embedded in. While this may seem like a convenient way to track items, it's also a convenient way to do something less benign: track people and their activities through their belongings. EFF is working to ensure that embrace of this technology does not erode your right to privacy.

Stopping the FBI from creating surveillance backdoors on the Internet. EFF is part of a coalition opposing the FBI's expansion of the Communications Assistance for Law Enforcement Act (CALEA), which would require that the wiretap capabilities built into the phone system be extended to the Internet, forcing ISPs to build backdoors for law enforcement.

Providing you with a means by which you can contact key decision-makers on cyber-liberties issues. EFF maintains an action center that provides alerts on technology, civil liberties issues and pending legislation to more than 50,000 subscribers. EFF also generates a weekly online newsletter, EFFector, and a blog that provides up-to-the minute information and commentary.

Defending your right to listen to and copy digital music and movies. The entertainment industry has been overzealous in trying to protect its copyrights, often decimating fair use rights in the process. EFF is standing up to the movie and music industries on several fronts.

Check out all of the things we're working on at http://www.eff.org and join today or make a donation to support the fight to defend freedom online.

ELECTRONIC FRONTIER FOUNDATION · 454 SHOTWELL STREET · SAN FRANCISCO, CA 94110 · 415.436.9333

More No-Nonsense Books from **NO STARCH PRESS**

HACKING
The Art of Exploitation

by JON ERICKSON

A comprehensive introduction to the techniques of exploitation and creative problem-solving methods commonly referred to as "hacking." Shows how hackers exploit programs and write exploits, instead of just how to run other people's exploits. Explains the technical aspects of hacking, including stack-based overflows, heap-based overflows, string exploits, return-into-libc, shellcode, and cryptographic attacks on 802.11b.

"From all the books I've read so far, I would consider this the seminal hacker's handbook."—Security Forums.com

NOVEMBER 2003, 264 PP., $39.95 ($59.95 CAN)
ISBN 1-59327-007-0

HACKING THE XBOX
An Introduction to Reverse Engineering

by ANDREW "BUNNIE" HUANG

Using the Xbox as a teaching tool, Huang introduces novices to basic hacking techniques, such as reverse engineering and debugging. *Hacking the Xbox* also covers Xbox security mechanisms and other advanced topics of interest to more seasoned hackers. A chapter contributed by the Electronic Frontier Foundation (EFF) rounds out the book with a discussion of the rights and responsibilities of hackers.

"Although it's a technical book, it unfolds like a spy novel."—Slashdot

JULY 2003, 288 PP., $24.99 ($37.99 CAN)
ISBN 1-59327-029-1

THE ART OF ASSEMBLY LANGUAGE

by RANDALL HYDE

The Art of Assembly Language presents assembly language from the high-level programmer's point of view, so programmers can start writing meaningful programs within days. The High Level Assembler that accompanies the book is the first assembler that allows programmers to write portable assembly language programs that run under either Linux or Windows with nothing more than a recompile.

SEPTEMBER 2003, 928 PP., W/CD-ROM, $59.95 ($89.95 CAN)
ISBN 1-886411-97-2

ENDING SPAM
Bayesian Content Filtering and the Art of Statistical Language Classification

by JONATHAN A. ZDZIARSKI

Considerable research and some brilliant minds have invented clever new ways to fight spam in all its nefarious forms. This landmark title describes, in depth, how statistical filtering is being used by next-generation spam filters to identify and filter spam. The author explains how spam filtering works and how language classification and machine learning combine to produce remarkably accurate spam filters. Readers gain a complete understanding of the mathematical approaches used in today's spam filters, as well as decoding, tokenization, the use of various algorithms (including Bayesian analysis and Markovian discrimination), and the benefits of using open-source solutions to end spam. Interviews with the creators of many of the best spam filters provide further insight into the anti-spam crusade.

APRIL 2005, 448 PP., $39.95 ($53.95 CAN)
ISBN 1-59327-052-6

THE TCP/IP GUIDE

by CHARLES M. KOZIEROK

An encyclopedic and comprehensible guide to the TCP/IP protocol suite for newcomers and seasoned professionals. Details the core protocols that make TCP/IP internetworks function, as well as the most important TCP/IP applications. Full coverage of PPP, ARP, IP, IPv6, IP NAT, IPSec, Mobile IP, ICMP, and much more. Offers a detailed view of the TCP/IP protocol suite, and describes networking fundamentals and the important OSI Reference Model.

MAY 2005, 1200 PP., $69.95 ($94.95 CAN)
ISBN 1-59327-047-X

PHONE:
800.420.7240 OR
415.863.9900
MONDAY THROUGH FRIDAY,
9 A.M. TO 5 P.M. (PST)

FAX:
415.863.9950
24 HOURS A DAY,
7 DAYS A WEEK

EMAIL:
SALES@NOSTARCH.COM

WEB:
HTTP://WWW.NOSTARCH.COM

MAIL:
NO STARCH PRESS
555 DE HARO ST, SUITE 250
SAN FRANCISCO, CA 94107
USA

UPDATES

Visit **http://www.nostarch.com/silence.htm** for updates, errata, and other information.